Where Demons Hide

Executing the Judgment of Truth
(Zechariah 8:16 KJV)
Revealing Darkness

J. Woods

Predicated on the written Word of God

xulon
PRESS

Copyright © 2010 by J. Woods

Where Demons Hide
Executing the Judgment of Truth (Zechariah 8:16 KJV)
Predicated on the written Word of God
by J. Woods

Printed in the United States of America

ISBN 9781615799282

All rights reserved solely by the author. The author guarantees all contents are original and do not infringe upon the legal rights of any other person or work. No part of this book may be reproduced in any form without the permission of the author. The views expressed in this book are not necessarily those of the publisher.

All scripture quotations, unless otherwise indicated, are taken from The New King James Version®. Copyright © 1982 by Thomas Nelson, Inc. Used by permission.

Scripture quotations marked NLT are taken from The Holy Bible, New Living Translation. Copyright © 1996, 2004 by Tyndale House Publishers. Used by permission.

Scripture taken from The Holy Bible, New International Version®. Copyright © 1973, 1978, 1978 by Biblica International Bible Society. Used by permission of Zondervan.

Scripture taken from The King James Version. Copyright © 1993, 1994, 1995, 1996, 2000, 2001, 2002 by NavPress Publishing Group. Used by permission.

www.xulonpress.com

To The Reader

∽

The reader is encouraged to research scripture to study in depth God's Word, to come into enlightenment into the wisdom, knowledge, and understanding of truth and to learn what and who you really are. Scripture is presented for two reasons; first to verify the writings that are God's truth and secondly they are for you, that you may have the *willingness* and eagerness to yield to the truth and to read for yourself and begin to understand that the Bible is for you.

By reading and studying scripture, you will spiritually grow into the wisdom, knowledge and understanding of God and the truth of life.

The seriousness of life is beyond your moral and mortal comprehension. You are going to learn how your spirit, soul and mind are a conduit into the spiritual realm of righteousness or unrighteousness.

This book is written in truth according to God's Word with no speculation, assumptions, hypothesis, theories, and no philosophical rhetoric.

A spiritual gift prepared for you, is waiting for you if you want it, all you need to do is receive it and God will open your eyes.

These writings reflect the way God sees humanity, for his thoughts are not like our thoughts and his ways are not our ways. Isaiah 55:8

We are not to try to figure God out, we are just to believe.

How to study the Bible (See Appendix).

Contents

❧

To the Reader v

Preface xi

Introduction xiii

PART I   THE AWARENESS OF OUR JOURNEY

Chapter 1   Our Journey 19
- Learn this on your Journey 21
- Nearing your Journey's End 24
- A Little about You 27

Chapter 2   Help In Our Understanding 30
- People are Destroyed of lack of Knowledge 32
- The Value of Knowledge 35
- Fear God 37

Chapter 3   Our Will 43
- A New Light 45

PART II   IN THE VERY BEGINNING

Chapter 4   Creations – In Heaven 55
- The Very First Sin in the Universe 58
- The Very First War – In Heaven 59

Where Demons Hide

Chapter 5	Creations – On Earth, the Human Race 63
	• The Original Sin on Earth, The Fall of Man 65
	• What Happened..................................68
	• Visit the Garden................................69
Chapter 6	Our Spiritual Inheritance 76
	• The Dichotomy..................................77
	• 2/3 Complete
PART III	THE SPIRIT REALM, INVISIBLE AND VERY POWERFUL
Chapter 7	A Look into Hell..111
	• A Look Into Heaven...........................114
	• Heaven's Books 115
	• The Book of Life................................116
Chapter 8	Two Kingdoms 117
	• Satan 119
	• Names of Satan..................................121
	• Satan's Characteristics......................122
	• Satan's sin – God's Plan...................132
	• Facts about Satan...............................130
	• Satan's sin, God's plan....................132
	• Satan's Army, Demons....................132
	• Where Demons Hide 135
	• Expressions of Demonic Activity......139
	• A Person Under the Influence............142
	• Satan's Global Agenda.....................145
	• Ranking of Demons..........................152
	• Kingdom of God 152

viii

Part IV	MAN	
Chapter 9	Trilogy of Man	157
	• Our Spirit	161
	• Our Soul	162
	• Our Body	162
	• Our Conscience	169
	• Our Imagination	169
	• Our Heart	171
Chapter 10	They Infiltrate Our Mind	176
	• Out of Our Mind	181
	• Mistaken Identity	189
	• Attitudes	192
	• Behaviors	193
	• Thoughts	194
	• Self	197
Chapter 11	This World	201
	• The Worldly System	201
	• The Worlds Wisdom	208
	• The wrong message	211
Chapter 12	Living in the Spirit Realm	214
	• Satanic, Worldly, and Human	214
	• Darkness Revealed	215
	• Deception	218
	• Some tactics the devil uses in deception	218
	• Deceptive Tools	224
	• Who are these misguided pawns	230
	• The Two Simile Gates	232
	• The comparison	233
	• Blindness	235
	• Ignorance	236
	• Captive, enslaved	237
	• Dead because of sin	237

- Lost 238
- Death 239
- Your Choice 241
- Judgment 242

Chapter 13   Reality 245
- The Bible 246
- God's church 247
- Our Creator 248
- Through God's eyes 251
- A personal God 252
- Our Savior 252

Chapter 14   The Beauty of it All 255
- Examine yourself 256
- A Haunting Question 257
- Three Questions 257
- Do you really want to know 258
- Are you willing 260
- Sinner's Prayer 261
- A Prayer for Our Nation 262

Epilogue 263

Appendix 267

PREFACE

While growing up, I noticed people doing things that I thought were, oh let us say a bit abnormal, but then again we do live in a mixed-up society. I noticed there was lying, cheating, stealing, rebellion, disobedience, conniving, people selling themselves, people giving themselves away, people sharing themselves with the same gender. There was a heavy usage of drugs, selling drugs, alcohol, hate crimes, prejudices, and killings. I noticed corruption in government at all levels.

As I grew older, it seemed things were getting worse and more of it and at a much higher-level of intensity. Now, I am more aware of things happening just not here but around the world. People are crazier than ever before, doing things and harming others with no remorse whatsoever. What is going on in this confused world? Do these actions balance out life, the good vs. the evil? Is this what makes the world go around?

The news media continually reporting negative issues going on in the world that seem to be escalating to no end. Professionals, in areas of the mind, in theology, in diplomacy giving their opinions why people in countries around the world are so full of evil, anger, deceit, perversion, and immorality. This is truly an angry world.

Before I came into an understanding of these and other bizarre acts, my life became altered toward a spiritual awareness. Within this spiritual awareness came spiritual knowledge and spiritual understanding. Answers to carnal acts are in the spirit realm, where they originate.

To gain spiritual understand, we need to gain spiritual knowledge. To gain spiritual knowledge, our life must be, transformed, regenerated, converted, altered, and then, comes spiritual awareness. What is this spiritual awareness, spiritual knowledge, and this converted life? Let us see into it to help in our understanding of the spiritual realm.

There is another realm to our lives beside the physical. It will exceedingly propel you into another dimension of knowledge and understanding, if you are *willing*, and want it. If not, you will remain in this realm, which is the same realm in which you were born. In this dimension, is where deception, discouragement, depression, disobedience, delusion, untruth, no absolute truth, false religions, a life of error that permeate the human soul.

These writings are here to help show you the way to the "truth" of life, who you are, what you are and your final destination in life, pending on the decision you make here in the now.

INTRODUCTION

It would take all of eternity to get to the tip of knowing God, knowing His ways, knowing the mysteries of God, knowing His master plan for this universe, knowing the Deity, gaining His knowledge, learning of Him and that is exactly what we have, eternity. We have a God given eternal life to learn, understand and gain knowledge of Him. We can receive knowledge of God and from God while we are here on Earth, this is essential in growing in our relationship with our Lord. Growing in spiritual knowledge, is knowing what is truth, because God is truth, (Deut. 32:4) the absolute truth. Spiritual knowledge He wants us to have, Hosea will expound.

We are going back before the human race, back to the creations in heaven. We must know where it all began. Even though this will take us back somewhere in an eon of time, it affects us today because **sin does not die with age,** and through the ages, everything pertaining to man has been, perverted.

In our history we have read the annals of time of our ancestors and the history they made and the price, they paid to make this country what it is. Our ancestors founded this country on Judeo Christian principles and in God, we trust. There were times in the past that were difficult and many people died in that difficulty defending this belief. That put people in very stressful situations in their life because of rebuke, resentment, rejection, unbelief and unfortunately it has carried over into our present day lives.

It seems now this stress has evolved into an evil mentality, it is likening to an evil psychological psychosis virus that is sweeping the face of the Earth. It affects the minds of the human race and the worse part is that it robs and hinders humans of the knowledge of truth and it is done intentionally. This evil virus maintains a separation from God and it endeavors to exert untruth into the human mind. It feeds on negative destroying factors of life that has intensified and multiplied greatly. It manifest itself in the mislead vessels of the human race, which are the unbelievers, the unsaved, ungodly, the infidels, the agnostics, the unrighteous who prefer not to know nor want to have the knowledge of true God in their lives. They prefer to live continually in the lust and the untruth of the world with their own beliefs, theories and philosophies.

This evil mind-robbing virus consumes and influences billions of individuals around the world in their daily activities and throughout their life. One out of one people are subject to demonic forces and influences. Sure, there may be different levels of their intensity or should I say weakness or sickness, but that evil thinking, rapidly spreading malevolent malignant virus comes from one source. Let us look at this closer and understand why there is so much debauchery, perversion and so much evil in the world and where it comes from.

We are going right to the source that tells us what this evil is and how it is consuming this world and the human mind. We have to understand, we must understand where this sickness originated and how it affects the world and the people within. To do this in a rightful manner, we will look at this world as it truly is and look at humankind through God's eyes, according to God's word and from God's heart.

There is an unrelenting battle between the spirit of truth and the spirit of error going on in the spirit realm. The spirit of truth collides with the status-quo of the world, which opposes the absolute truth.

WHERE DEMONS HIDE

PART I

AWARENESS
OF
OUR JOURNEY

**YOUR JOURNEY BEGAN AT CONCEPTION
FROM ONE STAGE TO ANOTHER,**

**THROUGH THE COURSE AND PASSAGE
THAT YOU CHOSE TO LIVE,**

**YOU ARE APPROACHING
YOUR DESTINATION**
- J. Woods

PART I

Chapter 1

OUR JOURNEY

❦

Our lives are a journey, a physical journey but more so a spiritual journey. We are time travelers; we live in a time vacuum because our human lives are on a timetable. Physically we are locked in time the spirit world is not. Most travel through life knowing only the terrestrial realm in which they live and not experiencing any form of spiritual awareness. Reading this book will be a spiritual element of your journey through life.

Look back at the year you were born, through infancy, the time of adolescence, your growing up period, the years of education, your working status, your marital status, the years up until now. Where did the time go? During this time of your journey, what have you learned about yourself, your make-up, who you are, what have you learned about life, what are you here for, have you ever thought on these?

As you think about life as we know it in our generation, some would say it is wonderful, some say it is okay, some think that there is more to life than this, some may say I lived my life to its fullest, then there are those who cannot wait until it is over. There are those filled with worry and fear and some that do not have a care in the world. There are those who love life and those who have no respect for life one iota. Some just want to live a peaceful life and others that will fight you on a bet. There are those who see beauty in life and others want to make it as dirty, ugly and perverse as possible. There are those who hate with a passion and others that are forgiving. Some want to perform every evil act conceivable, others wish to do what is right. Some want to experience as much physical and sexual perverseness as possible and others want to stay pure. Some want a healthy life, some dump chemicals in their bodies in many different ways not knowing what the outcome will be, others, because of some sort of confusion, take their own life.

You have seen the beauty in this world and you have seen the ugliness of this world; you have seen the flourishing, you have seen the devastations. You have seen the wealth and you have seen the impoverished. You have seen the good and you have seen the evil; you have seen the fairness and you have seen the injustice; you have seen the love and you have seen the hatred.

Life may seem imbalanced with the rich and the poor, the good and the bad, the happy and the sad. Some ease right through life and others always seem to struggle no matter what. Some countries have those militant extremist causing havoc in their country and other countries throughout the world. There are those poor souls living in third world countries with no food, weeks and months of drought, wells of dust, contaminated rivers and streams filled with diseases killing hundreds if not thousands a day, and there are those of us living in comfort. This is the visible world with spiritual applications attached to it.

You will learn that our journey inherently began as a diversion, a diversion from what is truth. Our journey, the inherited path we take through life, known as the wide gate, designed before our birth, through a system of pleasure allurements; and then we were born and entered the world, born, and continue with no awareness of absolute truth. Down through the centuries millions before us have journeyed this same path of life and some found, ran across, were introduced to the proverbial fork in the road, or the crossroad of life, this leads to the altered life, the converted life, the regenerated life, the life of truth.

At times, your journey may not always be to your liking or your expectations; does it not seem like there is always something that interrupts your plans or your life. Situations and circumstances can change your demeanor and your hope for that day or a time, or a lifetime because of severe situations and circumstances that fall upon you, that may lead to hopelessness. Paths on your journey can change in a moment and then you can experience up and down emotions that possibly can be unbearable. At these times of discouragement what do you do? Where is your hope?

Our journey through the physical life, which is a substandard life, is a phase that we all must travel. Within this journey lay all the rudiments of a self-absorbed selfish-life because of the fallen nature. Through your journey, if you do not know by now, you will learn that we live in a world of moral decay.

Learn this on Your Journey

What we experience in life depends on what path of life we journey. We can travel one of two paths. One path is of **truth** the other is the path of **error**, our inherited path. Our experiences on the path of truth will be much different than traveling the path of error. Our knowledge on the path of truth will be much different than the knowledge gained on the path of error. The path of truth is much straighter, narrower, and stringent than the wide path of error. These two paths of life have their own nature and our lives conducted according to what nature we live in, which path of life we take on our journey.

The Bible teaches that there are only two ways to live life, and to live either life, we must travel through one of two gates because we cannot live both ways at the same time, it is one, or the other. A passage in Matthew 7:13,14 [NIV], tells of these two-ways of life. One is through a narrow gate; the right way, the other is through a wide gate, the wrong way, these ways represent ways of conduct, life styles, and thinking. The narrow gate, which will lead on the narrow path of life, represents righteousness, and the wide gate, leading down the wide path of life represents unrighteousness, life is either the way of righteousness or the way of unrighteousness. These are the terms of the populous of the world.

To enter the Kingdom of God, one must travel through the **narrow gate**; this is the **gateway to life**. The gate is small, the road is narrow, and only a few ever find it. In addition, there is the **highway to hell**, its gate is wide, and the road is broad to accommodate the many of the world who choose this way to live, this road breeds sin, leads to destruction, and death.

These two paths of life are ways of thinking; the narrow road of life is a way of austere thinking, living, and being sober minded, clear-headed in thought, a sound mind, this is the way through God's word, this is the way to follow God. Through the wide gate of open-mindedness, this way of thinking the world's population exercises freedoms given to them by the devil who they follow like the pied piper down the wide road leading them to fulfillment of any desire, a freedom that leads to further corruption. Here the self-life is selfishly developed and conformed to the worldly system, while they live a spiritually distorted life.

This passage in Matthew is saying the majority of the population on the planet is following the wrong path of life, their thinking, their thoughts; their actions, the way they live are wrong, with wrong beliefs, wrong teachings, and wrong doctrines and wrong motives, telling lies and believing lies and because of this, they are being lead astray.

The wide gate, the highway to hell is the way of death or through the narrow gate, the Gateway to life, are the only two courses to travel our life's journey. These pathways of life, the wide road or the narrow road are our only ways of thinking. The appealing pathway, through the wide gate caters to our physical life, our fleshly desires verses the spiritual pathway, which caters to our spirit, our spiritual desires like really wanting to know the truth, knowing God, reading the Bible, etc.. Truth can only be found in the spirit realm. We can say that the wide road is the road to nowhere, the road to death, the way of foolish living, and the narrow road the road to life, the highway to heaven, the way of the wise and living wisely.

Those that travel the wide road of life, their minds are pre-occupied in a world full of human and nonhuman networking systems that entice, flatter, intrigues, capture, corrupt, interrupt, feed you with sensual and immoral-desires leading to actions that surely will defile you, and add in there a chaotic world that is in such disorder. This path will lead you further away from the truth and addicts you with desires that your mind and flesh have appetites for, all by deceiving you. Our enemy cleverly laid this path before us, attempting to pollute our minds immediately after birth and as I said, to keep our minds pre-occupied from thinking and wanting to know what is truth, where to find it and it is in reality, within your reach.

We are to live our lives wisely, and skillfully in wisdom, if not it will be a life filled with folly. We are lost creatures living on a cursed planet where eternal treasures do not exist. Every one of us is somebody special in this lost world. Our life is more than a flickering-candle, when it goes out, it's over. Yes, we are lost but we can be found. We do not think of ourselves anything other than just passing through; we do not know what awaits us ahead. Therefore, we live aimlessly with a not caring attitude. The great old hymn Amazing Grace written by John Newton starts out with a verse, "Amazing Grace how sweet the sound that sav'd a wretch like me. I once was lost, but now am found, was blind, but now I see." This does not mean that the person was lost in the woods or in a big city somewhere and was found by a search party, nor does it mean that this person was physically blind and had an operation and now sees in the physical. No, this person is saying that he was spiritually lost, lost to all God's truth, because of the condition of darkness, darkness is a lost condition. Darkness is a metaphor for sin, for lies, for error. He did not have any spiritual knowledge or understanding, but because of his spiritual conversion, which is a miracle, the darkness removed from his eyes and now he sees, knows and understands the truth, spiritual truth.

We are to stop, and think, and learn, before we leave this planet. It is up to us to <u>want</u> to know who we are; we <u>must</u> be *willing* to seek out this knowledge. Even though we are God's creations and he loves every one of us, the fact remains that we **must** make an effort, strive to find our way out of this world of sin. If not we will be like that vapor, that flame that disappears and forgotten, or we break through the lost deadly disease.

We get so involved in the world's enticements and the affairs of this world that we do not have or take time in finding our way out. It is up to us, *willingly* reach out, open the celestial door, and go through, you are immediately confronted with truth. Because of sin and the blindness and within the world's enticements we remain naive of our spiritual life and continue without knowledge of it. Our own waywardness will lead us to our own demise. When we die, it is not the end, it is a new beginning, even for the sinner and unfortunately, his new beginning, he will not enjoy.

As you have read our lives are eternal, we do not die an endless death and disappear although our bones are at the foot of the grave our eternal consciousness lives.

Nearing Your Journey's End

In the spiritual realm, there are two spiritual destinations where your journey will come to a near end. Only one of those destinations will be your final abode and that, determined by a decision you make in the now physical realm. Once we are in the spiritual realm after our physical death, there is no decision making concerning our destination.

During your physical journey, some time in your life you will have an opportunity to enter through this narrow mind-gate of life, the fork in the road, or the crossroad of life by being introduced to a change of life, an altered life, a converted life, a new life by accepting Jesus Christ as your personal savior. Taking this opportunity and making this choice is highly recommended, it is a matter of life or death.

Sometime during your life's journey, this opportunity will arise in your life to make a choice, to continue living in the world's ways or accepting Jesus Christ as your personal savior by entering through the narrow mind-gate of thinking. By accepting Christ, you are now living in a spiritual/physical realm.

The narrow gate, narrow way of thinking, is a controlled way, a governed way, a biblical way of thinking which will lead to the spiritual awareness realm of thinking and the truth that you are seeking will be revealed unto you. You will now live in a spiritual/physical dimension while on this earth rather than living only in the mere physical realm.

Millions believe there are other ways to eternal life, to God, to heaven. There is not, Jesus is the only way. Jesus is the Mediator. *"For there is one God and one Mediator between God and men, the Man Christ Jesus"* (1st Tim. 2:5) we must accept Jesus first before we go to God.

You were born in the physical realm, now you are born in the spiritual realm. Your spirit, heart, soul, and mind are brought into a realization, an awareness of absolute truth, because you are set-free from the premeditated lies, false doctrines, worldly philosophies, in the physical realm, absorbed in the world's system, hence, worldly wisdom, the path that was maliciously laid before you.

Now you are born into the spirit realm, or being born again, born from above, converted, transformed, regenerated, your spirit now resurrected, which was void in you from birth, you are now born of God. The feeling of emptiness or the feeling of something was missing in your life is now complete the void is now filled.

Not being happy, or feeling odd, a feeling of incompleteness comes from this void that we carry around in us and try to fill with what the world, Satan, has to offer, those mundane evil desires. The void is our missing spirit, God in our spirit.

Living in the spiritual/physical realm because of being converted of God (John 1:12, 13), one is aware of truth, the absolute truth and continues to learn of it. You become a believer, a believer in absolute truth. Truth's are revealed to you, you become a believer in life after death, because Jesus Christ died for your sins, rose from the dead, and are made aware of this fact, believer that you are a triune being destined for a life of eternity, in heaven. You will believe and know the choice is yours for that destiny, you will know that what you believed in the past because of being-programmed, conformed of the worldly ways was a lie of deception and that you believed those lies. You will realize that your spirit is alive but because of sin, realize it was dead. You will begin a brand new path of life that you will walk, the narrow road; you will think, talk and behave differently, you will have joy and peace in your soul and you will have an exciting new joyous journey from that time on in your spirit.

The individual who rejects Jesus Christ, which is rejecting God's forgiveness of sins, is rejecting God's invitation of eternal life in heaven. With this rejection of salvation, he will not know the truth no matter how hard he tries to understand, because of spiritual blindness, spiritual deafness, and spiritual dullness from living only in the physical realm. His lack of knowledge and of all the years of believing the lies of the **spirit of error**, unable to understand spiritual matters (Matt. 13:13) this is because he is **self**-absorbed. The individual will not experience the spiritual/physical life while here, but only the mere physical and presuppose spiritual life, and immediately be aware of his spiritual life and of truth upon his death, when he awakens, trembling and bowing in the presence of the Lord at his judgment. No one should want to experience this, you see, dying is not the worst thing that can happen to you, being judged, condemned and losing an eternal life with God is far worse.

A Little about You

Do you know you have three lives? You have your physical, your spiritual and your eternal life. This is our creative make-up; we all have this in common and on our journey, we will experience life in this order because we are chronological creatures. We will experience these stages in our life's journey. First, you will live in the physical realm, the body that you know so well. Within this physical journey, you will have the opportunity to enter through the narrow mind-gate to live the spiritual/physical life. Second, you will die from the physical realm. The body will last only so long no matter what is done to try to preserve it. Third, you will live again in the spirit realm, the eternal spirit world with a spiritual resurrected body.

Our lives have a beginning, the physical, an ending, also physical and another beginning, the spiritual/eternal life; this is because our lives are spiritual and supernatural, and possibly depending upon your decision you make now or do not make now, in the physical realm, there can be a second death. Our physical life has a beginning and an ending; our spiritual life has a beginning and never ends. Our spiritual/eternal life comes from our physical death.

Here your journey is near the end; the path separates for eternity in His presents. If you have accepted Jesus Christ into your life as your personal savior, which is being born again, saved, regenerated, being-redeemed, converted by your spirit made alive through your faith in Jesus, then you shall not come into judgment but pass into everlasting life. By accepting Christ you pass from death into eternal life and enter into the Kingdom of God (John 5:24). You have just made a reservation to get into heaven.

What does it mean you pass from death? You pass from judgment, from hell, the second death. If you rejected Christ while on earth, which by the way, you are called a coward, and continue living your vile unbelieving ways, living without Christ in your life you will face judgment and experience a second death. Here are those who will experience the second, *"the cowardly, the unbelieving, the murderers, the sexually immoral, those who practice magic arts, (sorcerers), the idolaters, and all liars-their place will be in the lake of burning sulfur. This is the second death"* (Rev. 21:8 NIV). Going to hell is the second death. That is far worse than the first physical death. Listen to what Revelation 20:13-15 NIV says; *"The sea gave up the dead that were in it, and death and* **Hades** *gave up the dead that were in them, and each person was judged according to what he had done."* *"then death and Hades were thrown into the lake of fire. The lake of fire is the second death."* *"If anyone's name was not found written in the book of life, he was thrown into the lake of fire."* Those not written in the book of life are those on earth that rejected the truth, rejected God, rejected his Son, rejected salvation, rejected the Word, rejected the spiritual knowledge of God, all this rejection they signed their own death certificate. These, lived their lives unknowingly for Satan who kept them in bondage by blinding their minds with sin and by their own-selves, *willingly* living in the sin nature, unable of knowing any spiritual truth.

The second death is the eternal separation from God. Separated from any loved ones that have gone on to heaven before you and you are sent to the chambers of death, a place of sulfur burning stench, a vile smelling, repulsive cell, with weeping and gnashing of teeth. Heat beyond your comprehension; a fire that never goes out; dryness and thirst with no quenching, total darkness and you, will be alienated for eternity, this is the end of your journey, not the end of your life. You see what is also built into our spiritual DNA is eternal life. God made the human being, that upon conception, that seed has eternal life written into it. This is one reason why abortion is so horrific. Those aborted defenseless babies had God's eternal design in their DNA. All pro-choicers are going to pay for their choice of abortion.

Our life's journey is in reality a supernatural spiritual journey, because we are spirit eternal beings. Steven Covery wrote, "We are not human beings on a spiritual journey, we are spiritual beings on a human journey." If you are not aware of the spiritual aspect of your life, your journey is meaningless, it is physical only, carnally minded, full of **self, self**-adorations, **self**-endearment, **self**-exhalations, **self**-righteous, **self**-expectations, **self**-absorbed, **self**-centeredness, so full of prideful-**self** and so full of the world.

On this leg of your journey, you should learn who you are, and what you are here for, you see, what you do on earth today affects your eternity. It is of extreme importance for your eternal life how you finish your physical journey.

Your physical journey began at conception; your spiritual journey began before you were born. You are not an accident; you are here at this time in this millennium for a reason, you are here to learn who you are, what you are, and what you are here for and what course in life you will choose. Listen to Psalm 119:59,105 ᴺᴸᵀ "*I pondered the direction of my life, and I turned to follow your laws.*" "*Your word is a lamp to guide my feet and a light for my path.*" Light is a metaphor for truth. Turn to the right path of life. Everyone has the opportunity to choose, everyone has the resilience to say, I *will* change my path, my way of life for the better. It is discouraging to the unbeliever to turn from his wicked ways. I heard a man say, "The journey through the wide gate can take you to places you do not want to be, where you do not want to stay, with people you do not know. It can shrink your horizon to where everyday has no sunrise, where gloom hangs over you with despair lurking in every thought."

Chapter 2

HELP IN OUR UNDERSTANDING

"What we want is to see the child in pursuit of knowledge, not knowledge in pursuit of the child." — George Bernard Shaw

To capture the full essence of this book's topic, to grasp truth, spiritual knowledge is required. Worldly knowledge has no discernment in spiritual matters. However, I pray since you are reading this book that your spiritual eyes will be opened and in your heart *willing* to learn the truth.

If in your heart, you desire spiritual knowledge for knowing truth, the truth about life, knowing the truth of who you really are, knowing scripture, knowing God, truth for discerning and distinguishing between spirits (1 Corinthians 12:10c) then you will seek out this knowledge. You will learn that your life's desires are all in the heart. Are you a prudent person? Are you a disciplined person in your conduct? The person with the prudent heart, the person with the discerning heart acquires knowledge, and the ear of the wise seeks out this spiritual knowledge (Prov. 8:15).

What does it mean discerning and distinguishing between spirits? There are two spirits governing in this world. One is **the spirit of truth, of good;** the other is **the spirit of error, of**

evil. In them, their ways, their personalities, their characteristics, their natures and their attitudes are valid or invalid activities. Either valid in truth, or invalid of untruth, read 1st John 4:1-3;5-6 [NIV] to learn what constitutes **the spirit of truth** and of **error**. Please read these scriptures in the New Testament and fix those in your mind know them. Also in Hebrews 5:14 [NIV] the Bible is telling us that the mature Christian, who is a student of the Bible with spiritual knowledge, spiritual wisdom and spiritual understanding who by constant use of the Word (this is his food feeding his spirit) have trained himself to distinguish good and evil.

We gain spiritual knowledge by digesting God's word, by digesting God's word we gain wisdom and knowledge. Be *willing*, be enthusiastic, to open your spiritual senses so that you can see what is truly of God and what is satanic. Recognizing the works of the devil, some are so evident; others call for spiritual vigilance, spiritual discernment, not carnal thinking, not intelligence, not philosophical discernment, nor through psychological methods, not through **the spirit of error** but **the Holy Spirit**, the Spirit of truth, the Word (knowledge) is the instrument through which the Holy Spirit operates in us, bringing discernment. God will open your mind so you can understand scripture (Ps. 119:130 [NLT]).

Luke 24:45 [NIV], will tell you, God, will open your mind so you can understand scripture. You have heard it said, *"Knowledge is strength"*, or power this is, **truth**, and it is biblical truth, you will find it in the book of Proverbs, 24:5. God puts a high value on having spiritual knowledge; the Bible says that it is more valuable than gold (Prov. 8:10), you will find that it leads to life, it gives life if you have it (Eccles. 7:12b).

Spiritual knowledge comes through reading God's word, through confessions of your sins, through repentance, and the forgiveness of sins, through salvation, with God's mercy and grace (Luke 1:77 [NIV]). Salvation comes through faith and believing in and accepting Jesus Christ as your personal savior. We will expound on this at the end of the book. Faith comes from hearing God's word (Rom. 10:17 [NLT]), hearing

God's word comes from someone telling you of the Word or you reading the Word by which you will hear what it says to you. The more you read the more you grow.

Those who choose not to have spiritual knowledge; God calls them *"the simpletons," "simpleminded," "mockers," "fools,"* because they are biblically naïve (Prov. 1:22 [NLT]). They hate knowledge and since they hate spiritual knowledge, which would free them from untruth, from the lies of the world, from the untruth of darkness, from **the spirit of error,** and from making fools of themselves, they do not fear the Lord (Prov. 1:29 [NLT]). Their waywardness and their complacency will destroy them and they will perish (Hos. 4:6a). Jesus was saying in the book of Mark 12:24 [NIV], that they were in error, in other words, they were living the spirit of error, because they did not know the scripture, did not know God's word, or the power of God, and did not fear God. They had spiritual ignorance, ignorance of the Word, no spiritual knowledge, no spiritual understanding. All those who hate Jesus love death.

Because of the great sin, our spirit is dead; leaving a void within us and that void is filled with the components of the sin nature, which must be relinquished and filled with the Spirit and knowledge of our Savior and not of man. You see, the beginning of knowledge is having fear of the Lord; this is the foundation of true knowledge, but fools despise wisdom and discipline (Prov. 1:7 [NIV]).

"My People are destroyed For Lack Of Knowledge"

HOSEA 4:6

God said; *"My people are destroyed for lack of knowledge,"* Think about this, it is profound. Why should people be destroyed, or perish for lack of knowledge? Drop the pronoun my and read, People are destroyed for lack of knowledge. In reality, this is happening; people are destroyed from lack of spiritual knowledge. Let us take a closer look at this account.

<u>My</u> people: Not a distinction of Christians, or the Israelites as the people of God, but people in general. God created all things through Him and for Him whether they are visible or invisible (Col. 1:16) that is <u>all</u> things, including us, the human race, His people. He has the right to say, 'my people,' because he made us, which includes you. (See Appendix)

are <u>destroyed</u>: signifies to destroy, are destroyed within themselves. The idea is not extinction, but ruin, spiritual damnation, impoverishment, the unsaved, to depart, to be lost; this verb implies the completion of the process of spiritual destruction, spiritual death.

<u>for lack of knowledge</u>: what kind of knowledge? Knowledge of God, because God is knowledge and truth, and without injustice, (1St Sam. 2:3c; Deut. 32:4c) knowledge of the **truth** (1st Tim. 2:4) the truth that you are seeking, knowledge of knowing Him. Knowing the scripture, the doctrine, the Word, is knowledge, biblical principles, our code of conduct of life.

Why was there a lack of knowledge? There was not a lack of knowledge per-se, the knowledge was there, the word was there, all they had to do was read it, study it, believe it, and accept it as it is today, but there was a lack of wanting this spiritual knowledge again, as it is today. People did not have godly knowledge because they did not want the knowledge; hence, the lack of knowledge, again as it is today. No godly knowledge, wisdom, understanding, nor truth was found in these people. They *willingly* rejected the word of God and left themselves spiritually blinded by idolatry, pleasures of lust and sinful passions of the world, even as it is today.

People, who are living for the world, through the wide mind-gate, the world's ways, they are not interested in the knowledge of God or knowing Him. It does not matter if it was four thousand years ago or today; humans are the same no matter what millennium it is. This is where for some, religion takes hold and nourishes them with that religion or church, then they are appeased but this does not give them salvation.

Therefore, God's people, the human race perish, are lost, have spiritual destruction, **self**-destruction, are spiritually dead, eternal damnation for lack of knowledge, they did not want the knowledge of God. They *willingly* made their choice not to have God in their lives; they turned their back on his knowledge and refused to recognize God's revelations. They rejected God's knowledge and by this rejection, they do not know what is right and true, as it is today. Call this spiritual suicide.

This was their attitude and their demise, again, the *willing* negative attitude. If one stays in this way of life, through the wide mind-gate, open mindedness, in this sin nature, in the spirit of error, the nature of untruth, in this frame of mind that rejects God's salvation then this person becomes depraved, immoral, corrupted, lost in their sin and their sins are rejected by God, and excluded from salvation. Just look at the many different beliefs today. Look at the atheists, humanist, the agnostics, the unbelievers, and look at the radical terrorist, the extremist with their beliefs and mind sets, these people are depraved and void of God's spiritual knowledge, they will perish.

God does not send people to hell; people send themselves to hell. Look for example what the book of Romans 13:2 [NIV] says; *"Consequently, he who rebels against the authority is rebelling against what God has instituted, and those who do so will bring judgment on themselves."*

Why does the human race prefer the world and its evil ways to wanting to believe in, knowing and learning of their God, their Creator, their heavenly Father, the one who gave them life in the first place and the only one who can give them eternal life with Him? Why is this gift of eternal life rejected, why is spiritual knowledge rejected?

To answer this we must investigate our make-up. Who are we that we would turn our backs on our God? The God who sent his Son to this world to die for our sins that we may believe in Him and <u>not</u> <u>perish</u> but have ever lasting life (John 3:16 ^{NLT}- 1 John 4:9). What do we have or what do we not have inside us that draw us further and further away from our Creator. It is our sin; we love our deeds of darkness, of evil rather than of light, judgment will be based on this fact. We prefer the world and its ways its evil deeds (John 3:19 ^{NIV}), their self-centered deeds and they prefer not to believe because they want to enjoy their sin, live in that sin, believe what they want and not answer to a higher power to surrender to and answer to. This may be the biggest reason, they do not want to surrender to a higher power they cannot see, or believe in and another may be that they may not believe in an alternate life, an afterlife that they are just passing through this one and there is nothing else. This is a deceptive scheme of the devil.

The world does not know what sin is; they would rather deny the truth than believe the truth. It is easier to deny and believe that there is no authority higher to answer to, to be accountable to, and they just enjoy their sin and bask in their ignorance of lies of untruth.

Let us look into the creation of the visible and the invisible world with God's wisdom and knowledge, that we may bring a focus to our understanding.

The Value of Knowledge

Wise people store up knowledge (Prov. 10:14a) in their hearts, wisdom will be spoken from their lips the Bible says. God's knowledge is a treasure and will be our preservation. The Bible says, do not seek worldly wisdom nor your own understanding (Prov. 3:5b), we must believe God is able to do what he wills in our lives. Conceitedness of our own understanding is a great enemy of God, because it comes from the carnal mind and serves **self,** in other words the heart is overflowing with and serving **self**. We must be wise to do what is best and good according to His promises. God's knowledge will lead you to good judgment, (Ps. 119:66a) and the right principles of life. It will give a clear perception of fact, and truth. This is infinite understanding and knowledge of God with a spiritual perception of divine things (Col. 1:9). God wants **all** to be **saved** and come into the **knowledge of the truth** (1st Timothy 2:4).

The Bible says that knowledge is easy to him who understands (Prov. 14:6b NLT), he that understands departs from evil and does good (Ps. 34:14a) you stop your worldly living and stop accepting all that it has to offer, in this process, our behavior changes. Do you see the simplicity here? If you have this Godly knowledge, you will not perish but have everlasting life. God gave, to get us back from Satan. It cost Jesus his life, it cost us our confession our full repentance and the giving of our lives to Christ. Now comes all assurance of understanding the mysteries and treasures of wisdom and knowledge of God in whom are hidden. He gives them to us (Col. 2:2, 3).

"Happy is the man who finds wisdom, and the man who gains understanding" (Prov. 3:13). *"Wisdom is the principle thing; therefore get wisdom and all your getting, get understanding"* (Prov. 4:7). Wisdom and knowledge are linked together like spirit and soul. Wisdom is knowing and having knowledge of the truth and how to apply it to any given situation. Understanding is knowledge modified by wisdom, because wisdom is first, insight, knowledge knows what you have, and wisdom knows what to do with what you have. Do you want understanding in spiritual matters? Get spiritual wisdom. Wisdom, knowledge, and understanding are amalgamated, as are the spirit, soul and mind.

In the Bible, without God, man's worldly wisdom, man's worldly knowledge, his understanding in matters is vanity, all vanity. All we do without God is vanity the Bible tells us; it is meaningless in God's eyes (Eccles. 1:2). Solomon is simply saying that worldly wisdom is empty and frustrating. What we think is wise is not always wise from God's viewpoint. When we attempt being wise and not take God into consideration it is folly of the worse sort. The world by its wisdom, its intelligence knows not God. Those living in the sin nature traveling the wide road of life with no faith or hope of an eternal life after this are dying. Those with open-mindedness to the world's ways and closed minded to spiritual matters, those that are unrighteous, the unconverted, those with worldly thinking, carnal thinking, carnal minds through their worldly intelligence, through their reasoning cannot and do not know God.

Fear God

> *"The fear of the Lord is the beginning of wisdom"...*
> Psalm 111:10 NLT

Does not it make sense to think and live by Godly principles? Knowledge begins with the **fear** of the Lord (Prov. 1:7) and therefore godly knowledge always includes Him as the primary factory. Knowledge is the foundation in understanding. With wisdom, knowledge comes, and because of its divine source, it comes with understanding embedded in it.

Why fear the Lord? Judgment, no one will escape it. The Bible says that we will die once, physically, (no reincarnation) and then the judgment (Heb. 9:27). *"Now all has been heard; here is the conclusion of the matter: Fear God and keep his commandments, for this is the whole duty of man." "For God will bring every deed into judgment, including every hidden* (secret) *thing, whether it is good or evil." "There is nothing concealed that will not be disclosed, or hidden that will not be made known"* (Eccles. 12:13, 14- Matt. 10:26b NIV). Every secret act or thought will be judged.

Why fear God? You will not make it into heaven. Respecting Him, in reverence, and worship for the mighty God He is, is our duty. Being a child of God, we are to fear God, and keep His commandments. *"Fear of the Lord lengthens one's life."* Proverbs 10:27a NLT tells us. This should reign in our hearts. The fear of God will give us a reverence of His majesty, a reverence to His authority and a dread of His wrath. Jesus said, *"And do not fear those who kill the body, but cannot kill the soul. But rather **fear** Him who is able to destroy both soul and body in hell"* (Matt.

10:28). Only God has the power over life, death and hell...To fear God means to revere, respect and honor Him. His word needs to be read and studied. Look at Proverbs 13:13 *"he who despises the word will be destroyed, but he who fears the commandment will be rewarded."* In Proverbs 1:22, it is the fools who hate knowledge, and the fool is known by what he hates, it is the lack of knowledge that is man's problem, it is not the shortage of information but rather the rejection of information, it is not intelligence but wisdom that is available and offered to man. With the rejection of God's knowledge they are in captivity (Isa. 5:13a) of their enemy and they are destroyed from that lack of knowledge.

Those held captive in the sin nature have no idea what is holy and unholy, they have no idea what is clean and unclean, they have no idea what sin is. This is because they have *willingly* hid their eyes, their mind from the truth and in doing so have shown God's words disrespect and makes them unholy to him. Also in Proverbs 8:13 *"To fear the LORD is to hate evil."* God says right there that he hates pride and arrogance, evil behavior and perverse speech. These are instructions for us to heed, in Proverbs 13:14 *"the instruction of the wise is like a life-giving fountain; those who accept it avoid the snares of death."*

The Christian is to walk worthy; we are to take this knowledge, and wisdom and understanding in our daily walk in life, take it on our journey. We are to increase in the knowledge of God. We are to gain knowledge by reading his word, gain wisdom by having knowledge, gain spiritual understanding by having wisdom, and again increasing in the knowledge of God in our daily living, this is spiritual growth. We need spiritual knowledge that we may have spiritual understanding in the affairs of this life. The Bible is the most important book you will every read, our journey should be a spiritual growing cycle, if not it will be a worldly growing cycle.

Knowledge of God refers to intimate fellowship with Him and to true happiness, and real meaning of life, try it!

Those who are of the world, those who fall back into the world, those who refuse God, refuse to retain God in their knowledge, in their heart, those who refuse to acknowledge Him and did not give God glory, they became futile in their thoughts and their foolish hearts will darken. In the carnal mind, what they think is what they are, if you believe a lie you will live that lie, if you know the truth you will live the truth and not the lies of the world. If they are Christians, then they are Christians, if they are unbelievers they are unbelievers and will live accordingly. God gave the unbelievers up to a reprobated, a debased, and a depraved mind (Rom. 1:28). Knowledge being rejected, in turn, God was rejected. A grave consequence, not what God wants for his people, God's wish is <u>none</u> to perish (2nd Pet. 3:9b), he is patient for your sake, waiting for you, for your repentance.

Remember, knowledge is what you know and people will go to heaven or hell according to how they respond to what they know. The more we expose ourselves to the Bible, the Word, which is gaining godly wisdom and knowledge, the more we grow in faith. The more we expose ourselves to sin, the less we know about sin. The less we know of the spirit life the more ignorant we are toward knowing God. This is the design of the sin nature, to hold you in untruth, literally with a lack of spiritual knowledge that you may not advance to your potential as a child of God. No matter what your belief, you were not a puddle of slime developed from some outer-space protoplasm, in reality we are all children of the living God, who created the human race, and the human race are the children of God, God is our heavenly Father. Nevertheless, some of the human race is lost, unsaved, living the mere physical realm and not experiencing the spiritual because they have not accepted Christ as their Savior.

If we do not have spiritual knowledge, then what knowledge do we have? We have worldly knowledge, worldly understanding, worldly wisdom, worldly feelings, worldly understanding of creation, or no creation, worldly knowledge of religion, of love, of government, of everything and these are meaningless in the spiritual world. If we do not have spiritual knowledge, then we are ignorant to the knowledge of God and God does not bless ignorance. No spiritual knowledge equals ignorance.

When one is ignorant of spiritual knowledge, their worldly religious acts are bias, and their motives are wrong. Listen to what David says to Solomon his son. "*And you, my son Solomon, acknowledge the God of your father, and serve him with wholehearted devotion and with a **willing** mind, **for the Lord searches every heart** and **understands every motive** behind the thoughts. If you seek Him, he will be found by you; but if you forsake him, he will reject you forever*" (1st Chron. 28:9 NIV). "*But if from there you will search again for the Lord your God. And if you search for him with all your heart (your mind) and soul, you will find him*" (Deut. 4:29 NLT). God says, "*If you look for me wholeheartedly, you will find me*" (Jer. 29:13 NLT). God gives us ample opportunity to seek him, do not pass up this opportunity, do not be foolish any longer. Our stubborn will says this is foolishness, but search deeper in your heart. Reach down into your soul past the darkness of lies and pull the real you up to reality.

"A longing for God, is a gift from God" – Max Lucado

How important is it to Him that you have His knowledge? God says in Hosea 6:6 "*For I desire mercy, and not sacrifice; and the **knowledge** of God more than burnt offerings.*" In the New Living Translation it says, "*I want you to show love, not offer sacrifices. **I want you to know me** more than I want burnt offerings.*" To know Him we must accept Him, read and study about Him, there is only one place on this planet to learn and know about God, and that is the Holy Bible. Remember, reading the Bible gives you knowledge about God; obeying the Bible gives you knowledge of God. God will become real to you. With Godly, understanding comes a behavioral change.

God knows if you do not have spiritual knowledge. Your perception will be faulty in life and misleading to your soul and to Him. The people on this planet that have given their life to Christ, also know your lack of spiritual knowledge, your faulty perception of yourself and others and worldly matters, it is very evident of those who are unbelievers. Reading his word is the most powerful weapon you can use to change your heart. I heard a preacher say that, "we are changed by what we know and we are changed by what we do not know." As we gain knowledge we grow in spiritual maturity, we will also grow in God's grace and peace (2nd Pet. 1:2).

Without spiritual knowledge, your perception of the worldly affairs and the affairs of man will be faulty and misleading.

In Hosea, the people were not admitting their sins because they did not want to give them up.

"WITHOUT FREE WILL

MAN WOULD HAVE BEEN

A MERE PUPPET"

       -Unknown

Chapter 3

OUR WILL

❦

I am going to mention this subject at times throughout these writings because of the importance of the will. By italicizing the word will *(will)* it will indicate an emphasis that the will was "*willfully,*" intentionally used in making decisions in obedience or disobedience toward God. The will is a vital element of the human and spiritual life, a component of our soul, a requisite of being a total person in spirit, soul and body. It means the human being has the ability and the capability of being in complete control of his total being. Complete in the sense that one realizes that to become the most mature human being, to become a total person, in spirit, soul and body, to be the person God intended us to be, one must be *willing* to surrender his will, his life over to God.

Your will, will control your thought process and your actions. If your mind takes action on your thought process, your body will follow. If you have a thought of entering a relationship that you know you should not because of obvious reasons but you are *willing* to take a chance, your body will take you there. As you have just read in Hosea 4:6 about the attitude of the will in decision making, those who didn't pursue God didn't have the knowledge of God, didn't want the knowledge of God, lacked that knowledge, and they made a *willful* decision not to pursue the knowledge of God.

Their *willful* decisions lead them into damnation and separating them eternally from God. Their *willful* decisions lead them into willful spiritual blindness, meaning they chose to live in darkness, in sin, because in the natural our will and heart bends toward evil.

With our will we have the ability to make up our own minds. We have the ability to do right or do wrong, to do good or to do evil, to choose heaven or hell. We have the will to choose Jesus Christ as our personal savior or not to choose him when that opportunity is presented to us. It lies within the province of man's will to accept or reject Jesus Christ as personal savior. The sinner is in a lost condition, and when or if he has heard the Gospel it is within his power to yield toward God or toward the world.

Inadvertently this will determine our final destination in life, our journey's end as you have just read above. This decision can only be made while we are living here on earth. When we make decisions in life they are made through the thought process of the will. If we make a choice to do something good, we *willfully* made a choice to do something good, if we choose to do something evil, we *willfully* choose to do something evil. Either way we willfully make that decision. You are in charge of your will; you are in charge of your decision-making. The ones that are tempted must understand the true force of the will. The will is the governing power of our natural man, here is where we have the power of decision making and the power of choice.

God gave man the dignity of free will (Ezra 7:13 KJV). We are "free-moral agents," meaning, you are not a puppet, a robot, neither were we created self-sufficient; everything comes from God, we were made to think, we are capable of making up our own minds when making decisions. Angels have this same freedom and can think for themselves and to choose right or wrong; good or evil; heaven or hell; to obey or disobey God. You will read this in Part II, Creations in Heaven.

Throughout your lifetime, you will make numerous decisions. We make decisions hastily, we make them under pressure, we make decisions without really thinking, and we make decisions from a nature that is already erroneous from our meant-to-be creative thinking. You will use your will to choose which way to go in life when you come to that crossroads. In your conscience, you will make that decision, meaning heaven or hell as your final destination. At the end of the book are <u>three</u> of the most important decisions you will ever make in your life, they are at the top of your decision-making list, whether you now know it or not.

When you hear or feel God is calling in your life, answer that call in your heart, the call from within, remember, **it is all in the heart** and prayerfully you will choose eternal life, through the narrow gate, the narrow way of thinking, the strait path, by accepting Him. You will know in your heart, in your conscience, in your spirit that either you *willfully* made that choice or you *willfully* did not.

God will not interfere in your decision-making; he will not make up your mind for you. He will not make you do good, he will not make you do right, and he will not make you choose heaven. He will through his Spirit offer Christ to you. We must *willingly* want Christ in our life; we must prove ourselves to Him. We have to take control of our thoughts, and taking control of our thoughts, we take control of our will, taking control of our will, our conscience, our imagination, we surrender it to God then it is God's will that we do and not our will. If we stand steadfast in our thinking and take control of our will and making the right decisions, we will be strong disciplined human beings by having power over our will (1st Cor. 7:37ab ^{NIV}), self-control, and show we are worthy of His blessings. Going against your will to do what is right is initiating self-control.

A New Light

In doing this we unlock the inner most part of our will, the entrance to our spirit and open the door for the Holy Spirit to come in and work in us. Our will lays deep within us, but what lies deeper within the will is our spirit, our true identity, our connection with God. Our spirit lays dormant, it is the sin nature as a dark curtain pulled over our spirit, covered with darkness, which dulls our spiritual understanding. We cannot see what is spiritually before us.

The will is the gateway to our spirit. The will is very strong in the sin nature of unrighteousness and stands at the gate of your heart to stop God from entering through that gate to your heart. The will is the gatekeeper. Have you heard people described as being strong-willed or bullheaded, stubborn etc? Sure, you have. They are so programmed to the world and their beliefs that their freewill is dominated and influenced by those negative forces from **the spirit of error** the sprit that is of the world and their lives are lived more of a negative way through decision-making. They stop God from coming into their lives by having a negative *will* through the negative thought process and saying no, they do not want God in their lives, and for some they may say at least not now. This is a trick of the devil to keep them from giving their life to the Lord at that time.

What Satan is doing, he is buying time and hoping that you will die before you make the decision to ask Jesus Christ into your heart, because then, you will not make it into heaven. This is the spirit of unrighteousness, spirit of disobedience, spirit of rebellion, of deceptiveness talking through them. This is what Hosea 4:6 is saying, "My people are destroyed for lack of knowledge," saying no to God is saying no to spiritual knowledge. You receive this lack of knowledge by *willfully* rejecting it.

God will not force Himself upon you, but he will stand at that door and knock at (Rev. 3:20) the door of your heart, he will call out to you. The door of your heart is naturally closed by the sin nature; it covers your heart with the dark cloak of selfishness and unrighteousness and is closed to God. Your *will*, stands at the door and guards against the Lord from entering because you are a free-moral agent and can make decisions on your own, you have been programmed to a self-life and you are not going to accept or answer to anything invisible. Nevertheless, he is so patient and gracious that he stands at the door of your heart and knocks, calling you, waiting, that you will accept him and that you will *willingly* make the decision to ask Christ into your life, into your heart, this is at the crossroads. He wishes none to perish, but that <u>all</u> men be saved and come unto the knowledge of the truth (1st Tim. 2:4).

Offering or surrendering your will, you *will* be accepting him with your mind, your heart, and with your soul to what he is about to give you. Receiving Him, you will have and enjoy an intimate relationship and fellowship with the Lord Jesus Christ. Notice He says, "*Behold I stand at the door,*" He is waiting for you to open your heart to Him. This shows the paradox of grace of our Savior, he offers this opportunity because He wishes none to perish and it shows our personal responsibility by taking control-of-self and come into the reality of who you really are. Mentioned earlier that the entrance of your heart being closed by the sin nature, but He does not immediately withdraw. He wants to be gracious, although God <u>desires</u> the salvation of all men. He will not violate their opportunity to choose.

To answer God's knock at the door humble yourself, look into your soul, feel your soul, do you feel that void, an emptiness. Your soul is a lost and bewildered component of your being. It is out there being absorbed and conformed to a godless system that lacks God's truth. We are born with ideas, concepts, influences from the wrong side of the tracks and that disobedience to God will leave the sinner lost.

Be *willing* to surrender yourself, your will, to God, to truth. Be *willing* to push and reach through the darkness for the Lord and he will pull you through. By doing so, your spirit will burst past your will and His Spirit will come into you, and you will enjoy His presence and His graciousness. When you open the door of your heart and receive Christ, you become a child of God. Listen to what the book of Romans 8:16 says; "*The Spirit Himself* (that is His Spirit, the Holy Spirit, the third element of the Trinity) *bears witness with our spirit that we are the children of God."* His Holy Spirit speaks to our heart, our spirit and tells us that we truly are God's children.

If you do not want God in your life, the door of your heart, because of your will, in the sin-nature will remain closed to the truth, the truth of life, you will live the rest of your days an incomplete person, not knowing the truth of life, or who really you are. Without God in your life, without Jesus Christ as your personal savior, your destination will not be heaven nor will you have real life. When one *willfully* makes a choice to live the world's ways rather than to choose life, which is light to man through God's word, they choose to live in unrighteousness, in darkness, in sin, in unbelief. They chose not to be saved, because they prefer the deeds of evil they are doing, this fills the void. Through this, the unbeliever will be judged. *"And the **judgment** is based on this fact: God's light (Jesus) came into the world, but people loved the darkness more than the light, for their actions were evil"* (John 3:19 NLT).

We have what we think is freewill but our will lies in our choice of thought. The power of making a reasoned choice or decision of controlling one's own actions is in the power of the will. The will has and is power; we must exercise and control this power. We have the freedom of choice and the freedom of decision. Our flesh is under great submission of the sin nature and we are running away from God. We must direct this power to the higher power of God and surrender our will and ourselves to Him. As we take power over our will, over self, which is taking power over our flesh, this is settled in the mind (1st Cor. 7:37 NIV). Not our will, but His will must be done. This is why so many individuals struggle when trying to break bad habits. Years of trying to control dieting, stop smoking, stop cheating, stop drinking, stop drugs, stop perverted sexual acts and the like, the flesh is very weak. All you really want is victory over these habits, if you really want to know the truth, if you really want God in your life and want to know him then you must determine to do your part. Your part is surrendering your will over to Him. Do not your will, but do His will; His will, will be done in your life. Now He can work in your life according to His good pleasure.

In Isaiah 1:18-19 ᴷᴶⱽ the Lord says he wants us to be _willing_ to reason with Him and _willingly_ be obedient to Him and repent of our sins, we will be forgiven. We need to be _willing_ and obedient. Is that too much to ask for the forgiveness of our sins and eternal life?

If we yield not to God's will, our human will, will yield to the _will_ of the flesh, in the sin nature. You will remain in darkness, living the ways of the world and it will leave you to fulfill your sexual fantasies, desires and all the lust of the flesh. You will be filled with the pride of life and linger in untruth, and doubt, and be separated from the Spirit of God and continue to live a life of pride and telling lies and believing lies like evolution, humanism, atheism, agnosticism, and secularism that sway you in a false delusional world until your last breath. You will remain disillusioned, depressed and lost.

Freewill is the ability to choose what you want, you not only have the ability to choose what you want but you exercise that ability every moment of your life. "Man's choices are determined by his desires or inclinations and he always chooses in harmony with his strongest desire of inclination of his choosing." This is freewill, for the very essence of freedom is to be able to choose what you should not what you want.

God gave us freewill for our independence, even if that means not wanting to know him, and even if that means rejecting him, the choice is ours.

Without God, man is free to choose what he wants but he is in bondage to the sin nature and the sinful desires and inclinations of his heart and his life remains infected with the sin nature, so he chooses in harmony with his sinful desires and his sinful inclinations, _willfully_. Reality of the freedom of will in the sin nature is this, you think you have freedom in the sin nature, but you are choosing the carrot dangling from a string in front of you, and holding the string is the devil.

In our human nature, when a desire reaches a certain degree of passion, our will becomes involved. The will controls your moods, attitudes, habits, and even your relationships that will cater to your willful desires. Control the carnal mind, you will control the flesh, then surrender the will. The less we know of this, the more ignorant we become.

We are to get to know God, worship and serve him with a clean heart and a *willing* mind. The Lord sees every heart, understands, and knows every thought. If you seek him, you will find him; but if you forsake him, he will permanently throw you aside.

Pertaining to this book, you *will* believe, or you *will* not believe. "Your will is the facility of choice; it decides the course that you will take." You must understand that in the natural your will is the governing power of decision-making, the determining factor in making your choices in life. Everything in your life will depend on the right or wrong action of your will. The right or wrong decision you make *willingly*, will determine your final destination in life

You make the choice of what you want to believe in life, you make this choice on what you hear, read and see. No one is going to force you; you *willing* make the choice of what you want to be. If you want to be a believer or a unbeliever, an atheist, an evolutionist, a skeptic, a secularist, a humanist the choice is yours, the latter there is a consequence to this, judgment. Your will, will determine the path you take in life, through the wide gate or the narrow gate.

"NOTHING IN THE WORLD IS MORE DANGEROUS THAN THE SINCERE IGNORANCE AND CONSCIENTIOUS STUPIDITY"

— Martin Luther King Jr.

PART II

IN THE VERY BEGINNING

Chapter 4

Creations in the Heavens

Before humans inhabited the world, the only life that existed in the universe was God, the Word of God and the Spirit of God (Gen. 1:1–John 1:1), and God created the heavens. The Word of God refers to his Son, Jesus, the second person of the Trinity. It is hard for us to think or understand that at one point in the history of the universe in this vast celestial harmonious order, there was absolutely no one else, no angels, except God, this Trinity of God, but so the Bible says.

Creation is the act of God whereby he called into existence what did not before exist, He created the heavens, and stretched them out, and He created the earth. He knows the number of stars and gave every star a name. God created all the worlds, our sun and moon, all the heavenly host, these are the formation of the universe, and He created the winds (Gen. 1:1-Psa. 147:4-Heb. 1:2c-Gen. 1:14-18-Ps. 148:1-5-Amos 4:13b NIV).

If you notice, it says that God created the heavens, plural, and the earth. The Bible speaks of three heavens. First is the visible sky, our starry heaven, next to and around the earth. It is the atmosphere in which clouds float, where rain descends and where the birds fly.

The second heaven is the home of the sun and moon, the stars and the planets. The third heaven is the highest; here is

God's dwelling place, where God's throne is. It is where the angels are, and where the redeemed shall ultimately be (John 14:2).

In Ephesians 4:10 Paul tells us of the One who ascended far above the heavens and was caught up to the third heaven, speaking of Jesus at His ascension.

At some point God created His living pleasures. He created heavenly creatures for His glory, whether they are angels, or creatures called cherubs, cherubim's, seraphim's or other angelic host of God's creations of creatures, those majestic beings in the spiritual realm.

Angels we ordinarily understand as a race of supernatural spiritual beings of a nature exalted above man. Messengers of God and they are our defenders while we are here on earth. Billy Graham wrote, "Christians should never fail to sense the operation of an angelic glory. It forever eclipses the world of demonic powers, as the sun does a candle's light."

They have their individual personalities, their intelligence is superior to man, and they are ministers of the supernatural providences of God. Angels do have emotions, and under God's rule, they guide us, they care for us, they are agents in the great scheme of the spiritual blessings, redemption and sanctification of man. Angels do not die, they are spirits and they have spiritual heavenly bodies. They were never humans.

Cherubs, Cherubim's, Seraphim's (Ezek. 10:2, 7 [NIV]) are an order of celestial beings. Seraphim are whom Isaiah beheld in a vision standing above Jehovah God as He sat upon His throne. As majestic, as these creatures are Isaiah 6:2 has an infinitesimal description of their outward appearance. These celestial beings are closely related to the throne of God, they stood guard of the Deity. God mightily uses Cherubim's, in guarding the Throne of God (Ps. 99:1c). God did ride upon a Cherub (2nd Sam. 22:11-Palms 18:10).

Within the angelic realm, there are rankings or orders of these angelic creatures. They have responsibilities and are faithful, loyal and thankful to perform them. There are also heavenly angels on earth that encamp around them that fear God and love God, those that fear God these are his children. In God's kingdom, angels typify many corporate acts, some are ministering spirits to us on our human level, and of course, they are messengers to us. In the unseen spiritual realm, these angels execute the command of God when called upon. Three of these angelic hosts were the archangel Michael; there is Gabriel, and Lucifer.

In Jude verse nine, Michael is noted as an archangel, his high-ranking authority over the angels, and they rank down from him. His tremendous authority means to be the first in political rank and power. He and other angels warred victoriously against the enemies of the people of God. These enemies are the devil and his angels (Rev. 12:7).

Gabriel the messenger, was commissioned to Mary, to tell her she was chosen to the high privilege of being mother of the Messiah (Luke 1:26, 27, 28, 31). He was sent to interpret a vision to the prophet Daniel, and again he was sent to Daniel to give him skill and understanding and reveal to him the prophecy of his people. He was sent to Zacharias to announce the birth of his son; he was to name him John this child would become John the Baptist (Luke 1:13), Gabriel is customarily standing in the presence of God (Luke 1:19).

These angels have special places and task in heaven including the Holy Mountain of God, where God's throne resides.

We are going to focus our celestial spiritual telescope in on Lucifer, the one angel who was perfect in all aspects of completion (Ezek. 28:12c) that God himself did give him a special place upon the Holy Mountain (Ezek. 28:14b) to bring glory to God. Lucifer was the most powerful of God's creatures, perfect in beauty and full of wisdom (Ezek. 28:12b). Lucifer in Hebrew means, son of the morning, or star of the morning (Isa. 14:12 [NIV]). He was created to be a servant of God. He was an anointed angel, indicating his high office with authority and responsibility. This was a high order and specific placement by God himself, with a unique opportunity to bring glory to God with harmonious crescendos of worship.

Angel in the Greek: means messenger, envoy. Angels are celestial beings; spiritual beings, God made His angels spirits (Ps. 104:4-Heb. 1:7), eternal living spirits.

The Original Sin In Heaven

This is Why there is evil

This anointed angel became jealous of God because of the glory, honor, worship and reverence that was bestowed Him. This jealousy puffed up Lucifer with pride and power (Ezek. 28:17 ^{NLT}), and with self-exaltation, this was the original sin and it took place in heaven. Because of his beauty, because of his power, because of his wisdom, because of his authority, he believed he and other angels could dethrone God and take over God's throne, the heavenly Kingdom, and the entire heavenly host would worship him.

Lucifer had authority and power over other angels and in a subtle, deceiving, cunning, lying manner approached other angels with this misguided attempt and told them what he believed they could do. Sin started to compound, it got worse and lead into more lies. The Bible says that he is the father of lies (John 8:44b), meaning he was the first who told a lie. Here in heaven, as hard as this is to comprehend, sin originated from pride, covetousness, he wanted what God had, and lies evolved as rebellion and disobediences came from Lucifer.

Lucifer made his choice, he *willingly* choose to go against God. He made his decision on his own and the other angels that followed him *willingly* made the same choice, the same mistake, to *willingly* follow Lucifer and *willingly* go against God. *Willful* sins; they misused their God given freedom of will.

Lucifer made this statement, a bold announcement, his declaration against God. He was asked, *"How art thou fallen from heaven O Lucifer, son of the morning?"* (Isa. 14:12a) meaning he was asked why he was cast out of heaven, *"For thou said in thine heart"* (Isaiah 14:13, 14), evil originates in the heart; rebellion comes from the heart, Lucifer's declaration against God.

"I *will* ascend in heaven

I *will* exalt my throne above the stars of God

I *will* sit also upon the mount of the congregation, on the sides of the North,

I *will* ascend above the heights of the clouds,

I *will* be like the most-high God," is this narcissism or what? Lucifer performed blasphemy at its highest degree. This is the same thing as saying today, I do not need God in my life, or, there is no God, I *will* do my own thing, and I *will* do it my way. He made his choice. Can you see all the pride here, look at the five vain "I *wills*." This will lead him into eternal damnation.

The First War
Heaven Filled With Violence

In this passage God is speaking directly to Lucifer, he is in his face, *"Thus saith the Lord God, thou sealest up the sum, full of wisdom, perfect in beauty." "Thou are the anointed angel that coverth, and I have set thee so, thou was upon the holy mountain of God." "Thou was perfect in thy ways from the day that thou was created, til iniquity,* (Heb. perversion, evil, fault, mischief, sin, lawlessness) *was found in thee"* (Ezek. 28:12b, 14a, 15 [KJV]). Lucifer misused his God given will, tempting himself and other angels to go against God, their Creator. The sin of pride lifted him up, puffed him up. Lucifer wanted to be praised and worshipped by the entire heavenly host; he *willingly* chose to go against God.

Lucifer led an organized army of angels against God and His Kingdom in an ill fail attempt to overthrow Him, but they failed. God said, *"By the multitude of thy merchandise thy have filled the mist of thee with violence, and thou hath sinned: therefore I will cast thee as profane,* (unrighteous) *out of the mountain of God: and I will destroy thee"* (Ezek. 28:16 KJV).

The number of angels that followed him is uncertain, but in the book of Revelation 12:4a, here the stars are symbolic with angels. The Bible says, *"His tail drew a third of the stars of heaven, and threw them to the earth."* Here you see Lucifer and the immoral hostile angels were cast to earth. They are now Satan and the demonic forces on this planet. Whatever the total amount of angels there were in heaven, no doubt multiple of millions possibly billions, one third of them are now with us. The Bible says that the angels are innumerable (Heb. 12:22).

They *willfully* choose to war against God, to go against Him and they lost. Lucifer and his angels fell from high honor and power to an abyss of shame and misery. At this time in heaven's history, Lucifer became Satan and the angels that followed him became his demon angels. They became the dark side of the spirit life.

FROM THIS POINT, LUCIFER WILL NOW BE CALLED SATAN FOR HE IS NO LONGER AN HONORABLE ARCHANGEL

Chapter 5

CREATION OF THE HUMAN RACE

❦

The Bible says that man was made in the image and the likeness of God (Gen. 1:26). *"And the Lord God formed man of the dust of the ground, and **breathed** into his nostrils the **breath of life**; and man became a living soul"* (Gen 2:7 KJV) a living person, a living being. God first formed man with all his intricacies, and the man was no doubt standing and then God breathed life into him thus man being a total person, spirit, soul and body. How awesome, God breathed breath, His life, His spirit into man; man became a living human being, by God breathing the breath of life into man. Other translations write, *"became a living person, a living soul."* What does it mean, to be made in the image of God? Man created in the complete image of God, as a living breathing and immortal soul and in true holiness, righteousness, with the ability to think and reason and, filled with knowledge. God made woman, blessed them, and said to them, *"Be fruitful and multiple and replenish the earth, and subdue it: and have dominion over the fish of the sea, and over the fowl of the air, and over every living thing that moveth upon the earth."* This gave them authority of all the earth and ruled over living creatures (Gen 1:28 KJV).

They were complete, in spirit, soul and body, their lives were set before them, they were to start raising a family, and multiply that family. They were rulers, king and queen of this world. They lived in paradise, there was no kind of contamination, everything and everywhere was pure, even their innocent thoughts and minds. They were both naked and were not ashamed, (Gen 2:25) nakedness was natural to them, this was their pure state, they were complete, perfect in spirit, soul and body and with a freewill, they were created in a mind-state of innocence. Their knowledge was of their surroundings and as God walked with them, their purity was a natural thing, and their knowledge was of all good, not of good verses evil, they knew no evil to compare good with they were not ashamed.

Adam's job was to dress and keep the garden in order (Gen 2:15) Eve, his wife was made to be his helpmate (Gen 2:18). There was one stipulation, that they neither touch nor eat of the fruit of the tree of knowledge of good and evil, this tree was their test in a form of a commandant, *"for in the day that thou eatest thereof thou shall surely die"* (Gen 2:17). God set forth a command, (Gen 2:16, 17) in the nature of a covenant of life and death. It was not that the fruit of the tree was bad or poisonous, it was a simple meaning of trust, and obedience and He wanted them to remain obedient. God blessed all that was before them, all they had to do was obey Him. God was protecting them from evil because He loved them. It is the same way for man today, he wants to protect us but man is too rebellious, too stubborn and too independent to trust and obey God.

Our Adversary

The enemy of the human race is the devil, Satan, our adversary and his demons. Satan entered a serpent used this serpent as his mouthpiece and was more cunning than any other beast of the field (Gen 3:1) he was smarter, craftier, more subtle than any other. He is a liar and the father of it, the Bible says, he is out to destroy the human race, because we are made in the image and likeness of God, and he hates God, but he cannot get to God but he can get to us and he hates us with a passion. This is a characteristic of spirit beings they have the capability of entering our realm, and we being spirit beings ourselves they can penetrate our souls but not as easy as they can the animal world. Animals do not have spirits, but we can see here if the devil or demons find a need to enter the animal kingdom, it shows they can do it by Satan entering a serpent.

A serpent, overcome by the indwelling of Satan told Eve that the fruit of the tree was good, they could eat of it, and they would not die (Gen. 3:4). He told her that God wants to keep them away from the tree because if they ate of it they would become like God (Gen. 3:5). We were not made to be demigods, Satan deceived Eve and after the sin of disobedience, she knew that she and Adam we deceived, they immediately knew.

The Very First Sin,
On Earth
The fall of Man,

Eve saw that the fruit was good for food, it was pretty, and pleasant to the eyes (Gen 3:6), and it was desired to make one wise, so she did eat, she was so focused on advancing herself she did not consider the consequences and repercussions from disobeying God (Gen. 3:1-19). She *willfully* made the decision to go against God's command, she gave it to Adam, and he did eat of it. He *willfully* made his decision and their eyes were open. Their mind was open to the knowledge of evil, because they did evil through disobedience, which they never knew, and they knew they were naked and tried to cover themselves, they knew they did wrong (Gen 3:7). Here you can see the familiarity just as the first sin in heaven where iniquity was found in Satan, here it is found in our first humans, because of pride and vain deceit because of Satan's' invasion into their mind. In reality, they yielded to their fleshly appetite, their desire to be something other than what they were created to be. Through the selfish act of disobedience, they forfeited their dominion, their rule of earth over to Satan; they fell from the state of innocence and being sinless and because of their disobedience entered the state of consciousness and corruption.

This was the fall of man; this was the first sin on earth that turned man to a slave, a slave to Satan and the demonic forces of darkness all because of pride, vain deceit and disobedience, the same that Satan used when he was Lucifer and carried out his rebellious act in heaven. Sin started compounding from this time on. The earth is a huge ball of dust and totally contaminated with sin.

They *willfully* disobeyed God, *willfully* used their will by actually saying, I *will* eat, in essence they were saying I *will* do what I want, which lead to disobedience. They broke the covenant and they made their choice to do what they wanted to do. They were free to make up their own minds and when they had that disobedient thought and acted on it, at that point, they sinned; they died a spiritual death and set forth great judgment on man. Physically at that moment they were fine, they did not die physically, but they set in motion for the body to die because of their sin, they brought this spiritual and physical death upon themselves and the entire human race. In addition, do not forget about the curse of the earth also from the sin.

One of Satan's tactics is to lead us into rationalization and making a rash decision in order for immediate benefits could be hurtful. Here you can see Adam and Eve rationalizing between these two. One saying, if you disobey you will surely die, the other saying, it would be okay, you will become as gods, and you will not die. When the serpent confronted Eve, she initially answered him in pure innocence; she did not consider the outcome of her actions. As you will see, it was their fleshly desires, (one of Satan's targets) that lead them astray.

Before the fall, man's nature rested on earth in its pure state of innocence, in all aspects of their lives, when God told them they would surely die, dying did mean physical death, which would take place later in their lives but more so it meant spiritual death which took place immediately. Their spiritual death meant they separated themselves from God, also inadvertently separated their spirit of eternal life with Him, the spirit of God in them. They were no longer total beings, now they were incomplete. They were now body and soul, minus the spirit, two-thirds of being complete, they were now living a two dimensional life. This is where we are today we live a two-dimensional life, body and soul. The great fall of man in the garden, who tripped over the snare of the devil, succumbed to the second most powerful intelligence in the universe a diabolical spirit that man is no match against him, and man is its spiritual slave.

The first humans lived under the covering of the divine nature. They had a privilege, a right and were capable of making up their own minds on how they wanted to live their lives. Unfortunately, for them and us, they *willingly* made the wrong choice. By sinning, they gave up their authority of the earth to Satan. They were free to choose and they *willingly* chose to disobey the command, rebelled and broke God's covenant and this act of disobedience ushered sin into the world corrupting humanity. Since they sinned they gave up their spirit, their spirit life, their communion with God, this was another penalty, consequence for their disobedience. They lost their spirituality and sent man into a whirlwind of sorrow. Now their children and <u>all</u> humankind inherited the sin nature. This original sin has conveyed posterity by natural generation, through man's linage. All humans are <u>conceived and born</u> in sin we are born sinners (Ps. 51:5, NLT-Rom. 5:12). We are sinners because sinners produced us.

You would surely die, did not just mean a physical and spiritual death for Adam and Eve, it meant every human ever born would be born spiritually dead, born an incomplete person, and born with physical death waiting them. In addition, we inherited the curse of this ball of dirt. God sent them out of the garden, multiplied their sorrow, and cursed the ground (Gen. 3:16-19). We live on a cursed planet, sin fills its air, hence we all have the capability of doing horrific things, this is why there are horrific things done, and we live in a sin-filled world.

When Adam sinned, sin entered the world, sin brought death, and sin and death spread to everyone, everyone is a sinner and everyone will experience death. Death is the removal, the separation of the soul from the body, it is a place of no return, and it can be a land of gloom, deep regret, deep sorrow and deep darkness (Job 10:21 ^{NIV}). Our physical death is losing that God given gift, the breath of life.

Man is still a spiritual being; he will live forever in eternity somewhere. Eternity does not necessarily mean heaven when man dies. Man's spirit is not alive in him, it is inactive, it is dormant, and it is asleep, or spiritually dead. Man lost his spiritually, his connection with God because of the first sin in the garden and only God can make your spirit come alive. This is done by being born again. Being born again is your spirit brought to life through the grace and mercy of God. Being born means new life does it not? In reality, the choice is yours to receive eternal life.

We all came from these first humans, and we all inherited the sin-nature of darkness, of unrighteousness and its consequences of sinning. From this first sin came death, unrighteousness, murder followed shortly after this between two-brothers. Satan immediately went to work in these souls; one of their sons killed the other. Suffering, wrongdoing, chaos, confusion, rebellion, disease, killings, wars, troubled-minds and on and on and continues in this world today, all, from yielding to temptation because of pride.

What happened?

There has always been a physical and spiritual aspect of the human life. The first humans lived their physical lives in the covering of the divine nature, for the spirit of God was in them. They lived a spiritual/physical life, God breathed life into them and they became living beings. Their spirit was alive, active toward God. This was their purity. The divine nature has no dark side, no darkness of corruption, and no evil. The dark side of the spirit world is its own identity. When Satan and his cohorts were cast to earth, they became the dark side of the spirit realm, where evil lives.

Those first humans co-existed with the dark forces of evil, but were seriously unaware, oblivious of their existence. We also co-existed with these dark forces of evil and ignorant of their power and their potential evil capabilities and some still doubt their existence.

They being pure in innocence were vulnerable to the deceptiveness of lies from the craftiest, slyest, and most cunning master deceiver himself, the devil. We cannot imagine an evil super intelligent supernatural spirit from the depths of darkness, covertly entering a reptile manifesting itself and conversing with the humans, but this is exactly what happened. A supernatural being can do things you cannot imagine. Think about this, Satan and his demon angels have the capability of entering any living being they choose, animals, mammals, and especially the mind of the human race. They thrive on living organisms. I personally believe they can enter wild carnivorous animals and those vicious flesh eating dogs, that so many use for watch dogs, or for protection that have killed or maimed so many beautiful innocent children, demons will use any means of killing, and destroying the human soul. I determine this from a passage in Matthew where demons were cast out of a demon-possessed man, and when they left that man, the evil demon spirits went into a herd of swine. They find rest in the souls of man, but man finds unrest.

Visit the garden.

These humans were living in a paradise, experiencing something new every day. Satan, who roams the earth watching everything that goes on (Job 1:7b NLT) looking for prey, human souls, as he does today, sought them out and he indwelt a serpent, stood upright, and talked with them. We cannot phantom this, but to them in their innocent minds it was another divinely creative creature, living with them in their newly created garden like world. Satan is the master of disguise, as you will learn. The cunning, deceptive dialogue began.

Satan had an ulterior motive. First, he wanted to get them from God, from the covering of the divine nature of purity, by sinning, by being disobedient, in doing so, they would secondly, die the spiritual death, give up their spirit and they would spiritually relinquish their authority of the earth, over to him, and third, the sin nature would prevail. It happened in just that manner. Satan deceived the humans. In Genesis 3:13 the woman admitted to God that the serpent deceived her. What is interesting here is that she did not know Satan as he talked through the serpent; she told God the serpent deceived her. I have read testimonies of people who have committed horrible crimes; they have said, "the devil made me do it." They sensed an evil about them. She realized immediately that she was deceived; she also realized immediately when God's Spirit left her. They lived in innocence, their minds lived in purity and they knew no evil, life was innocent to them up to that time but then, they sinned. They broke the covenant with God, lost their authority of the earth to Satan, lost their spiritual purity and their decency, lost their communion with God, and now were only body, soul, and slaves to Satan.

At this stage of their life's journey, for the first time they now knew good and evil. Now an antichrist spirit is the authority of this world. He is the god of this world (2 Cor. 4:4 NLT). His sinister master plan worked, he sent man into whirlwind of sin, he has taken over the planet, and the sin nature is very much active in the world today and working its elements of evil throughout the planet but his plan does not end there.

His spirit runs the course of this world. His plan is to deceive, destroy every person he possibly can. He is striking with intense blows, malevolent forces, with the same craftiness, honed to perfection in deceptiveness, implanting delusions of grandeur, evil imaginations, and personal fantasies at the very young to the very old. Age groups do not matter to him, he will attack humans of any age, what he wants is their soul. He wants to take the soul down before that soul becomes a Christian; he wants to ruin your life, that you may spend eternity with him in hell.

Satan is after our young people, he knows that the very young are susceptible and very easily bent-towards darkness, of the sin nature. Their minds are like sponges, sopping up every doctrine of error that comes along. They believe what they hear and it embeds deeply in their mind. Our young are showing us this today. He has many on alcohol, many hooked on drugs, many smoking and ingesting things they should not, perverse sexual activity he tempts them with, he has pierced bodies with objects of no meaning and inked fleshly bodies of individuals with sadistic drawings. They will carry these bent attitudes into their adulthood and grow into a dangerous obsessive fixation with the self within them. Growing more obsessive with power, power freaks they are known as control freaks. The devil will use any means that interest man, whether physically, emotionally or psychologically. With all the cultish books and movies, capturing our young in promoting witchcraft with their twisted idles in believing demons are friendly and their soul is a demon in the form of an animal, this path leads to hell.

Satan knows what you do not know. As evil, and as diabolical as he is, he does know what the truth is and he knows the natural man does not know the truth because man lives in the sin nature where spiritual truth can not be obtained, he severed this vessel of living truth when he persuaded man to sin. He wants to keep you from the truth and he does a very good job in keeping you, your mind, your thoughts, and your imagination literally in spiritual darkness where he will influence and even possess if permitted. He can do this and he does do this to human minds and the hearts of man, this is a way that he infiltrates us.

The truth is this; there is the divine nature, which is accessible to us while we live in the sinister sin nature that governs this world and deceives the people of the world. We have a choice, either live in the sin nature of unrighteousness, down the wide path of life, the carnal way of thinking with open mindedness or the divine nature of righteousness, the narrow path, living the spiritual/physical life, the choice is ours.

In the sin nature, a penalty comes with sinning. In the divine nature, there are rewards and blessings for those walking in the divine nature, how about the reward and blessing of immortality. There is no other way out of sins darkness into immorality than through the Light, (Jesus) which penetrates darkness, man cannot approach immortality any other way, and for Jesus is the only way.

You can understand if a light is shut off, what do you have, darkness. Without the Spirit living in you, you are considered dead because you live in darkness, a condition without spiritual understanding, in the sin nature. Living in darkness is living with no spiritual understanding because of the lack of knowledge. You have no light in you, no spiritual light; this is why there is no discernment in spiritual matters. We are like spiritual zombies, we walk around like we own this world and that it owes us something in all the while we are incomplete beings. The Bible explains in 1st Timothy 5:6 [NLT] that even though we live here in this world with all its pleasures that we love, that we are spiritually dead, asleep, even though we live, we are like the walking dead.

We live physically but are dead spiritually. If you have the Spirit, the Holy Spirit of God in you, you would have life because you would have spiritual light, *"In him (Jesus) was life, and that life was the light of men"* (John 1:4 [NIV]). Jesus came *"to open their eyes, and to turn them from darkness to light, and from the power of Satan unto God, that they may receive forgiveness of sins, and inheritance among them which are sanctified* (set apart, set apart from non believers) *by faith that is in me."* (Acts 26:18) Therefore, He says: *"Awake, you who sleep,* (who are spiritually dead) *arise from the dead, and Christ will give you light,"* (Eph. 5:14) this light makes everything visible, (e.g. understanding, discernment, and truth). This light is the Holy Spirit that will shed light, upon your spirit, and illuminate your understanding.

> **"In each of us there is a little of all of us."**
> **— George Christopher Lichtenberg**

We were born in the ancient sin nature of old; we are <u>all</u> born in sin, and not the divine nature of spiritual purity, and being born in sin, we are sinners. We were in spiritual darkness, a delusion from the very beginning of our lives, spiritually that is. Every human is born in sin and that of course is because of the contamination of that first sin, we all have this in common, it is a natural characteristic of the human life, from one man, then from generation to generation resulting in condemnation. The Bible says that the wages of sin is death, and it says that the gift of God is eternal life in Christ Jesus our Lord. Death is from this first sin, and death is from the devil.

Unless you had born again Christian parents or grandparents, or some other loving caring person in your life when growing up and showing you the way to the truth and Christian principles at a very young age, you were lost in having spiritual knowledge.

The sin nature holds our minds back from the truth; our minds are in spiritual bondage without us knowing it, this is the condition of darkness. This is why Jesus says when you are born again, *"then you will know the truth, and the truth will set you free"* (John 8:32 ^{NIV}), until when? Until you are born again, converted, regenerated you are not at liberty to know the truth.

You must get this

Having God's knowledge knows what truth is, it is having knowledge of the truth, you must have God's knowledge, to have God's knowledge you <u>must</u> be born again and then be a student of the Bible. When you are born again, converted,

God's Spirit comes alive in you, you have your own personal miracle, he gives us his Spirit (1st John 4:13 NIV). The way to God, the way to truth is through Jesus, for Jesus is the way and the truth (John 14:6). He is the spirit of truth. Jesus will break the chains of bondage and release the truth unto you, because the truth is in the Spirit and the Spirit dwells in you. No longer are we ruled or controlled by the sin nature, but by the Spirit of God because we now belong to him. Those without the Spirit, the sinner, the unbeliever are not his (Rom. 8:9 NLT).

When this happens, you will know that you have been living a very sin filled and sinful life, and you will realize that life, and the world, are sinful and sin filled. You will know that you have been living a life of spiritual blindness, a life of disobedience toward God, *willful* disobedience and you will know that you have been obedient to Satan while you were doing the things of the world, because the workings of his kingdom will be revealed to you.

Your mind was deceived, darkness held it in bondage and captivity. When one is converted, he gains knowledge of Jesus and he gains knowledge of Satan, he gets to know them both but now, has a relationship with Jesus and not with the devil's sin nature.

While doing worldly things, you may know deep within you that you are doing things that you should not be doing or saying things, you should not be saying according to the goodness of life. Maybe you did not realize you were going against God and you certainly did not realize that a satanic identity was leading you further and deeper in a downward spiral into a deeper inky darkness away from God, away from the truth and away from life. You probably think you are being your own person, doing what you want in life and not having to answer to anyone and not realizing the sin nature is deceiving you in the captivity of your mind. These mysteries are hidden from unbelievers because they *willfully* choose not to believe and receive Christ and God's knowledge. Only to born again believers are mysteries revealed. The Bible says that "*you* (believers) *are permitted to understand the secrets, but others are not* (Matt. 13:11 ᴺᴸᵀ). The others are the unsaved, the unbelievers the rebellious ones that have not accepted him.

The mystery of God's will also is revealed to us (Eph. 1:9). These Bible mysteries are hidden, requiring special revelation from God that people of the world could never know by depending on the world and their own understanding.

Chapter 6

OUR SPIRITUAL INHERITANCE

Became a
Dichotomy

As we continue on our journey, remember what you are reading in this book is biblical truth, biblical knowledge predicated on the written word of God, which is spiritual truth, absolute truth from the Holy Bible, given by God.

When Satan took over authority of this planet, the human race was inherently born into a sinful nature that no one escapes. We all, with no exceptions are influenced by it and we all possess it. It influences us to sin and we sin, our fleshly desires rise up in this sin nature because man is weak and give into its temptation. This sin nature blinds and binds our thoughts and understanding of the spirit realm where discernment of right and wrong come to mind. Adam and Eve were born in innocence; but their children were born into this sin nature, because of their parents' sin and every generation since, we are sons and daughters of Adam. When they yielded to sin and acted out the sin, their innocence left them, sin came in the world and with the sin, spiritual blindness bound their and our understanding, consequently, this is our spiritual inheritance. In the beginning, their human nature was in covenant with God's divine nature, now because of the fall the human nature is in covenant with the sin nature.

The Dichotomy

Planet earth belongs to God, but, because of the fall of man, earth is temporarily ruled by Satan, which means this, God owns the universe as far as it extends and all that is within, including all living matter. Satan is the temporary ruler, prince, and the god of this world, which leaves us with **two** natures, the sin nature, because he rules the world, in addition to this shadow of darkness there is a gleam of light, the divine nature, and the divine nature is God's nature, in which God created the world and us. Within these two natures, the population is separated and within these two natures, all of us are being watched. One is our enemy, the god of this world and the other is our friend, the God of the universe.

This is our inheritance, the sin nature and all the evil baggage that comes with it. The sin nature is the dark segment of the spirit world that has access to our spiritual, physical, mental, and material world; the most diabolical creature in the universe, put the souls of the planet into a division, like a sadistic strike of lighting, cutting us away from God.

Within these two natures are two supernatural forces, invisible, and intellectually superior to man. They are the governing forces encompassing this world, God and Satan. Because of these **two** different and conflicting natures, they leave us with only **two** kinds of people on the planet, and only **two** ways to live life. We were left with a **two** dimensional life, on a plane of incompleteness and **two**, only **two** destinations waiting us after death.

These **two** authorities of power rule their own nature. God rules the divine nature Satan rules the sin nature. God's kingdom is the visible and the invisible universe not just the heavens where the planets, stars and galaxies are, and beyond but here, in man's spirit.

Satan's kingdom is the first heaven, the air, where clouds are, where planes and birds fly, where hurricanes, typhoons, cyclones, tornadoes originate and his kingdom includes the earth, which means he is not in hell, which many believe. These are the two supernatural powers, invisible, intellectual, governing forces, controlling their kingdoms, and encompassing this world. This is all taking place in the invisible spirit realm.

Swirling around us in the spirit realm are fierce demon spirits waiting for the right opportunity to devour a human soul. In the movie "Raiders of the Lost Ark" by Steven Spielberg at the latter part of the movie he showed evil spirits swirling around and tormenting humans, a small glimpse of spiritual terrorism. You cannot see television airwaves, radio airwaves, you cannot see microwaves, you cannot see the source of power for cell phones, you cannot see gravity but you know these are out there and they are working.

A note here, the devil does not travel from hell to earth to menace us, he lives here, and rules here.

The invisible power sources in our world are very real; they are more real than this physical life. One is on a mission to destroy and destruct through deceptive ways, to kill and to steal in any possible way imaginable and in ways you cannot imagine. The other wants to save you from this evil, save your soul and give you eternal life, if, you are *willing*. Which would you prefer? You do have the power of choice, to believe or not to believe, to live or to die.

The more powerful of these two is the power of God he is omnipotent, all-powerful. His is the divine nature, the light of the world. The power from Satan is not omnipotent his power is limited and controlled by his Creator. He is the sin nature, the darkness of the world; he is the spirit of error, he is the anti-Christ spirit. Both of these represent the **two** paths of life we can take; they have an affect on our physical, our psychological and our spiritual journey. Squeezed between the two is our human nature, looming out there in the spirit world, that will be attacked, devoured and destroyed or, will be saved. The choice is yours.

The **two** kinds of people are the righteous or the unrighteous, known as the believers or the unbelievers. The **two** ways of life are two behaviors of thinking, two styles of life through the wide gate, of open mindedness, a free for-all in the mind, any thing goes, or the narrow gate, the straight and narrow path in life focused on the Lord. The **two** dimensional life is living life in an incomplete state, the body and soul minus the spirit; the **two** destinations are heaven or hell, eternal peace or eternal torment. We will talk about hell in a bit, but one thing you should know about hell, God made it for the devil and his demons, not for people; but, man chooses to be evil and do evil and in doing so, man sends <u>himself</u> to hell.

In the beginning of earth's history when God created everything by speaking the Word, the Word (Jesus) gave life to everything, plants, animals, and yes, humans, everything that has life. There was no corruption on earth; this period is known as the dispensation of Innocence. The life given them also brought spiritual light unto them, spiritual understanding. This light brought understanding, enlightened their understanding and knowledge with wisdom of intellectual superiority. This light was the light of man. This dispensation lasted until the man and woman sinned by being in rebellion against God and his covenant and died a spiritual death (Gen. 2:17b) this sin of disobedience ushered in the dispensation of Conscience. Now they were conscious of their sin, and now they knew evil.

When they died spiritually, the Spirit of God left them, the Light left them, now darkness set in and entered man's life on earth. The passage of John 1:4 tells us that Jesus is life and in the life is the light. *"The Word gave life to everything that was created and his life brought light to everyone."* Without light, there is darkness, without life there is death. Here we are in darkness with physical death and now you know why. The Bible says we are blinded by darkness; we are born spiritually blind, spiritually dead because there is no Light (Jesus) in us. Without spiritual Light (Jesus) we live in spiritual darkness, spiritual darkness comes from not having God and Jesus Christ (life and light) in our lives.

Those first humans were created in light, in, enlightenment, they did not know any darkness, because there was no darkness, and there was no corruption, no sin, and no evil. They, because of the great sin, went from light to darkness, went from spiritual enlightenment to spiritual darkness, no enlightenment, to spiritual blindness, we on the other hand are born in spiritual darkness, born in sin, born in spiritual blindness, born in a corrupt nature and do not know the Light, we do not know spiritual enlightenment and never did. When they sinned, the Spirit of the Lord left them because a Holy God cannot live in unholy man, leaving them in a dark depraved state, this depraved nature this is what we inherited. Within this inheritance of darkness, our minds are naturally closed and our hearts are naturally hardened against God in unbelief. When an individual experiences the miracle of being born again that individual's spirit comes alive by the Spirit entering him. His spirit, his soul, moves from unbelief to truth, from darkness, to spiritual enlightenment, and spiritual understanding.

The Two natures

The Sin Nature

In God's eyes, if you are of the sin nature, of the world you are dead, spiritually dead, because you are in a sinful state. The sin nature is the nature of this world, hence, born is sin, (born in the sin nature) it oppresses us; it literally becomes part of us. It operates in the soul of man and is appealing to the carnal mind, it prohibits entry of our understanding into the spiritual realm and it closes God out of our lives.

Born in the sin nature we are born in sin, we are born as sinners. We all possess and are influenced to sin and this is the source of our sinful lust. This negative force stimulates our mind to the alertness of deeds of darkness. The enemy can attack us in mild areas of our life such as our eating habits, fleshly pleasures; smoking, drinking and even sleeping. He will take advantage of us, keep our minds lethargic, and render us useless in spiritual matters because the truth is not in us. *But people who aren't spiritual can't receive these truths from God's Spirit. It all sounds foolish to them and they can't understand it, for only those who are spiritual can understand what the Spirit means* (1st Cor. 2:14 NLT).

Those of the world think through their prideful carnal reasoning, which is opposed to spiritual truth. They are strangers to God and his word and enable their lives in sensuality. They are disconnected from the real meaning of life. They are like zombies in the sin nature, non-existent, with unconsciousness, deadness toward Godly matters because of the power of darkness. We humans are dead in our spirit but still with conscious awareness. God considers us dead while we live, spiritually dead while we physically live. Earlier mentioned 1st Timothy 5:6 this passage is referring to a widow, but refers to people in general, living in the world and not in the Spirit. *But the widow* (all those) *who lives only for pleasure is spiritually dead* (dead in trespasses and sins) *even while she lives*. Because of the sin nature, we are prodigals of our heavenly Father, our Creator. We are prodigals of our true identity, of who we really are. We are living a reckless and damaging life. We live in the sin nature and this sin nature rules us until we die as a sinner, or until we become followers of Christ.

Our sin nature sides with the devil's lie instead of God's truth, because we are sinners. We would rather believe the devils lie than God's truth. Sin is a disease that pulsates through the veins of the human race, it is part of us and we are part of it, we breathe its evil that circulates through the heart and digest its nature. The disease of sin is at the heart of the troubles of the world. No matter where you live on the planet, man is stricken by the sin nature; the sin nature is a disease of the heart.

Our human nature lives within the sin nature; here is where our daily lives exist. Unbeknown to us that our nature is first a sin nature and secondly controlled under the very keen and intense evil eye of the devil himself. By this nature, we are physically and spiritually doomed. Physically by physical death and spiritually by spiritual death, the second death, and that suits the devil just fine. For he knows the sinner living in the sin nature will go straight to Hades at death, then the judgment, then hell, not to die, but to live in torment for ever and ever and ever and never ending. This is because the sinner refused the gospel, refused the truth and God's invitation of salvation, so he remains a sinner as he passes through his physical death into the realm of forever-land. The devil knows this and it is a motivation for him to see a human soul go to the lake of fire.

The divine nature and the sin nature translate into good, and evil, righteous and unrighteous, and every human on the face of the earth whoever was, and is and yet to come, will live their days under the influence and power of God's Spirit the Holy Spirit, or the spirit of darkness, the antichrist spirit governed by Satan. This is a supernatural spiritual life and we are naturally born into the sin nature, but also while in the sin nature we are offered sometime in our lives while on our life's journey the opportunity to move into the divine nature, from darkness to light.

These two natures consist of two ways of life, two styles of life to travel as you have previously read. They both have their own distinctions. The divine nature is the narrow and straightforward path of life to travel. The traveler has his eyes fixed on one thing only and few travel this road with him. The sin nature is known as the wide path or wide road of life where the Bible says many do accompany this traveler. Between the two, man is found to be moral or immoral, in his qualities and activities of his life are determined. Think of his moral activities, his personality, his attitudes, how moral can his qualities be if he is only two-thirds complete and living in a sinful nature, without the Spirit of God and living in a world ruled by the devil himself. What a dark journey that is, but that is exactly how life is. He can only be and only do so much; his possibilities are limited according to the powers within the sin nature.

The irony is, those living in the divine nature know the truth of the sin nature, it has been revealed to them, they lived it, they been there and they have done it, shamefully. Those living in the sin nature traveling the wide road of life do not recognize where they are or not knowing where they are going, their mask has been removed and their identity, their individuality and their characteristics have been revealed by their life style, we know them. We know them by their ways, their actions, their speech and who they follower, by the path they travel.

The sin nature is a path that is not known as a path to death. Within its nature lie its allurements of sin. It encompasses the earth and is undetected like a stealth enemy and we are unaware, unknowingly consumed by its spiritual darkness of immorality. The world is impregnated by its evil. We live in the belly of this beast.

The sin nature is filled with wickedness, perverseness, filthiness, faithlessness, evil beyond your imagination. It is deliberately deceiving us and gives us an illusion of life in relationships, in religion, it takes away hope and leaves our hearts barren. It tells you money, material things, wealth will bring you happiness, and this can very easily put one in financial bondage and destroy one's future, family and at various times in one's life.

In the sin nature lives a life of unrighteousness, it is a life of uncertainties, unbelief's, and it keeps us from the truth, the truth of this life and eternal life. It keeps us from the knowledge of the truth. When the bible speaks of the last days it says in 2nd Timothy 3:1-4 *"that man will be lovers of themselves, lovers of money, boasters, proud people, blasphemers, the disobedient to parents, unthankful, unholy, unloving, unforgiving, slanders, people without self control, brutal people, despisers of good, betrayers, headstrong people, haughty people, lovers of pleasures rather than lovers of God."* These are God deniers, the unsaved, the unbelievers, and the unrighteous. Does this remind you of the mentality of this nation and the increase of evil in the world today?

In the sin nature, people are characterized by all kinds of self-centeredness and unnatural perversions. They will have a strong desire and intense craving for physical lust, and lust for things. Gratifying sensual cravings, desiring the forbidden, longing for evil, wanting what belongs to someone else. They will be striving for things, persons, and experiences contrary in opposition to God's will and want to justify what they are doing to what they believe is right, or, their right, in all the while they are fatally wrong.

In Matthew 15:19-20a the Bible says, *"for out of the heart proceed evil thoughts, murders, adulteries, fornications, thefts, false witness, blasphemies," "these are the things which defile a man."* The thoughts of the wicked are an abomination to the Lord. The Lord knows the thoughts of man, that they are vanity, how long vain thoughts shall lodge within the thoughts of the foolish, this is sin, we must wash our hearts from wickedness, that we may be saved. *"If you confess with your mouth that Jesus is Lord and believe in your heart that God raised him from the dead, you will be saved"* (Rom. 10:9). They are always looking in the wrong direction for answers to life, never learning spiritual knowledge and never able to come to grasp the understanding of the truth.

Doomed

We are already doomed to perish just by living; living in the sin nature lays the potential of being demon possessed by *willingly* living a life of evil, from this doomed vault. Choosing to live a ruthless life, a perverted life, living a life without any remorse towards others, living a life of self-openness towards evil, invites satanic forces to charge into the decaying soul.

The sin nature and the world is the domain of the devil, his playground, as well as anyone *willingly* who delves into sin, he is giving Satan and demons legal right to enter his soul, the sinner's mind, because the sinner *willfully* sinned. Habitually sinning in the sin nature, is inviting satanic activity to take place in the soul, now the sinner is possessed. Satan has the sinner legally; he has him by his *willful* actions.

In the sin nature, our minds and hearts are shaped in iniquity, basking under the cloud of darkness. Because of the sin nature, sin is twisted in our spiritual DNA. Everyone that is ever born is born into a corrupt nature, wretchedly degenerated from spiritual purity, honesty and truth, and God's truth is nowhere to found in the sin nature.

The sin nature is meant to keep us from God and if we are a child of God, born again it is bent to lead us into backsliding from God. Born in the sin nature we are born estranged from God, born with a wicked heart, born to work wickedness, alienated from divine life and of its principles, powers, pleasures and blessings. We proceed from evil, to evil. We adopt the sin nature's nature, naturally. Corruption is built into it; at birth, corruption is built into us. We soon learn to speak lies and we learn malice at a very young age. A person that tells a lie is not called a liar because he told a lie, he told a lie, because he is a liar. A thief is not a thief because he stole; he stole, because he is a thief and so it goes. We do what we do because we are what we are, sinners.

We are these things naturally; because we are born and live in the sin nature. Corruption is built into the sin nature that we adopt naturally. It is like a hallucinogenic drug of the worse kind, blowing in the wind, breathed and absorbed in our soul, lethal and very detrimental.

Although we do not know, what awaits us around every turn, every corner, but every step is calculated, cleverly laid to seduce you and lead you astray. It is a chartered course; it has been cleverly, ingeniously designed that you would not recognize its dangers, its allurements, its lies, its false teaching, its false religions, its philosophies, and its darkness and most of all, not knowing whose kingdom is secretly keeping you in its clutches. By what it has to offer, you want more of it.

Your journey through the sin nature is a maze of abominations, fornications, idolatries disguised as pleasures, warm acquaintances, experiences, allurements, and the dark side is attached to all these. These allurements from the dark side will lead you down dark slopes deeper into the dark of darkness with demons at every turn, every corner of life awaiting every opportunity to seduce your soul, and lead you from the heat to the oven. Demons are messengers of death.

Living in the sin nature, the world's ways, you are systemized; the Bible calls it being conformed, to the world's ways. Good people living in the sin nature doing what they think are good deeds are doing them for the wrong reason, the wrong motive, this is a trick, and a scheme of the devil, for the road to hell is paved with good intentions, and unaware to you that your journey is steadily declining into the abyss. Remember the path of your journey, was cleverly laid before you, and disguised as a normal place to be with doors that can be opened with loose morals and a *willing* attitude. Satan will come in with unleashed evil and because sinners have deliberately forfeited the truth so that they would be saved, deception is their life and deception is their future,

The sin nature feeds our fleshly nature and our human nature with passions and desires with physical appetites that prompt gross immorality and in this sin nature, it is all for **self**, nothing spiritual and certainly not for Jesus. People *willingly* living in a **self**-absorbed world, God has very little patience with because of their denial of His Son. This passage comes from the book of Romans 1:26-32 the New Living Translation. *"That is why God abandoned them to their shameful desires. Even the women turned against the natural way to have sex and instead indulged in sex with each other. And the men, instead of having normal sexual relations with women, burned with lust for each other. Men did shameful things with other men, and as a result of this sin, they suffered within themselves the penalty they deserved. Since they thought it foolish to acknowledge God, he abandoned them to their foolish thinking and let them do things that should never be done. Their lives became full of every kind of wick-*

edness, sin, greed, hate, envy, murder, quarreling, deception, malicious behavior, and gossip. They are backstabbers, haters of God, insolent, proud, and boastful. They invent new ways of sinning, and they disobey their parents. They refuse to understand, break their promises, are heartless, and have no mercy. They know God's justice requires that those who do these things deserve to die, yet they do them anyway. Worse yet, they encourage others to do them, too." People appear to be what they are not going through society with seemingly concern in their heart, but on the inside lays wolves in sheep's clothing.

The devil takes the sinner captive by the allurements of the sin nature. God has little tolerance for *willful* sinners, he loves them because they are his creation but they are foolish, they turn their backs on God, they are hardhearted and insensitive to God and His word. They live a godless life style, in opposition to God. Instead of praying and asking God for direction they are reliable on their own ideas of achieving things, they are dependent on their own **self**.

In the sin nature, we are born physically alive but spiritually dead, spiritually stagnated, without understanding. There is no dependence on the Spirit one iota. The sin nature is our lifeline and we feed from its nature, filled with its corrupted nature that wraps itself around your *will* like a chrysalis casting forming a cocoon, an amniotic sac entrapping your will feeding you stimuli from darkness from birth, we are in conformity with spiritual error and this darkness within holds our will captive. Within this entrapping state, we are alienated from God, our understandings of spiritual matters are blinded and our heart becomes corrupted with sin. Our will chooses what it chooses because of the condition of the heart.

Those who do not know Satan would not be aware by his subtleties. The sin nature is fully clothed with Satan's behaviors, his traits, his characteristics and even his personality. Satan, his nature we are born in, these behaviors, traits, his characteristics, and his personality birthed the sin nature, which promotes ungodly global-culture values, which captures man's desires and being ungodly man is totally in depravity. This is why greed is glorified by the ungodly; this is why idols are worshiped by the lost, this is why the seeking of personal pleasures, desires of the flesh and of the mind takes precedence over true spiritual matters.

Within the deep darkness of the sin nature, all humans are prone to this nature. It starts out with the human's first breath because the baby is born into the programs of its nature, the sin nature, and becomes part of it and it becomes part of the human. It continues with the child as the child grows and if left unattended, spiritually, with no spiritual growth, the child's whole life will be programmed into a godless system of untruth.

It is no accident that children spend hours in front of the television, as their life develops from watching cartoons to watching video games, movies with violent and sexual content and programs with filthy language and murderous plots, they are being programmed into a life of vicious uncertainties. Pornography has a huge grip on children and they carrier that into adulthood and you know what results this can bring, they are endless. Pornography, sexual perversion is a vicious tool that the devil uses to keep man's soul in a lost state.

In the sin nature you will never know the real you, you will never know the truth about life. Living in the sin nature will have a destructive impact on you. This sinful fallen nature leads to *willful* sins against God; these sins shut God out of your life. In the sin nature we are enemies of God, he is not our enemy we are his.

In the sin nature, reality and truth are absent. Kept from those living without reality and truth is a lost society, and without their knowledge, it will ripple down to devastation. The sin nature will lure the human soul to the pleasure sensing pathways of alcohol, drugs, food, crime, sex, perverted sex any pleasurable desire that attracts humans, we can call these addictions.

This is the adolescence of the sin nature; it continues pressuring the young to participate in its temptations, inclinations and its excitements.

This sin nature is your natural source, your only source of spiritual energy, which leaves you spiritual empty, from forces that rule in darkness, they will inject false spirituality. Living in the sin nature without Christ in your life, your life will be in harms-way, and also pitiless, and fruitless. The unseen, unknowing, and unbelieving forces in your life cannot be differentiated between them and your own self. This unseen force and you live in the sin nature, which are your natural inheritance, habitat and weakness. You inherited this by being born; we live in devil-land.

In the sin nature, we have developed a spirit of rebellion, a spirit of mythologies, and a spirit of no absolutes. This is because we are born blind spiritually blind with no godly insight. You have heard that there are only two-things for sure; taxes and death are these absolute truths? Oh yes, you will forever pay taxes and your day of dying is approaching. These are etched in terrestrial and celestial stones. Uncle Sam will not miss you; there is coming more after you to contribute to our deficit. When you experience death, which you know you will, your spiritual blinders will be removed, not by eye surgery but by physical death. It will now be too late for the sinner, but for the first time in his life, he will now see what he refused to see on earth, is the truth, the absolute truth.

The sin nature is a godless nature, it is a counterfeit, its façade is of untruth, and religious idolatry propaganda bent toward self. When a *willing* choice is determined to stay in the sin nature by turning away from the truth, a life corrupted with unrighteousness and vile ways uproar in the fools' heart that say there is no God.

The sin nature's nature is antichrist; it shows a strong emotion against anyone who believes in Christ and with this emotional attachment to the soul of the unbeliever. The unbeliever is persuaded, influenced, convinced to live a godless life, to believe lies, to indulge in appetites that feed **self**. The dark spirit that permeates the sin nature is the spirit of Satan, anti-god, antichrist, anti-truth, an antichristian spirit that breeds in the mind of the unbelievers. This antichrist spirit is the devils character personified throughout the sin nature. It is a spirit of oppression, of opposing, of antagonism, of possession against the things of God. The spirit of the antichrist is the most repulsive influence in this world and Satan is honing his perfection for the physical antichrist when he appears. The sin nature is as its name implies a nature contaminated with sin; and Satan takes every unfair advantage in our weaknesses, situations and circumstances in every one of us when there is a breach in our heart.

Occupying the sin nature

The sin nature is the abode of the devil and his demons; they will not enter a soul until there is an invitation by that soul who *willfully* chooses to live an evil life. When choosing to live an evil life the individual comes into agreement with the law of the spiritual nature. Satanic forces enter, set up camp, conquer the foothold, the sinner's weakness, create a stronghold, and possess the mind. They will harass, influence, persuade, badger, torment by their own means or by means of others that they influence and under their control. Satan unleashes his tactics, his strategies, and his tools of deception, of discouragement, of depression, his negative attitudes of un-forgiveness, bitterness, resentment, anger, and hatred and so on. Building a stronghold, they gain incredible power in one's life. At this point, the demons will use us; take advantage of us, to do horrific things to others and to our selves. All negative attitudes are demonically inspired and planted in the minds of the unbeliever. Hence, we do evil things because it is our nature. These are some acts of the sinful nature that man participates in, *"The acts of the sinful nature are obvious: sexual immorality, impurity and debauchery;* (lustful pleasures) *idolatry and witchcraft;* (sorcery) *hatred,* (hostility) *discord, jealousy, fits of rage,* (outburst of anger) *selfish ambition, dissensions, factions and envy; drunkenness, orgies,*(wild parties) *and the like. I warn you, as I did before, that those who live like this will not inherit the kingdom of God"* (Gal. 5:19-21 NIV). These are in disobedience to Godly values and Satan works on the sinner to lead a life of gratifying the cravings, the passionate desires and inclinations of our sinful nature and following its thoughts of the carnal mind.

The journey for the unsaved is a journey through spiritual darkness, a journey of evil wickedness, spiritual criminal unrighteousness, and a society of cold-blooded murderers, and for some, living a sin-filled life leaving regrets that cannot be taken away. In the sin nature, there are brainwashed people, who brainwash others that cause harm in the world, destroying families, marriages, societies, with no remorse.

Without Christ human nature can be diabolically stimulated with pride, selfishness, self-centeredness, huge-egos, a rebellious and stubborn spirit, cold and hardheartedness, anxiety and depression, fear and worry, sadness, doubts, lies, and superstition. Satan can bring on a state of loneliness, sadness, denying the truth, believing in abortion, pro-choice, evolution, atheisms, secular humanism, male and female homosexuality. You can withdraw from family, from society, you have a love of evil, living with wrong motives and wrong morals, living in idolatry, and adultery, envy, jealousy, drugs, drunkenness, bitterness, anger, liberal secularism, lust of the flesh and of the material world. There are defiantly God-haters, enemies of God with confusion and unbelief in their minds, unbelievers, because they believe lies that have no bases for their weak foundation.

The sin nature is a worldly nature that naturally separates us from God. We are restricted from him, we are opposed to him, we are in rebellion against him (Matt. 12:30a NLT), we are alienated from the only one true God, (Col. 1:21) and the inability to receive, comprehend or understand spiritual matters because of ignorance (the lack of spiritual knowledge) and spiritual blindness of the heart. You will learn that what drives you is all in the heart, in the mind. Sinners, the unsaved, the unbelievers are hopelessly confused, because their minds are full of darkness; they wander far from the life God gives because they have closed their minds and hardened their hearts against him (Eph. 4:17,18 ^{NLT}).

In the sin-nature, we think with the carnal mind. This is of the flesh, sensual, governed by human nature, the fleshly-nature instead of by the Spirit of God, which is the divine nature. The people of the world live by the sin nature and are controlled by the sin nature, this leads to negative and harmful attitudes of the sin nature as, jealously and quarrellings with one another. (1st Cor. 3:3a ^{NLT}). Carnality pertains to the sources of man's corrupt and fallen nature. Carnally minded thinking is death; death to the spirit. Those traveling the wide path of life have carnal souls. Within this carnal soul is carnal thinking, carnal imaginations, carnal rationalization, and carnality rules **self** who is on the throne of the sinner, the unbeliever. Letting your sinful nature control your mind, will lead you down the path to death, but letting the Holy Spirit control your mind, will lead you to life and peace (Rom. 8:6,8 ^{NLT}). Spiritually minded is life and peace, this is through the narrow gate, the narrow path of life.

What is keeping us in this frame of mind, holding us in this carnal way of thinking? It is the nature of sin twisted into our spiritual DNA. Without spiritual awareness, the spirit of God in us, we try drawing life from an empty-well, our journey is meaningless to God, and its endeavors are self-made ambitions with the wrong motives.

Being in a world filled with chaos, living in the sin nature of confusion, people's minds are so mixed up that they do absolutely anything to bring them joy. They are looking for peace, pleasures, satisfactions, giving themselves away with no care, giving themselves any means of an adrenaline rush, these are temporal and counterfeit, they are from the pit of darkness, they are fake at the most, and sadly, at times, it can cost some their lives and this style of living is designed to do just that. They are doing these things trying to find contentment, trying to fill that void within them that is missing, called, their spirit. Those who exceedingly live a godless life show their activities, without question. It is overly obvious that people who live a sinful and sinned filled life demonstrate a life fueled from the dark side of the spiritual realm. Others demonstrate a more delicate manner of living to hide their dark side, but do come out at appropriate times, and then there are those who think they live a good life and do not bother or hurt anyone, but all live under a cloud of deception. We are sinners just by living.

The darkness that blankets the face of the earth is a spirit, it is an antichrist spirit, anti-righteous, anti anything that leads to truth, to good and to God. This is our inheritance and it lives with us in this sin-nature.

The world's inhabitants, over. 6.7 billion of us, the ratio is, one birth every seven seconds and one death every thirteen seconds (See Appendix). We are separated into two groups, the righteous and the unrighteous, the saved and the unsaved, the believers and the unbelievers. The unbelievers camp with Satan, the spirit of error; and the believers of divine nature is of God.

The sin nature emanates into the worldly system, its wisdom, worldly knowledge, worldly understanding, the life of secular humanism; this is where the children (people) of disobedience live. They are called children because of their immaturity, their lack of and limited wisdom, understanding, beliefs and spiritual knowledge, and being so they are responsive to false teachings, they are teachable with counterfeit standards. This is where you will find atheist, evolutionist, agnostics; believers of false religions, believers of manmade religions, these are the products of those traveling the wide road of life.

In God's eyes, people of the world are known as the 'children of wrath' and children of disobedience because they choose to do what they want instead of what they should, and they are also called the children of the prince of this world (John 14:30-Eph. 2:2), which is Satan the devil. They are called the children of wrath and of disobedience because they will fall under God's wrath for being disobedient to God and His calling. This spiritual darkness that blankets the face of the earth, is a spirit, it is a anti-Christ spirit, anti-God spirit, anti-Bible spirit, anti-spiritual knowledge spirit, anti anything that leads to God or Christ, which Christ, leads to God. This is our inheritance and it lives with us.

High speed cultures, busy, busy, busy, rush, rush, rush, hurry, hurry, hurry not enough time in a day feelings of something or someone is chasing them, our minds can only think the way it has been conformed toward, programmed into deception and in the error of life. This is carnal thinking and it is of the natural man, the sin nature influenced by **the spirit of error** in the spirit realm from birth. Designed to keep us preoccupied and so busy that we do not have time to stop and smell those fading roses.

Looking at this carnal way of thinking in the physical realm with the natural man, from the spiritual viewpoint, many live this way and follow this way of thinking.

Everything and anything of the world's system that excites us, influences us, entertains us, thrills us is bent on deceiving us, controlling us, fogging our minds with lies, deceptions, illusions, false hope or, no hope.

If you drift away from God's word, or if you were never in it at all, your life gets very crowded with worldly mundane desires, infectious cravings, and a life that is heading for the morgue. There is only the highway to hell or the Gateway to life, one or the other there is no third alterative, no middle ground. By the millions, many travel the wide road, the mental path, lead by the spirit of error that travels as your partner on the edge of darkness, and this is the reason our society and the world is careening out of control.

The mighty fallen angel and his demons control the sin nature of this planet and they are determined with all their forces, with all the ammunition of deceptive lies, to bring on destruction of families, bring evil imaginations and inclinations into the minds of unbelievers. Satan will fill their minds with fantasies, selfish-thoughts, selfish-ambitions, selfish-pleasures that bring on an array of disguises believed to be truth. The sinner knows no difference between truth and error of spiritual matters; they follow the status-quo of the sin nature through the wide gate leading the blind into the inky-blackness of sin.

Living in the sin nature brings glory and joy to Satan, he lives for glory and worship and the lost human gives him just that, and to Satan that lost sinner has no worth. This is where Satan reigns and this is where the lost show their allegiance to the devil even though they do not realize what they are spiritually doing because of their ignorance and lack of biblical knowledge. The pity is that the lost are kept in hopelessness because of the blindness in their heart, their *willingness* to remain there. In our fallen sinful nature, lies, deceit, trickery, that leads to a life style of self-centeredness, of unrest, a life of confusion and no real meaning, no real joy, no real peace and no real purpose. All humans are bound to be lost and doomed who occupy this nature of sin.

The Divine Nature

Entering into the divine nature is the result of accepting God's Son, through faith in Jesus Christ. God reveals himself to man through his word. The Bible says in 2nd Peter 1:3, 4. *"as His divine power has given to us all things that pertain to life and godliness, through the <u>knowledge</u> of Him who called us by glory and virtue," by which have been given to us exceedingly great and precious promises, that through these you may be partakers of the **divine nature**, having escaped the corruption that is in the world through lust."* This corruption in the world is the sin nature; we only escaped it by accepting Jesus Christ and by the grace of God. Those living in the light, those living in the divine nature, those living a righteous life, are those who are born again, saved by the blood of Christ, are living in the kingdom of God here on earth and are God's children.

The divine nature is the Spirit of truth (1st John 4:6) is akin to the Spirit of God and the spirit of error is akin to the sin nature, the spirit of Satan. The Spirit of good verses the spirit of evil; this is the conflict in the world. The nature of the Spirit of truth is righteousness, truth, honesty, honorable things, things that are just, right, pure and lovely, things that are admirable. The Bible says for us to dwell on these things, think on these things. This way of thinking will determine our thought life, and not depending on others. If you practiced self-control and cause yourself to think on these things, and not depending on others, peers or the philosophies and theories in our culture you will find that these will result in right living and right thinking of the mind and that, will develop our character and conduct and will strengthen your life and faith. This is through the narrow gate.

The journey of the saved person travels the highway to heaven, the narrow road. Their lives have meaning and purpose, mercy and blessings and forgiveness of sins. The Lord has revealed in Scripture how we are to live. He wants us to base our decisions on biblical principles rather than on our own thinking.

The Holy Spirit helps us replace sinful behavior with godly conduct. *"Get rid of all bitterness, rage, anger, harsh words, and slander, as well as all types of evil behavior. Instead, be kind to each other, tenderhearted, forgiving one another, just as God through Christ has forgiven you* (Eph. 4:31-32 [NLT]). We have the Spirit, which is of God in us, not the spirit that is in the world, *"And we have received God's Spirit* (not the world's spirit), *so we can know the wonderful things God has freely given us"* (1st Cor. 2:12 [NLT]).

Bottom Line

The sin nature or the divine nature, there is no other; our will is under the dominance of the devil, or God, no other. As often as 'free-will' is used, our will is not free. We serve either God or Satan, we serve self indirectly, we are not free, and we serve one or the other. We come out of the sin nature and serve God or we remain in the sin nature and serve Satan.

The musician, songwriter, Bob Dylan's song, "Gotta Serve Somebody" has a lyric saying, "you're gonna have to serve somebody, well, it my be the devil or it may be the Lord, but you're gonna have to serve somebody." In short, we either serve the devil of we serve God, we do what we do because of the condition of our heart. If you are an unbeliever, a sinner, you serve the devil. You may think you just serve yourself but you do not, spiritually, you are not in the equation.

Everyone's life falls under one of these two natures, these authorities these supernatural powers of governing bodies of all things. These two natures represent the two kinds of people on the planet, the cultures, the ways of life, wisdoms, thoughts and knowledge. The divine-nature is the spirit of truth. Here spiritual knowledge, spiritual wisdom, spiritual understanding, are found and the blessings from God, where God's children live. This is the journey on the narrow road of life.

Our human nature

Our human physical nature is a dimension in which we were born; we live in while we are on this planet. In this physical dimension, we are restricted to this realm only; we think with the carnal mind, and we are held captive in our own mind. Imprisoned in our own inability to move out of the carnal way of thinking into the true spiritual way of thinking, being incarcerated it is beyond our human potential, the restriction cannot be lifted without divine Grace, it cannot be done any other way. The physical nature is also called the fleshly nature. Carnal thinking is natural in the sin nature. Being natural, is being worldly, in the physical dimension and thinking from the carnal mind. A passage in Eph. 2:3 the writer is expressing the conduct of the carnal way of thinking. It is of the world and the fleshly nature we were born in, where Christians came out. *"Among whom also we all once conducted ourselves in the lust of the flesh, fulfilling the desires of the flesh,* (the fleshly nature) *and of the mind, and were by nature* (the sin-nature) *children of wrath, just as the others."* We by nature, that is, the sin nature, the fleshly nature, are children of wrath. We were born in the sin nature we were born as sinners. In the sin nature, the carnal way of thinking, dominates you.

Our inheritance is the sin nature, we are bound to the sin nature, and we are under the dominion of sin. Nevertheless, because of the birth, death, and resurrection of Christ we have the divine nature at hand if we want it, our entrance into eternal life. We were born in the sin nature, but we can be born spiritually into the divine nature. The choice is ours. Through the narrow gate is the path to salvation, redemption, to Jesus Christ, to God, to life. Satan targets our human fleshly nature because of its appetites, it is easily taken under enemy control, our flesh is weak, and through our flesh, he invades the mind with allurements. Our inheritance continues.

Our Two Dimensional Lives

Our generation is no different from others, when the sin nature raised its ugly evil head into humanity; it changed man's spiritual situation of life because of its many variable factors. We lack the main component of our being and yet we are still able to function, in humanity not in spirituality. We try to pacify ourselves with worldly and fleshly pleasures but without the Spirit alive in us, we are considered spiritually dead. We are like living, fleshing breathing mannequins functioning without our spirit alive in us.

The unique creatures that we are we walk the planet as incomplete beings feeding from substandard influences because we lack that spiritual component, we are only two-thirds complete. Without our spirit, we are separated souls from our Creator. We lack internal direction, we now live without any contact with our Maker; we lack any inner guidance or direction from him.

Unrighteousness, injustice, morally wrong, doing unjust-acts filled with iniquity these are the opposite of our intended nature. The reason we have difficulty being what we were meant to be is due to our inheritance, our spirit missing in our wholeness. We are not whole; we are two-thirds of being complete. In this incompleteness, our thinking is off; it has become dull by spiritual darkness that leaves us with no perceptivity toward spiritual matters. Being incomplete, we naturally inherit a hardened callousness swaying us in the opposite direction away from an unknown God of the universe, our Creator. Darkness takes over our void and we live a life of error. It happens like this; when we take our first breath out of the loving protected womb, we inherit a sinful nature. We breathe darkness into our soul that instantly fills the void in us with sin.

Our minds became slaves to the fulfillment of our selfish desires, our physical needs, and the allurements of the world's system; this has twisted the way our minds, emotions, and our physical bodies were meant to operate. We have become utterly dependent on people, and circumstances, we roam through life driven by these circumstances and others' opinions and the external world of things, to provide for our needs and not depending on our Creator. To our Creator we most likely look like a mass of little blind neurotic creatures trying to survive in a dark world without him. We live in a twisted narcissistic nature ran by a demonic force with an evil intention of destroying you, before you, find out about him.

We are not aware that we live on a two dimensional plane. Man's existence is on a level one-third lower or one-third less than what God created him to be. Meaning we live in a body, first dimension, and we have soul, second dimension, but minus our living spirit, hence the void, which would be our third dimension that would make us whole, complete, make us what we were created to be, spirit, soul and body. The body and soul relates to the world, the spirit to God.

We are born literally into a sin-filled world; this leaves us extremely vulnerable to the advancements of darkness towards our soul. Without our spirit, we live on a two-dimensional plane; this is why we are considered spiritually dead. We have no spiritual knowledge, with no spiritual knowledge we have no perspicacity of absolute truth, eternal truth, spiritual truth, and we have no idea what is going on in the spirit realm with no spiritual discernment. We have no draw towards the Creator, towards his Son, towards truth, matter of fact we turn our back around to them.

The void within us is there because our spirit is not alive with the Spirit of God; it is inactive because we are sinners. This is why we are only two-thirds complete. Born in this state and we will remain in this state until we are born again or, if we die in this state we will forever remain in this state, not a happy place to be.

Being spiritually dead, spiritually asleep, or only two-thirds complete, leaves us with this **void** in us that we try to fill it with things that seem right to us, or see things in a way that seem practical for our needs, for instance the lie of evolution. This lie has lead millions into eternal abyss for there is no spiritual knowledge in those who believe that one time man was a fish. We have a yearning for something or things to please **self** because our soul is missing the Spirit, meant to indwell us. We seek things to help make us feel complete, to feel better than what we feel, we seek things to make us smarter to learn what is missing in our lives. The Spirit of God is to live in man with man's spirit, making him complete, we are missing this Spirit. Without the Spirit, man is incomplete. The Spirit of God left man when man left God. Man is spiritually dead leaving him with a void from the great fall in the garden and subject to the deeds of darkness.

We live with no spiritual discernment. The mind of the natural man, his thoughts cannot penetrate beyond the human nature. He cannot understand the divine nature or the sin nature in the spirit realm. Discernment works in distinguishing between an actualization of evil and the convicting power of the Holy Spirit, which God gives. Spiritual discernment is not possible from the sin nature, those of the sin nature think with the carnal mind and the carnal mind impairs discernment. The spirit of the world does not give spiritual discernment; it gives hunches, intuitions, spontaneous feeling, sixth sense, guessing, assumptions, but discernment is a gift given to the born again man from God (John 3:27 ^{KJV}). This gift from God comes from God's word and through God's Spirit, with the word comes knowledge, and through knowledge comes depth of insight (Phil. 1:9). This is another reason why God requires the reading and studying of his word. Christians cannot close their eyes to the matter of discernment, we must truly know what is of God and what is of Satan, and it takes constant vigilance.

We are ignorantly unaware because the nature of the sin nature is to keep spiritual matters from us, to keep us in the dark. In the sin nature, it is normal being two-thirds complete, you cannot have a born again spiritual experience and be incomplete. There are such strong delusions and lies in the sin nature that they hold the spiritless man captive by their pleasures and allurements and the secular humanistic life style. Satan rules the sin nature and you are doing what he wants you to do, even though you may think you are doing good works, but what truly is your motive? You cannot have the right motive being only two-thirds complete, you cannot. The missing Spirit in man is the common factor that invites dark demonic influence and drives man to do evil.

For instance, on a global scale, unscrupulous leaders of countries are so dementedly obsessed with power, power to destroy, power in weapons, having the power in nuclear weapons, chemical weapons, threatening other nations and countries with destruction, threatening international peace. They create the ability and power to annihilate anything on the face of the earth and running their government and people with an iron fist. The leaders that are evil driven are *willingly*, consumed with that negative evil virus of the mind. The attitude of dictators with these obsessions is one thing to try to understand and dissect, but trying to understand what is happening to individuals in the world that live a life full of lust, sexual perversions, racism, hate crimes, a life that drives them to self destruction through drugs, alcohol and perform insidious and senseless murders. They live a life with such viciousness, cold-blooded excess cruelty, and heinous methods of torture and slaughter of one another mercilessly. Those who hurt us most lightly have been hurt some way in their lives and as it stays inside and festers, it builds to hatred and hatred leads to violence. There is the sadness of suicides; these individuals may think that they are helping someone else by their death, possibly emotionally, financially, or maybe wanting to hurt someone emotionally, or financially. Whatever the case darkness sunk its vicious venomous fangs into the sinner's mind and shrunk their thinking to a desperate state of loneliness where nothing matters. Brainwashed suicide bombers, their belief in an ideology that they are doing something special for their god but are destroying their soul just as the devil has lead them to do and all along, they are being sent to hell because they believe lies. These individuals do these acts without knowing what is awaiting them on the other side, and it is not a fantasy of awaiting virgins. Spousal abuse is on the increase, divorces, parents killing one another, parents killing their children, children killing their parents, children killing children and the massacres of the cold-blooded killings in our schools, and universities, churches, and in public areas. Children having babies, approximately fifty million aborted babies to date, thirty seven hundred a day in this country and forty-two million a year worldwide, one-hundred and fifteen thousand a day worldwide and on and on are all negative perversions of life (See Appendix). So much unexplained fatal incidences and senseless deaths. These are terrible atrocities and many more have occurred without our knowledge and all influenced by darkness.

What drives people to be like this? The commonality here in these individuals is the factor of being an incomplete person, missing the Spirit of God to make us whole making us complete, giving us understanding, and absolute truth. Man is thinking on his own, influenced by the devil in his pitiful carnal mind. The characterization of being incomplete means the minds of unbelievers are missing that vital ingredient. With our spirit dead to sin, our human nature living in the sin nature is subject to physical and spiritual criminal activity. Spiritual criminal activity comes in when one rejects the gospel, rejects Christ, as what is happening around the world. As mentioned above, the missing spirit in man is the common factor that invites demonic influence and drives man to do evil by filling the void where our spirit should be alive. Instead of man being-filled with the Spirit of God, he is filled with the spirit of error of the sin nature, the spirit of Satan, that may be a chilling thought, but it is absolute truth. The *willing* attitude to do these wicked and wretched things comes from the sin nature. Remember, sin consumes and encompasses the world, and sin is the child of the devil. Individuals opening their mind to wicked thoughts, they open the door to Satan and he rushes in like a high-powered projectile penetrating the soul and takes a foothold, by the victims weaknesses and in that weakness he determines a stronghold and finds himself a home in the mind of the unsaved. The unsaved, the incomplete soul whether ruling a nation or a household lives a life motivated mostly by his selfish fleshly desires, and the pride of life which brings a sense of deceitful invincible power which the sin nature feeds him and he is capable of committing any sin.

They Fill the Void

Pride and ignorance fill the void in the unbelievers' soul and surface to the top of his/her emptiness, and floating with pride and ignorance is a generous amount of arrogance. Through their life's journey, their pride and ignorance will grow into a height of arrogance and self-exaltation. The more that the unbeliever's life yields to the affairs of the world the more lies, the more false doctrines, idiosyncrasies of character are developed, with more false thrills, are dabbled into to fill the very deep and personal yearning of feelings of loathness, of loneliness, of hopelessness, the feeling that something is missing in the life of the unbeliever. The emptiness fully disguised as happiness, attempts to fill the void. Does there seem like something is missing in your life, do you feel there must be more to life than this, do you feel incomplete? The missing link is not a jawbone, or a primitive skull, the missing link is the truth.

Worldly intellectualism is the wise man of the world; but he is a spiritually ignorant man. When the spirit, is absent from our personality, our moods and attitudes flip-flop and darkness creeps into the soul with false love, with overwhelming anger, with a charismatic fun loving personality used in darkness and achieving evil. The emptiness we feel is because of the missing ingredient, which is spiritual. We do not know this so we try to feel that emptiness, that yearning for something fulfilling, the thing what will make us complete. We try sex, relationships, drugs, alcohol, craving success, the fastest car, money, wealth, material stuff; we even try to be a better moral person. Even church, religion, and entertainment do not seem to help. Your lack of satisfaction leaves you with feelings that you have missed something somewhere in life, but do not quite know what it is.

If we choose not to believe in God, in the gospel, in Jesus Christ, in life after death, which these thoughts come naturally in the sin nature, we turn our back on God and turn from the truth of life. When we turn form the truth, we face darkness and facing darkness, we are blinded from the truth. Truth illuminates our mind with understanding and discernment. Following darkness down the wide path of life, the prince of darkness usurps our thinking because now we are on his turf, his domain. Satan attempts to take control of the unbeliever's life when the unbeliever's is firm in his decision of denouncing Jesus Christ because then the unbelievers mind is susceptible to philosophies theories, and assumptions that make sense to him because of the spiritual void in his soul which is filled with lies. Satan knows that those living in the sin nature are void of the Spirit and void of truth and with his schemes and deceptions can give the unbeliever a feeling of completeness or satisfaction with those schemes and deceptions or philosophies and theories that someone else made up and assumes are correct. Satan attempts to fill the void with false truths and deceptions of life down the wide path, we, thinking with open mindedness, he drags us by our unbelief down the road of good intentions. Facing darkness we do not see the Son, facing the Son we do not see darkness.

With the spiritual void we are off balance in our thinking, we are off balance in our whole being. Apathy has set in; the spirit of error tips the scale and favors 'self' the self-life so much so that it weighs down the scale to the bottom measurement while the empty part of the scale, is unreachable. The weigh is the political correctness of the world, the legalism in our cultures; it is filled with lies and deceit, error of life, error of truth, error of who you really are, and all of the devil's lies that fills that void. It is filled and heavy with egotism; it is heavy with depravity that sends man into a downward spiral into the abyss. The unbalance in man's life is so far from God that God is the only one that can bring man into completeness. It is up to man to let God fill that void. Man must throw 'self' off the scale through repentance and let God bring life into balance, with truth, with forgiveness of sins, with eternal life, with the promises and blessings that he wants to give a repentant sinner and eliminate all excess weight of corruption. Man must be *willing* to let God fill that empty part of the scale, which is, man's incomplete life and bring it into balance.

This is why there are so many man made religions, theories of man's origin, beliefs in reincarnation, every unbeliever is searching for something, someone to fill that space in their life to fulfill there yearning. Only God can do that with the born again experience.

When one is willing to live in the sin nature and commit what they should not, even if it is not such wickedness this is an invitation for an evil spirit, or spirits, demons to take up residence in the mind and heart of that sinner who is without the Spirit. These evil spirits roam around the void and fill it with inferior deceptive authority, selfish-thoughts, beliefs, philosophies, a prideful heart and an ignorant soul towards spiritual matters. We are blindly ignorant of the truth, the absolute truth, we are ignorant of the truth about the gospel, we are ignorant of sin, we are ignorant of all that determines our eternal future and we are ignorant in our every day lives in how we should be living. Blatantly, we were born in ignorance.

This is the cause of crime, violence and frightful terror in the world and our human nature is a major contributor to the problem and to the suffering with unavoidable results because we *willingly* want to, choose to, relish in sin. This is because we are profoundly, and unknowing incomplete which is a deceptive-factor to our self-deceptiveness.

With our spirit dead or call it asleep, hence the void, we cannot understand the things of God, this holds us back from knowing ourselves, knowing the truths of life, knowing who we really are. We are lacking this key ingredient. According to God's Word, human beings are essentially selfish — concerned primarily with their own self-gratification. The Bible refers to this as being carnally minded which "the flesh" stimulates. *"For those who live according to the flesh set their minds on the things of the flesh, but those who live according to the Spirit, the things of the Spirit. For to be carnally minded is death, but to be spiritually minded is life and peace. Because the carnal mind is enmity against God; for it is not subject to the law of God, nor indeed can be. So then, those who are in the flesh cannot please God"* (Rom. 8:5-8). Believers live by the Spirit, since God's Spirit dwells in them. . . ." Verse nine of this passage reads; *"But you (believers) are not in the flesh but in the Spirit, if indeed the Spirit of God dwells in you. Now if anyone does not have the Spirit of Christ, he is not His."* Without God's Spirit, the essence of the sin nature's primary motivations toward the human soul is their selfish and fleshly desires.

When God's Spirit enters man, a remarkable change takes place, it is truly a miracle and man will have its vital missing ingredient, now he is complete and a new man, with a new heart, with a renewed mind and a new way of thinking. In the book of Ephesians 4:23, 24 the Bible says, *"and be renewed in the spirit of your mind, and that you put on the new man which was created according to God, in true righteousness and holiness."* We are renewed is the spirit of our mind, with new thoughts and new attitudes, a new life in a new nature. In the book of Colossians 3:10 *"and have put on the new man who is renewed in knowledge according to the image of Him who created him."* The new man is your spirit being born again with a new attitude and thoughts and the absolute truth about life.

To find wholeness, a person must start by receiving Jesus Christ as Savior; the sin that stands between him, and God, sin must be, removed. Without Jesus in your life, your life will be a pitiless, callous and a fruitless journey in the one-dimensional physical realm. The void is a spiritual inheritance that all humans have in common and God is the only one that can fill it and seal it with his Spirit of love and truth.

PART III

THE SPIRIT WORLD INVISIBLE AND VERY POWERFUL

Chapter 7

What are some elements in the spirit world? God's glorious and majestic kingdom and Satan's evil domain, heaven and hell, God's angels who surround us and minister to us, demon spirits who hunt and taunt us, the invisible part of man, his spirit, soul, mind and heart lives in the invisible world, and the paths that our thoughts travel.

The unseen realm is like an invisible curtain separating the physical life from the spiritual life. On our side of this invisible curtain is everything that you have experienced and can experience in life, everything you hear, see, touch, smell, taste and feel. This is the life you have only ever known. This curtain separates us from the spiritual realm which we are inescapably, unavoidably susceptible to. Go on, poke your head through the curtain and see how highly at risk we are with the activities sparring in the spiritual realm, where there are literally, millions of demon spirits, swirling around us that are ravenous for our souls. While you are caught up in a frenzied state of frightfulness, these demons are frantically swirling around our souls waiting for the right opportunity to devour that individual with a demonic stronghold. Do not be discouraged about this thought, they have been there forever you just have not known it. They intend to deceive us, corrupt us, discourage us, depress us, confuse us, inject wicked evil thoughts into our minds, lead us further down the wrong path of life, they keep us from truth, keep us from God, keep us from knowing God and keep us from knowing whom we are and what we are. They are mighty powers in the spirit realm and they can affect our whole being. There is much to learn about them and there is much to learn how they can avoid you.

A Look into Hell

Jesus pulled back the curtain to give us a glimpse what hell is like. This glimpse is not the depth of the lake of fire but of Hades, Hades is like a holding cell, an intermediate state between judgment and hell.

Jesus told of an unrighteous man and a righteous man, referring to Old Testament times. When death occurred, the righteous went to a place called Abraham's bosom, a type of paradise, not in heaven. When the unrighteous died they went to a place called *Sheol*, (Heb.) *Hades*, (Gr.) this is a place of suffering, burning, conviction with undying memories of a misspent life, and living in separation from God and with unbearable stench of sulfuric brimstone. The unrighteous will remain here until released for judgment. Jesus told of this unrighteous rich man and the poor righteous man in Luke 16:19-28. The rich man lived extravagantly every day, he lived in luxury and the poor man was a beggar and desiring to eat the crumbs, which fell from the rich man's table. He goes on to tell that they both died and angels carried the poor man away and the rich man was buried, saying nothing about angels comforting him.

Now, the curtain being pulled back to reveal a glimpse of the home for the unbeliever after death, is also telling us it is too late after we die to make a decision to repent and also revealing the constant torment, not torture, torment, loneliness, sorrow and grief in hell. You can read in verse twenty-three, the rich man now in Hades, looking up and saw Abraham and the beggar, he speaks of 'being in torments,' plural. In verse twenty-four, he is 'tormented by flames,' he wish that the poor man would dip the tip of his finger in water and cool his tongue, but the poor man can not because of a great gulf fixed between them, verse twenty-six. In verse twenty-five the torment is confirmed and verse twenty-eight he speaks again of it being a 'place of torment.' The rich man also request that the beggar be sent back from the dead to warn the rich man's five brothers who are still alive on earth that they may repent and not come to this place of torment, read verses twenty-seven through thirty-one.

You can see from verse twenty-four that the rich man was in torment from an extreme heat of hell's flames. This tells us that there will be sensual misery; our five senses will be susceptible to that hellish environment. This is not a place of joy and peace or a place of camaraderie. Hell is a painful, miserable existence, you keep dying and dying and dying and never able to die, a death that will go on and on and on forever, and ever dying. It is a place, an existence of unspeakable sorrow. You will feel like you are always near death but never dying.

It is an unending place of dark isolated torment, flames from the inextinguishable lake of fire, with a thirst that cannot be quenched what an incredibly bleak picture, an unhappy fate for the lost sinner. Hell is unending, hell is for those who do not believe in God, in Jesus Christ and this will be their reward for their rebellious heart. Billy Sunday said this; "Hell is the highest reward that the devil can offer you for being a servant of his."

They will experience a condition with no improvement, an existence of unspeakable sorrow, an unquenchable eternal fire, they will spend eternality in agony and despair, weeping and gnashing of teeth. Eternal hopelessness spans the width of the shore-less lake, everlasting and unending torment, taunts the perishing regretful sinner. Even some who do-good things will end up in hell, for their motives were generated with pride and these, the Lord calls evil doers, and whose names are not written in God's book of life, and there are great and eternal sorrows in hell.

The great gulf fixed is the final separation between good and evil, between the righteous and the unrighteous, between the believer and the unbeliever, between heaven and hell, which is the second and last death.

If you could experience just one second in hell, you would **run** to the alter, you could not get to the Lord fast enough, for hell is literally a location, and death is definitely a condition.

What does the sinner, the unsaved, the unbeliever the skeptic have to do to go to hell, nothing. Those in hell are there not because they sinned, they are there because they rejected God's Son. R.A. Torrey said this about hell. "Hell is the hospital of the incurables of the universe, where men exist in awful and perpetual pain." Hell is for unrepentant sinners.

"The vague and tenuous hope that God is too kind to punish the ungodly has become a deadly opiate for the consciences of millions." — A.W. Tozer

I heard the late Dr. Adrian Rogers say, "You can laugh your way into hell but you cannot laugh your way out." He explained Hades with this analogy. "When a person commits a horrible crime and caught he is taken away to some county jail and not released with bail or let back into society but held for trial, before sent to prison. This is comparable to the fate of the sinner who dies lost. He his held in Hades awaiting judgment before his sentence of being found guilty of rejecting Gods Son, guilty and sent to hell." Hades is like a spiritual holding cell.

Heaven

Heaven is more than the sky although the sky is a heaven; the eternal heaven is a place for the righteous. Those who are in heaven through faith and humility, been converted through repentance, have committed to the only way to enter heaven, our eternal home where he has prepared a place for those who are his. The kingdom of God is not heaven only; it is the entire spectrum of all existence. Heaven is a gift from God to all those who believe in Jesus. What we do in this life will determine to a great degree how God blesses us in the life to come, we should view each day on earth as an opportunity to invest for eternity. Heaven is a place of eternal living for those saved, the celestial abode and the eternal blessedness for the redeemed.

To the Christian, being with the Lord in heaven for eternity is such a powerful stimulant to do good, to live right and a deterrent from evil in this life and is a profound conviction as to the reality of the future life and that our position there will depend on our behavior here. The Christian whose eyes fixed on heaven as their final dwelling place will surely mean a more careful walk in this world. Here, this life has an end, the next lasts forever, we realize that we are strangers here and our home is there. As a sinner persuades a sinner to sin, ensuring damnation, a Christian attempts to persuade a sinner to be saved, ensuring heaven. You **must** make that reservation to get into heaven; it is not a place for doubters, skeptics, and unbelievers.

We do not know what heaven is like, we only know a glimpse of it, and we can only imagine the peacefulness of it. Its beauty is not important to us at this stage of our lives, the eternal home for the redeemed and the reality of the eternal Savior welcoming those who came to their senses, realized that they were sinners, and needed a Savior is enough beauty we can handle for now.

I heard this years ago at a much younger age, 'this earth is the only heaven the sinner will know and it is the only hell the believer will know.'

Heavens Books

We are not talking a library of books for the heavenly beings to occupy their time; no, we are talking about God revealing books of records of those who populate his earth. At the judgment seat of Christ recorded is the sinner's works of accountability on this planet and the sinner will be judged from books that will be opened. In heaven, there will be no big viewing screen of your earthly life, but there will be books opened at judgment revealing records of men's lives.

In heaven, there are two sets of books, one is the Book of Life it is of the saved, and the other is a set of books of recording of the unsaved. God tells us that in Revelation 20:12,13 *"And I saw the dead, great and small, standing before the throne, and books were opened. Another book was opened, which is the book of life. The dead were judged according to what they had done as recorded in the books."* If you are a rebellious sinner you will get away with nothing, no sin will go unnoticed no sin will be unpunished. *"The sea gave up the dead who were in it, and Death and Hades delivered up the dead who were in them. And they were judged, each one according to his works."*

The dead, great and small are those who never repented of their sins, but wait for judgment. The great are those who were intellectually superior above others, those with great power, royalty, those who ruled nations, the kings, queens and lords of their land, government officials, those in high places. The small are those under these and subservient in importance. The dead are given this name by God because they are dead, spiritually dead to God, not born again they did not repent and lived only the physical realm while on earth not the spiritual/physical realm. The books are many for the deceived sinners are many.

The Book of life

The Book of Life contains the names of those who while on earth accepted God's Son as their personal Savior, those who became God's children through repentance and their acceptance and faith in Jesus Christ, these are the true Christians. Here God records the names of the righteous. Recorded are those who are only worthy signifying the living redeemed, who shall awaken to everlasting life all others are doomed. *"And anyone whose name was not found recorded in the Book of Life was thrown into the lake of fire"* (Rev. 20:15 NLT). Those whose names are written in the Book of Life will not face the White Throne Judgment. They have passed from death to life.

Chapter 8

Two Kingdoms

"And if thou be not in the kingdom of Christ, it is certain that thou belonged to the kingdom of Satan, which is the evil world."–Martin Luther

Kingdom of Satan

Lucifer, the once archangel of the Holy Mountain of God held a predominant position in heaven until he rebelled and brought sin into the universe through munity in heaven and now is the archenemy of God and all humanity. Satan is the CEO, chief evil officer of his kingdom. He rules his kingdom with superior authority, as would a leader of a country or, as a leader of a nation a leader of his own world. His kingdom is a temporary kingdom, and will dissolve and disappear like a vapor. Satan rules this world like it is his but he knows it is not and he never ever stops destroying souls. He is directing his authority, maneuvering the world's governments to make way for his future human appearance. His armies of demons carry out his orders with intense severity maneuvering their human pawns further down the path of false impressions and away from truth and reality into the world of lies accomplishing his will.

Satan rules the planet even though you want to save it; he is the prince of the power of the air, the first heaven you see at day, not the second heaven you see at night. The atmosphere surrounding the earth he also rules and has this air space to set up emissaries, principalities to over watch countries that they may embark organized evil forces to instigate, prompt man into wars through pointless insurgencies that will kill off humans, in cold blood, murdered with the brutality and disregard of human life. This is the mentality of demons, they thrive on human souls, as a leech sucks blood from his victim, demons suck the life, and the truth, out of man.

We live on their turf and they do not like it but they just cannot throw us off into outer space, they must be what they are and do what they must to rid themselves of us. The kingdom of Satan has a two-fold ministry, first is to damn as many souls as they possibly can, as soon as they can and secondly make way for the soon coming one-world ruler, in which he himself will have an imposing investment.

The kingdom of Satan, a.k.a. the kingdom of darkness rules in unrighteousness. It rules in the spirit realm and it rules in our physical realm. There is nothing good in that kingdom, there is no feeling of warmth, there is no kindness, and there is no reasoning, no understanding, and no light. The kingdom of darkness is a place for assembling of renegade putrid angels that turned evil and they gather to plan to purge this planet of the human race even if that means destroying ourselves, which now in this twenty-first century we do have, the nuclear capability to blow this planet into smithereens.

The kingdom of Satan in our physical realm operates within the worldly system, full of deception, division and destruction, it is a humanistic society without God, it is a place without meaning, it is an invisible weapon that has it's crosshairs on your soul. This society is those living in the kingdom of darkness and is against God, pride and arrogance is their driver.

Satan

Satan, the lost, mighty, angelic creature that brought evil into the world, is a spiritual narcissist psychopath.

God does not use the word bad, as a behavior of ours, because there is no bad to God, we only use that word, to God all is evil, and we are either good or evil. All evil in the world comes from this pathological neurotic narcissist, Satan. He is a vicious and wicked foe with no respect, no remorse against the human soul that he destroys. He works in deception, he has been at it for six thousands years and he has honed it to perfection. He is an unconquerable spirit, he rules the world's system; his timing is impeccable unnoticed by the unsaved and attempts to deceive the God's children. His character threatens the human race, his ability to convey his characteristics into the human soul devastates that soul, and all that is around it and ripples throughout the world. He is the most diabolical, evil personified creature to walk the face of the earth. He hates God; he hates Christ and hates God's children, the Christians who stand in his way from devouring more souls.

Satan's characteristics are like that of man. In the book of Job 1:7 God asks Satan a question, so, he hears, in verse six he moves, in verse nine he talks, in verse ten he can rationalize, he knows us, see us, he knows how much we possess. In verse twelve, he has hands, and power. In verse sixteen he has enough power that he can use natural resources to cause natural disasters, he has power over people, in verse seventeen he uses humans to do harm to other humans,. He will use humans to steal, do harm to others in any evil way, he will use humans to kill humans. He will use nature and he himself will destroy man. In the fully revealed doctrine of Satan, which is seen in the New Testament he is the demon of this world who has access to the hearts of men, deceives them, and receives their witting or unwitting obedience (Acts 5:3). He can bring disease on man (Job 2:7); he can impoverish a soul, mentally, spiritually, physically and emotionally. He uses the world and sin to draw the believers away from God and to keep the unsaved away from the truth. We live in the sin nature and Satan exploits that nature in the souls of man taking every advantage and every situation and every circumstance for his own gain into the soul of the individual. The Bible says in 2nd Thessalonians 2:10 NLT that *"He will use every kind of evil deception to fool those on their way to destruction, because they refuse to love and accept the truth that would save them."* It cannot be any clearer than this passage. The unbeliever will be destroyed for his rejection of the truth. Because of this, they are very easily deceived by the devil. The devil will also go after the believers, in 1st Timothy 4:1, 2 NLT *"Now the Holy Spirit tells us clearly that in the last times some will turn away from the true faith; they will follow deceptive spirits and teachings that come from demons. These people are hypocrites and liars, and their consciences are dead."* The human race has been mislead by the devil's lies.

Satan is our adversary, his agenda is hostile to all goodness and the chief opponent to God and man, his aim is to undo the work of God, seeking to persuade men to sin, eager of leading them to renounce God, and endeavoring to prevent their acceptance and salvation by God. He is sometimes influential in bringing about financial loss, physical sickness, he can help to push someone over the edge, he can create stress, through job loss, traumatic events, and anger festers into hatred that is more powerful. In the sin nature, hate is a built in factor and is always there and he will take advantage of using it at any time, in any and every situation from road rage to neo-Nazi groups.

The thief's purpose, the devil's purpose is to steal and kill and destroy (John 10:10). He steals the word from the heart of the unaware and the inattentive hearer (Mark 4:15). The Satanic spirit that encompasses the earth is responsible for leading multitudes astray, leading them into believing lies, telling lies, he is responsible for all evil, the sins we commit the crimes we commit all for not believing and turning our backs on the truth. Men with hearts unchanged are under Satan's power (Acts 26:18). He is the real agent in the operations carried on by the man of sin nature (2nd Thess. 2:9,10 NLT).

Satan, the god of this world is determined to generate world-wide, a vast network of God haters in all nations, in all vocations, in all minds that reject God, reject Jesus Christ, reject the Word, reject the gospel, reject the truth and have no spiritual knowledge. He is accomplishing this through the unbelievers in the world, those with such great hatred toward Christianity and toward the name of Jesus Christ.

These unbelievers, the God haters, Satan already controls this portion of the human race, the ones called sinners, there is no need for him to seduce them into his family, he already has them through the sin nature, they are his pawns doing what he wishes. Satan zeros in on the souls that have turned their lives over to the Lord, they are the target that he wants to bring down because they pose an incredible threat to the kingdom of darkness because of their ability to do God's work against the kingdom of darkness through prayer, worshiping, fellowshipping, praising God which he hates us doing. Satan will do every thing possible to try to get you to destroy your faith in God. He targets the believers and he manipulates the sinner.

Names of Satan

The name Satan means 'adversary,' he is the adversary of goodness, the author of evil. He is our adversary (1st Pet. 5:8). He is the personification of evil influences in man's heart. You will learn that Satan has many names and the names encapsulate his character.

The name devil, one of Satan's names means accuser, a slander. This one maliciously slanders another for the purpose of injury, and personal gain (Job. 1:6-11; 2:1-5). He is called Abaddon in Hebrew; and Apollyon, in the Greek, the king of the tormenting locusts' (Rev. 9:7-10), and the angel of the abyss, the bottomless pit (Rev. 9:11), he is called Beelzebub, meaning prince of devils (Matt. 10:25; 12:27; Mark. 3:22; Luke

11:15). Accuser of the brethren (Rev. 12:10), he is Belial, (2nd Cor. 6:15) meaning ungodliness, worthless, an unbeliever, he is called the evil one (1st John 5:19b NIV). He is called the tempter (Matt. 4:3); (1st Thess. 3:5) he is the prince of this world (John 12:31 NIV) the god of this world. (2nd Cor. 4:4 NLT). He is the wicked one (Eph. 6:16), the evil one the prince of the power of the air (Eph. 2:2). He is the serpent from the garden (Gen. 3:1) the dragon of Revelation (Rev. 12:3), he can change into an angel of light. He is able to persuade men in churches to twist the truth and to believe lies (2nd Cor. 11:14). He is the father of lies (John. 8:44), he brought lying into the universe by his mutiny in heaven. He is the evil one (1st John 5:19 NIV), and others. Living in spiritual rebellion is opening the door for Satan and being the devil's slave. You will live under complete bondage, a slave to the devil and his demons and all his inclinations. These are his names and what he represents is the sin nature, the antichrist spirit that is in the world today and has been in the world since he became the devil. He is not the antichrist; he is the spirit of antichrist, for the antichrist will be a human being overcome by Satan as Satan overcame the serpent, Satan will overcome a human. Satan over came many world leaders throughout the ages, and he is still doing his evil bidding on lost foolish souls. Satan is a personal devil, meaning he will possess one soul at a time, he is at one place at a time, and there is one devil but many demons called devils. His characteristics are malignant to the highest degree.

Satan's characteristics

Satan characteristics are in relation with his aliases, he is a slander, he is a tormentor, he is an accuser, he is ungodly, and he is the personification of evil. He is the great tempter, and he is very wicked of his thoughts and actions. He can appear to be something he is not, i.e., an angel of light, false teachers in false religions leading millions astray. He has the characteristics of a serpent, cunning, sneaky like qualities, strikes faster then lighting speed. He is like a roaring lion, beyond vicious, with strength and power, seeking sinners to devoir. Satan is a liar; he is a persuader, with precise deceptive dialogue. He is an illusionist and he is a discourager. His vocabulary and his intelligence unmatched by anyone on the planet, no one human could stand up against him. Throughout life's history Satan indwelt leaders of countries, infiltrating their minds then their governments, their political, their economical, and their financial systems, cultures, religions, whole governmental systems with twisted concepts, and extreme ideologies, wicked purposes and intentions put in hearts of men that will reflect their sadistic personality and all that will affect their country.

He has very great power and creates conflicts on earth that are horrific to man, and man cannot understand how and why people on this earth are so thoughtless, insensitive and numb towards others.

Satan thrives on manipulation, control of others, being in command, giving orders, causing mayhem, confusion anywhere he possibly can with the purpose of destroying all who he can.

He is the great deceiver, and deception is one of his mightiest tools. It is used everywhere, on anyone, anytime, all the time to keep man in the dark and prevent man from knowing what is truth, keep man from wanting to know God, keep man from wanting Jesus Christ in his life.

He does not want you to know he is real; he tries to convince the world that he does not exist. He would rather you look at him as harmless, like the carton figure, fully clad in orange or red with a pitchfork and a pointed tail, forget that vision completely. If you envision him at all, envision him as the caricature of the Grim Reaper, death personified hiding under a deceptive cloak of darkness.

He executes his world dominance with his militia of demons that swarm on humans with no mercy, no compassion with their fiendish fangs at our jugulars. They want to destroy us as soon as possible, before we know what the truth is and that humanity has been living their life in a cesspool, living a wasted life.

Satan's diabolical plan against the human race is to cause death, to you, to your family, to friends, to everyone, to bring physical death, spiritual death, and eternal death. He wants to make you miserable, to steal your joy, steal your happiness; he wants to steal your purity, he wants to wreck your family, destroy your finances, he wants to ruin your life. As he makes life miserable for some, and keeping us in deceit and delusion until spiritual paralyses sets in. It is like a hypnotic state that we cannot detect as it captures our thinking by deception from darkness. It is bent on destroying the human race physically, spiritually, emotionally by breaking down relationships and friendships not only within our grasp but also with international leaders of countries and their people with intense dislike of our democracy.

As we see today with spiritual discernment in our time, what is taking place in countries around the world there is an association with the spirit of darkness. Evil everywhere is showing its face with the destruction of human lives, a hatred for humanity as if we are nothing.

The god of this age, Satan, blinds the minds of the unbeliever; there is a spiritual veil over the minds of those living in the sin nature. The truth is veiled; the gospel is veiled, oblique from those that reject the truth. Those in darkness do not know who they are (John 12:35c-1st John 2:11), where they came from or where they are going after death. Their journey is dismal, it is an outward show, a thin veneer, and they cannot see it. Look what is going on in Hollywood with some that could be inspiring to young people; their lives are out of control, spiraling downward at lightning rate of speed, just not Hollywood but everywhere.

Satan attacks the flesh through the senses, with your desires of the flesh, the imagination of sinful lust of the flesh, and lust of the eyes. He burns evil passions in your soul. He allures you with the love of money, of material possessions, he can entangle you with wealth and power, and of gambling, which can lead to loosing your home, family, marriage. He entices with an addiction of drugs, alcohol, and sex. He can turn you into a liar, a thief, a fraud, a killer, a murderer a mindless individual with no conscience towards another human.

Satan is the second highest intelligence in the universe. He has an agenda, he is a strategist, he has a plan, a root purpose for the human race, and it is for this reason. Even though he is anti God and anti Christ, he cannot get to them, but he can get to us whom God loves and this is why he is bent on destroying the human race, he will try to get to those who God loves. The human race was created to worship God and have a relationship with him; this is what Satan wants to stop, and stop you from finding out this truth. He is a reductionist; he attempts to miniscule the gospel, God's relationship with you and cannot feel his love for you or the importance of your salvation, and all truth. Remember his vain declaration in the very first sin, in heaven, in chapter four, he wanted to be like the most high and he, wanted to be worshiped and still does.

We are ignorant of Satan's devices, because we are ignorant of spiritual knowledge, the Word of God. You should know Satan is the oppressor, the originator of sickness and disease and of all evil in our lives.

Satan operates in the sensual realm, through our five senses, what we see, hear, what we touch or feel, what we smell and what we taste. This was the approach Satan used on the first humans. They saw the fruit was good, it was pleasing to the eyes, and they throught it would make them wise and they tasted it, verse six of Gen. 3. The five senses are areas of temptation the enemy uses to temp the flesh with an appealing hook to draw us in. We are weak in these areas and he knows it. By laying twisted paths of temptation before us, he leads us into a deeper lost condition, further away from the truth of spiritual life. Living in the realm of the five senses, he can dominate us through lust, illicit desires; unclean practices that lead a person to demonic influence. He has no feelings of warmth.

The original sin, the great fall of man was because of the "lust of the flesh," they saw the fruit was good, the "lust of the eyes," it was pleasing to the eyes and "the pride of life" they thought it would make them wise (1st John 2:16 NIV), this is how and where all sin originates. Satan appealed to Eve's senses besides her intellect. It was very deceptive and yet very alluring and successful. He lies to counter God's truth, he belittles the meaning of sin, denial and fear are tactics he uses, the whole world is under the power of the devil (1st John 5:19 NIV).

The book of Revelation 12:9 shows that Satan deceives the whole world, the whole world, do you get it, not some, but, the whole world. No one is exempt, meaning; all the societies, all cultures of the world are deceived into rejecting godly values. Satan is a spirit that can influence us; Satan's influence is so pervasive that it affects every area of life in every society, remember he deceives the whole world.

Satan initiated lying, hatred, murder, mass murdering, conniving and any negative erroneous act that you can imagine. He was the first terrorist, a cosmic terrorist, he being filled with violence; and jealousy because of pride exploited that violence in heaven.

Satan rules half of the dichotomized life. Remember life for the human is either righteous or unrighteous, he rules the unrighteous life. The unrighteous are those living in darkness, those whose minds are incapable of escaping that darkness, are incapable of understanding spiritual matters, those who do not realize they live in unrighteousness, those whom prefer to live without Christ in their life and their destiny is already determined.

Satan's aim is to undermine God's character and credibility. He and his demons infiltrate the world's political structures, bringing down governments by causing upheavals amongst the people. High-ranking demons can enter a world ruler, a leader of a country bent on destroying humans. These supernatural beings are superhuman and beyond our reach. They fill minds with lies and deceit.

When Satan usurped the kingdom of the world, that set in motion the spiritual warfare that is going on today. There are only two possibilities in the spirit world. Anything on the outside of the kingdom of God is inside the kingdom of Satan. We belong either to God or to Satan. Jesus said, "*those who are not with me are against me.*" The unrighteous, the unsaved, the unbeliever belong to the kingdom of Satan. Satan has human subjects in the world that are against the truth, against the population of the world learning the truth about the gospel of Jesus Christ.

Satan is the personification of evil influences in the mind, the heart. His personality rules in the sin nature and his personality injected into the minds of unbelievers. This is how they work; the spirit of darkness wants to remove Christian symbols from public places to push God from our society. The world finds the name Jesus, offensive.

Philosophies from darkness sound persuasive to the human nature, they are lies designed by Satan. The world does not know right from wrong. Satan is constantly trying to destroy and divert you from your appointed pathway of life. Satan attacks the mind on sexual development factors at a very young age. Spiritual wickedness and lust in the mind are special tools he uses to hook the young and carry over to their older generation.

He is the instigator of the whole world system, including the political, economical, educational systems at all levels, and financial structures worldwide. He embraces religions, spiritual philosophies that lead millions astray.

Satan's primary objective is human destruction; to destroy your spirit, soul, and body. By the conscience held captive, enslaved by darkness in the sin nature he has the ability to bend you towards a life of destruction. He has the tools to render you useless to society, to your family to God.

He can destroy a person, a family, a church, he can put false apostles is churches, and deceitful workers, masquerading as teachers of Christ (2nd Cor. 11:13 NIV), he can destroy a city, a government, a nation.

He is a conniver, a manipulator, a liar; he is a destroyer of families, friends, and relationships. He is a deceiver filled with sinister schemes, and thoughts of killing, of stealing your joy, with twisted ingenious and devious ways to where he will instill a terror of fear, of worry of anxiety to make one to ride on the edge of self-destruction. He can dull your mind with the evil of darkness to where you cannot discern what is right or wrong. The unbeliever thinks they are living and doing what they believe is right and doing it their way but what is taking place is they are being enticed and entrapped into satanic manipulation, because he is also the master of chess, he moves his pawns strategically. In this state of mind they are more apt to believe and accept lies and accept them as a way of life. Satan steals your joy, your sanity, your freedom, he will mess with your health, and he wants your eternal life. Anger creates a playground for Satan, if you are an angry person the devil will fill at home in your heart.

Satan is a cynic and we should be very cautious about cynicism in our lives, because cynicism and Satan go hand in hand. Some people believe anything and everything leaving them incredibly gullible. We do not want to be gullible, nor cynical, we should be people characterized by Godly discernments and Godly wisdom. Satan promotes, 'what is in it for me attitude.' He robs you of absolute truth, absolute reality, he drops confusion in your thinking and you do not know what truth is and do not know what is real. Satan convinces people that he does not exist. He can influence people and despitefully use others.

Reading in Job, you will learn the Satan has the power to afflict man with physical pain and suffering in Acts you can read that Jesus healed those who were under the power of the devil. Satan is himself a sinful spirit that sinned from the beginning (1st John 3:8 NIV). He will remain this way until his dark demise.

He raises individuals to a level that they will have a huge impact on the populous of the world, an even swaying others to follow their beliefs. Whether it be through false religions, through the political arena, through the media, through entertainment, through any public means, books, articles, government and world leaders etc... Karl Marks, Adolf Hitler, Charles Darwin believed that what they believed and were doing was for the betterment of the human race. The theory of evolution is a hypotheses looking for an answer. Charles Darwin traveled the wrong path of life and on his journey; satanic influence raised him up to set in place the grand illusion of man through the theory of evolution deceiving millions.

Miss Winfrey, who draws millions to her beliefs, says that Jesus cannot be the only way to God. Jose' Luis de Jesus Miranda and his growing sect, Growing in Grace Ministry and a host of others in our time are influencing and leading astray millions to believe either there is no God or there are many ways to God, or they are God. Jose' Luis de Jesus Miranda believes he is Jesus, he has a hundred thousand followers world wide. Those who have died in these beliefs are today, in a place of suffering because of whom they have followed down the wrong path of life.

Satan's character expresses the antagonistic, malicious and perverse nature of the enemy of God and of man. He designed an offensive nature of spiritual warfare toward God, his word and his people and the people of the world. Satan has an inborn hatred toward God and you and he is here on this planet to destroy you and all that belong to God and to ruin God's plans. He has a premeditated crusade against you and all of God's people and the sinners he will drag down with him. Satan is an immensely powerful invisible being who continually leads man down a path toward selfishness and self-destruction.

Satan is a spiritual person as you are a fleshly person, he is a spirit man as you are a physical man, and he is a spiritual creature as you are a physical creature. Upon your death, you will become a spiritual person with your spirit and soul in full contact.

He is a spirit, yet he is a person, a spiritual being, a constant threat immersed with evil, his essence is death, and there is complete boundlessness within his kingdom to destroy the human race. He is a murder, a lying deceiver to many, a destroyer of hope, and he is the evil, wicked ruler on earth.

Satan is in every aspect of humanity. He is involved in science, religions, cultures, governments, businesses, banking and financial institutions of the world; he is involved in the educational systems, parties of negotiations, the entertainment world, and the media of mass communications, which also involve the people of its productions and of these various organizations and academics of the world. He also tries putting his two-cents worth in all reading material, all viewing material, all hearing and all seeing. Satan's involvement in these can change the cultures of the world and has done just that, and that change has favored his kingdom.

He will use every kind of evil deception to fool those on their way to destruction, because by their own *will* they refuse to love and accept the truth that would save them.

Satan is a finite being. His history filled with deceitful actions, and these actions prophesied to continue until the time where there will be a day of judgment for him. He is a powerful evil force that tries to subtly trick-mankind into denouncing the way of truth.

More facts about Satan

He was the highest of the created beings in the universe, he is extraordinarily powerful, and extremely intellectually clever, and he is the ruler of this world, the first lie came from him, he is a hateful, vile, deceptive person, and he is filled with wrath. Satan hates God and he hates God's people, the Christians and the Jewish race, he sets into place anti-Semitism whom will turn against the Jewish race. This is Satan's personality, he is anti everything pertaining to God, he is anti good, anti truth, and he is anti Christian.

Satan brought evil into the world, and he will flood your soul with filth, with deceit, with perversion and illusions, with discouragement,

Satan takes advantage of us in the sin nature. He is obnoxious toward us; he is hostile in the spirit realm. Satan is a silent minded intruder, he enters in the mind through the interest the individual has in worldliness. He does not let you see him sitting near by while you are socializing at your favorite watering hole. He does not let you see him near by when an augment gets out of hand with your mate, with a family member, with a good friend, with your employer, with an employee. He does not let you see him in the car when rage roars up inside you against another motorist throwing gestures, profanity, acting insanely and edging you on in the direction of frustration, stress, and with an intolerable fury in all these instances. He is instigating the cause of destruction in any area of your life where he will wedge his evil spirit into your situations and circumstances. He will inject in you an irresponsible behavior, being inconsolable with a complete lack of reasoning, he is the mastermind of deception and Satan is the prince of pride.

Demons and the spirit of Satan encompass the planet. In the Old Testament Satan's spirit was anti-God, in the New Testament era he is the anti-Christ spirit. Antichrist spirit is the kingdom of darkness in the invisible spirit world. This antichrist spirit covers earth with all the characteristics and personality of Satan and the demons can mimic him and carry out his devious assault against the human race. Satan is not omniscient, all knowing like God is, he is not omnipresent, everywhere at all times, universal like God is, he is not omnipotent, invincible, unstoppable, supreme, almighty like God is. Satan's power is limited by the unlimited power of God and demons do have perimeters, controlled by their Creator also.

He can only be at one place at a time, we are not vital enough for Satan himself to indwell us but his demons also called devils are very interested in us. They are the ones that torment us. When satanic behavior works in your favor, he has your attention, he has the rest of you, and now you work in his favor.

Satan's Sin
God's Plan

When covetous entered Satan he was no longer doing God's will, but now his own and disorder rose immediately in him and pride turned this angel into a rebellious deceitful and defiant enemy of the God of this universe. When Satan sinned, he was not destroyed just as you are not when you *willfully* sin. Before you were created, before Satan (Lucifer) was created God set a plan into motion and that plan no man, no beast no spirit will derail and through all the ages, millenniums, dispensations including this one, God's plan is still in tack and right on course. You see my friend there is a time to live and a time to learn, a time to die and a time of judgment (See Appendix). Nothing will change this, nothing will change God's plan of law and order. This is our journey, we are given a time to live and during that living phase we are to learn, learn what this life is all about, and learn whom you are and we can even learn about the after-life and about God, to an extent.

Satan's lies misled us and he continues his manipulative, corrupting influence every opportunity he can in the weaker vessels of the human race. He has lead and tempted men and women to sin for thousands of years. He brought satanic influences into the universe when he rebelled against the will of God, and sought out his own will, this action of his flared his pride and he became a selfish egomaniacal tyrant.

Satan's army,
Demons

Demons are fallen angels, they are called fallen because they fell from their heavenly grace when they sinned by rebelling against God and teaming up with Lucifer to initiate a violent conflict in heaven, and because of this they will burn in hell.

Demons also called devils, can seduce humans into sinning, they know the human nature and they know the human is weak, and they know, our weaknesses. They are not mind readers, they are spies, and they are constantly watching us, learning our behaviors, observing our habits, moods, attitudes and personality. Besides being seducing spirits they are also deceiving spirits that have commandeered, seized the mind of some human ministers for their own purposes. These ministers of false religions now teach and preach satanic doctrines leading others astray. What a heavy anguish will come upon them at judgment.

They take advantage of our physical, our emotional, and our spiritual weaknesses. Navigating through our mind cleverly bombarding us with sinister thoughts of our desires, goals, wants, needs, in our activities, in our work environment, wealth, economics, in our society, in cultures, which is a huge target. They find ways to break-up marriages, families, relationships, partnerships, they twist minds where right is wrong and wrong is right.

Demons are a lower ranking of a higher anarchy under the authority of Satan and they truly do harass humans.

Their life is a life of terror centered on destroying humans with no remorse. They are here to inject harm into our lives. They are unclean spirits, they are also wicked spirits, and they are those fallen angels with a diabolical leader. They truly are spiritual terrorist. However, these spiritual creatures have a fear of their own. They fear the presence of the Lord, they know Jesus is the only one to fear, for He alone can and will, cause their end. They also fear the coming 'Day of the Lord' as they know their time is near damnation. Their final abode is the lake of fire.

Demon spirits are receptors of thoughts and interceptor of listening words to the mind, they are more sensitive to you then you are to them. Once you have turned your *will* over to darkness, which is turning from truth, now, you think you are in control of yourself, but in reality, you are not. Their stimuli will convert you into what they want you to be once that door is open to them.

They are unseen forces of evil, godless hecklers; erroneous manifestations of evil that infiltrate their way into occults, into minds that are turned off from God. They find their way into the hearts of men who are obsessed by lustful physical addictions, sexual orgies, homosexuality, lesbianism, trans-sexual behaviors, bi-sexual and any perverse sexual behavior. Sin justifiably forces evil into addictions of the body, of the mind, and brings on pride, conceitedness; they can control personalities and attitudes, they feast, feed and devour the souls of man, and they can inflict emotional torment, bring on clouds of depression and wicked, wicked prejudice.

Demons know there is only one God and when the Lord's name is mentioned, they shudder at his name (Jas. 2:19 NIV) and they know Jesus as Lord and as their future judge (Luke 4:41).

Wherever you are, they are. If you are at your home, in your car, at work, playing, at your leisure, on a plane, on vacation, where you should not be, they will even follow you to church. They can sneak in a prayer meeting, it does not matter where you are they are there also.

When they are disembodied from the human soul because that person has died or now saved they have no rest, they look for sinners to indwell, devour and torment and to work their dastardly deeds of evil through that sinner.

His armies of soul thirsty demons exert their spiritual strength as they are ordered to bring down and undermine the mind of the human race living in the sin nature and with a mind that does not function to its fullness we are at their beckoning. Satan is not just after pastors, preachers, evangelist, people that teach and preach the word of God, but his plan is to destroy the human race before they get knowledge of the truth.

His group of demonic spirits knows already what their fate and their destiny lays waiting. They have nothing to lose as far as extinction goes, they cannot help themselves, repentance is not written in their eternal future. They come after the human race with clandestine approaches that are unrecognizable by the unbeliever. They know the human nature, and all they have to do is to watch individuals, which will reveal their weaknesses. They will reveal their negative thoughts and circumstances, and situations in their life, their desires, their wants, their goals, their plans, their secret ambitions, their secret lives, their secret thoughts, because in the spiritual realm, these, are no secrets, all is revealed, all is visible.

Where Demons Hide

Demons hide behind a cloak of deception, behind an array of false lies, theories, assumptions, false religions, they hide behind earthly values, political correctness rather than biblical correctness and eternal values. They hide behind 'do your own thing,' "I'll do it my way," "be free-spirited," "I am my own boss," and they run rampant in cultures. They hide is false manmade religions, they hide in the political arenas, they hide in constitutions of governments.

They hide behind attitudes and moods, they hide in personalities, they fixate on your personality and run with the reckless inconsiderate person you are, they hide in perceptions; they hide and weave in and out our senses, they hide in our thoughts. They can lead a mind into the dominion of darkness, where feelings of loathness, hopelessness and an imposing feeling of being lost. They are in novels, they are in entertainment, they are in every aspect, every phase of our lives, and they are in people's minds. They hide in anti-Christ and anti-God organizations, groups, they hide in bigotry, they hide within supremacist, and they hide in religious and political dogmas.

Demons hide in the world's system structure to maneuver that structure and set people up that they may achieve their goals, to obtain their desires, to conquer their pursuits, which in turn keep them engrossed down the wide road to nowhere, and to lead them further from God.

They hide behind good intentions, behind attitudes, and moods. They hide in closets with their captives, keeping the captives thoughts alive by brainwashing the captive into believing that they are what they are because of what they feel is their right to believe what they believe or be what they want to be. These brainwashing techniques performed by seducing demon spirits, all that is needed is to open up to them, give them a foothold.

Demons have no authority on Christians but they have full dominance of the soul of the sinner. They can paralyze the sinner with fear, worry and high anxiety. In the book of Job, it shows they can cause physical disease or mental suffering. They can cause devastation from the weather, natural resources; they can cause some mental disorders. They have the ability to persuade individuals into immoral sins. They infiltrate false religions, originate and propagate false doctrines. Some sinners literally give themselves over to evil and demon possession takes place, demons are evil and bent to do evil.

Demons function in the will of Satan, they are to thwart the work of God here on earth. They have great strength is religions, mind-boggling the religious leaders that feed its people with false doctrine and the people end up having strong, programmed backgrounds in their religions of untruth. No one wants to hear that their beloved church or denomination is teaching false doctrines, with false idols or false philosophical and moral dogmas. You will learn what a true church of God is.

Demons hide in the world's governments; they hide in the sacred halls of justice, creating injustice through the devil's human-pawns. They pass laws that conflict with God's word, recruiting additional political-pawns to suppress Christian beliefs in the public arena that this country was founded on.

Demons have originated witchcraft, magic, astrology, necromancy, cults, Ouija boards, fortune telling, and many, many, enticing areas that lure the lost into further darkness by these enticing tactics. They rise up against us continually.

Demons promote divination, attempts to contact information from the spirit world. Soothsaying, sorcery, psychics, spiritualism, mediums, clairvoyance, animal sacrifice, all forms of mediumistic activity, and much other spiritual wizardry, of these they are masters. To consult mediums and to make contact with the dead, which is not possible, but making contact with demonic spirits acting as human spirits from the dead is possible. Exposing oneself to this darkness has serious risk, consequences and harm to one's soul and body. These types of spiritual wizardries are offered to unbelievers dabbling in the occults. Being an unbeliever in the first place shows the lack of belief and faith and confidence in God. To enter into this arena of demonic attacks will strip the soul of any moral and goodness one has. Demons are the spiritual agents in all idolatry. Every idol has a demon associated with it that induces idolatry. As seducing spirits, they deceive men into possibilities, that through mediums they can converse with the deceased.

Demons hide in addictions they will promote sadomasochism, any perverse sexual action, they promote child abuse, sexually abusing children, sexually assaulting children, when you see these assaults taking place in our society you are seeing individuals who are heavily demon influenced, or possessed. This is a thick-dark sickness in the mind.

Demons can implant discouragement, deception, confusion; they can cause impatience, anxiousness, they have no compassion for the heart, the soul, and mind of us humans, a thousand times the contrary. They are here to destroy us by any means they can and they will use every means they have.

Demons are evil spirited, inferior and subject to the Satan. They have ulterior motives toward us, they fill our mind with thoughts of sexual impurities, greed, anger, lust and any open ends in our lives are subject to them, like Christianity, is it true, creation verses evolution, they will lead you, push you, drag you towards evolution. Their purpose is to lead man away from God.

You will learn that demons pierce the mind with their tactics, they blaspheme God's name, even though demons take possessions of the wicked men they are subject to the devil. Demonic bondage is terrible torment and is destructible to the mind and body. When demons enter a person it is like poison, it spreads, it kills. A person influenced or possessed by a demon or demons, they cannot be detected from the outside world. His motives, attitudes, and personality can reveal his intensions to a discerner. This diminishes and dilutes the *will*, for wanting to know truth, wanting to know God. Demons hide their deadly force very well in secret places in the mind. "If you pour sugar into a bottle of poison, it is undetected but it will not keep the poison from being deadly." Demons or a demon will regress in a sick mind while that mind is being prognoses, probed by an interested party until they can be alone again.

> *"We are effectively destroying ourselves by violence, masquerading as love."*
> —R.D. Laing

Evil people are bent on your destruction. They are a highly organized force under the devil's control. They hide behind the great smiles and good gestures; they will stab you in the back while shaking your hand. They hide in cold calculated hearts with malicious tendencies to do great harm in our culture and our societies.

They can speak, which means they have voices (Mark 5:9-12), they also believe in Jesus (Jas. 2:19), they exercised their wills (Luke 11:24), they know about their future fate (Matt. 8:29), they know Jesus as the son of God (Mark 1:24) and they possess intelligence under God's will. They are spirits, evil spirits, they have personalities, and they are the devil's agents.

They are supernatural beings with mighty power, some with mightier strengths than others. There are different demons like there are different humans with different functions and capabilities they are of different levels of authority.

Demons have a mind-set of an assassin, they have the mind of the most horrific of terrorists, and they have the mind of a cold calculated deceitful enemy that seems as your friend. Let us look at this in reverse, assassins have the mind-set of a demon(s), terrorists have the mind of a demon(s) all that you have read is how they work in us. They hide in our mind.

Demons with satanic influence virtually cause all our problems, as individuals and as a society on the face of the earth. Demons work through man, pawns, who create wars, man, but in reality, satanic influence is behind it all.

The advantage they have over us is that they can see into our physical world. They know our physical and spiritual phases of life. They know who the real Christians are and who are not, they know ones who call themselves Christians and they know the believers and the unbelievers; they know this by our life styles. They know the human race very well they have had thousands of years to perfect their skills in deceiving and destroying us.

Expressions of demonic activity in humans

Ultimately, sin is of the sin nature, and the evil spirits of the sin nature dominate its goings on. We are sinners of the sin nature and are subject to demonic activity as we delve into experiences of deeper darkness. The deeper we go, the intenseness of evil strikes our soul like a viper injecting venomous thoughts that circumvent the humans reasoning and spreads through the mind as a noxious serum.

All forms of perversions and lust, hatred, bitterness, the practice of homosexuality, all grossly perverted sexual behaviors like sadomasochism, pedophilia, drunkenness, gluttony, witchcraft; these all have demonic roots deep within the sin nature.

They get deep in the soul and relate to your inner most being one on one and you think it is your own thoughts that are stirring things inside. They search the corridors of your mind; seek out your weak, dark and gray areas and the secrets of the heart and your hot spots of sensuality, trash through your dark closets and gently opening to bring out any dark characteristics that are hidden inside. Once in the open and now breathing fresh air you feel empowered by their release for the world to see. However, behind the curtain, a devouring snickering demon poisoning your thoughts with lies and very thick with evil deception that is undetectable by the victim leading that soul into the abyss because of believing lies.

Demons get in through our heart, our mind, our thoughts, our conscience, our senses entering our soul, and this is from the life style we live. When you hold grudges, if you have bitterness, are unforgiving and envy in your mind they will enter your soul, harden your heart, and vex your heart cold. It will open doors of your soul for deeper darkness to enter.

Pornography, sadistic and masochistic activities with demeaning, dehumanizing, desensitizing, and demoralizing its victims are lines of attack, tools that Satan uses to hold the sinner captive in the sensual realm. Child pornography with its curiosity will affect the perpetrators beliefs, values, and morals with the accessibility to explicit images, leading to becoming a child rapist, abusing a child sexually and physically, and child pedophilia, a parent sexually abusing their child, the lowest of the low. Jesus said; *"It would be better for him to be thrown into the sea with a millstone tied around his neck than for him to cause one of these little ones to sin"* (Luke 17:2 [NIV]). Woe to them, they will face their Creator at judgment. These people are bombarded externally and internally daily with sources of sexual images and messages driven in them from our culture.

Arsonist, sniper attacks, cold blooded excesses grotesque cruelty with viciousness, heinous methods of torture, and slaughter one another mercilessly any harm to others is satanic driven. Evil put into men's minds to drive them to commit such evil and devastating disgusting deeds snare them into situations where they feel compelled to commit such atrocities.

Desecrations of churches and cemeteries have been targets as long as there have been churches and cemeteries. The evil that emerges from darkness has no pity on the sacred things of man; a matter of fact, evil enjoys tormenting us. The pawns that the demons use to work through have no respect, no conscience, and no idea why they are doing what they are doing they just do it. They know that they are mischievous but have no clue that at the helm of their driving force that leads them to perform such deeds is a demonic influence. At every act of evil is a snickering demon at your control center guiding you toward damnation.

They do not rest until they indwell a human soul; they have no peace until they are free in the human mind where they set up a center of operations, a command center if you will. Here they persuade the ungodly to be extremist, suicide bombers that blast their victims into eternity. They convince the ungodly to seek attraction to the same gender, they convince the ungodly to pass laws that support adoration, and they convince the ungodly to kill the baby in the womb. They convince the ungodly to take God, and prayer out of our schools, they try to convince the ungodly to take "In God We Trust" off our money, to take God out of the 'Pledge of Allegiance.' They take the real meaning of life and the message of God and pervert them with a cloud of twisted darkness and the dark thick lies that lead millions astray. Our Creator gave our nation to us and our founders knew that and he choose us for this inheritance. The anti-God anti-Christ and anti-Christian citizens of this country are trying to ruin the land that God has his hand on and these demonic influenced pawns will not go unnoticed at judgment.

They know metaphysics; they feed you with philosophical rhetoric and theories, and convince you that you are your own god like being, that you came from a puddle of slime, that there is no absolute truth, and that there is nothing after this life. We can be drawn into the lust of the flesh, lust of our own humanism, which drives us to be spiritually lost selfish-ambitious creatures that do not know what they ought to do.

A person under the influence

All that we just talked about are demonic and satanic influenced and once they get a grip on a soul they merge into the personality and character of individuals completely undetected.

Think of the functioning alcoholic, he is able to work, drive, converse, socialize to an extent that some may not notice his condition. His mental and physical abilities may allow him to perform task to get him through the day while he resumes his addiction.

The same is true with the drug addict, the liar, the thief, the sex addict, the imposter, the adulterer, the murderer, the control freak, and any one who lives in the sin nature is under demonic influence of that nature.

Demon influence into our children's minds poisons them with deep roots of darkness. They target those who are off in their own-world, those who are not looking for eternal things, those who are not paying attention to what is going on in this world, those who are going backwards. In our young, demons can create liars, thieves, they teach young people to be teasers, bullies, antagonists, to be rebellious, they teach them to call others names that will hurt, diminish, and demoralize a child's self-esteem, put them down, and now they have created enemies. These bullies grow up and continue their antagonizing ways; the victims grow older feeling hurt, the demoralization turns from hurt and low self-esteem to self-pity, hatred and possibly an explosive action of vengeance.

Once they are in a soul their bombardment of heavy artillery, anger, hatred, violence, vengeance, murder, serial killings, deception, rape are for pathological criminals and liars.

Satan's unseen influence is always at work, though very few recognize it. Under his influence, our primary motivation is "gratifying the cravings of our sinful nature and following its desires and thoughts." Child molestation comes from demonic influence; it comes from the deep dark roots of darkness under the surface of the sin nature. You can expect anything when one lives in the sin nature, the capability of committing any sin, any crime, any act of violence, at any time. Satan attacks our moral views, our morality.

Demons influence, persuade, and lead man into a world of sinful acts from the very least of sins, stealing a pencil, or telling a little-white lie to the ultimate of taking a life whether by killing, first, second, or third degree murder, or even abortion. By the way, there is no such thing as a little-white lie.

When an individual is face to face with another individual telling him to commit an evil act, he would be able to determine this individual was influencing him with temptation. The demonic spiritual entity in the mind goes undetected with no discernment because of the lack of spiritual knowledge. The sinner's spiritual perceptivity is illogical in spiritual matters, his future hinges on him turning his heart toward God.

The darkness of the sin nature stimulates a person to be greedy, to be an accuser, a tempter, a flatterer, a discourager, living a life of deception, someone with excessive pleasure seeking, sexual perversion, a whoremonger, eating disorders, sleep disorders, guilt, anxiety, abuse, anger, frustration, boredom, depression, feelings of inferiority, philanthropy in disguise and with an ulterior motive. A person can be made a manipulator, a liar whose practice is deception, a person under satanic influence can be prideful, and full of anger, jealous and can be a murderer. His demons are discouragers, deceivers, liars, they are thieves, they are murderers, and they are destroyers. They attack our family, our friends; they attack our character through criticisms. They bring lofty images in our mind that cultivate lustful desires. Drugs, alcohol, sexual addiction, gambling, pornography, child pornography, rape, murder, embezzlement, gluttony, deception, slander, greed, and many others all have a commonality, the sin nature they live in. In demons, their primary agenda, to destroy you and behind them, is the devil.

You have heard as a description of a very fast driver called a 'speed-demon' or you have heard the expression, their demons, maybe referring to alcohol, drugs or whatever the case, the expression goes to show the personality and character of individuals acting in ways of noticeable change. If they get into the mind of the child, through medias like the computer with all its venues of addictive allurements, through the digital phenomenon it is a way of captivating the unknown. Videos and video games, i.e. **Dungeons and Dragons,** occult involvement, boards games, Ouija Board, fortunetelling, and they got his soul. Young and older people today cannot put their phone down for fear of missing something, a call, a text, a picture.

Demons observe your actions, they know your personality they know what turns you on and turns you off, they know what humanistic buttons to push to lead you into further sin and once the sin is committed they ferment that sin until it festers into desires of wanting more of that sin or sins. They will guide you into a life of worldliness that will offer the desires of your ego, your pride, your flesh they will enter your world of false religion with doctrinal defections and deficiencies that also feed the ego, the personality and the pride of life. They will create bickering, internal strife, power struggles, and squabbling in relationships.

They know humanity better then we do, they know we are power freaks, they know we are control freaks, they know we are egotistically driven, they know self-pride is a tool that everyone uses at some degree, they know we are opinionated creatures; they know that our religious views are as diverse as our cultures. In amongst all of humanities ill-proven drives they thrive on our young people, they want to capture our youth because they will be our future leaders, our future politicians, judges, lawyers, and worldly influential individuals that the satanic world can control. They invade every generation with their deeds of darkness.

Satan is a very cunning adversary, and he knows the human nature better than we do and he attacks at the first sign of our emotional weakness and devours any deep feelings we may have in over coming emotional weakness. He sets up strongholds, he injects strong illusions, strong influences and allurements tempting us to a point where resisting is out of the question and we succumb to the sins laid before us.

Demons are spirits and spirit attitudes, characteristics and they are personalities. Fear is a spirit; it is a spirit of slavery of bondage. In the book of Romans 8:15a demons enter a soul and if that soul's personality lacks spiritual knowledge phobia demons will create fear and superstition within that person and the person will succumb to those fears. This passage is referring to the believer, *"For you did not receive the spirit of bondage again to fear,"* fear is a demon spirit.

They have spiritual tyranny over man because they are unnoticed by the sinner. We cannot distinguish them by our senses, or their powers from natural causes or their presence known by doctors. We are no match towards these supernatural wicked creatures as you can see what evil is going on in the world, We are inherently unaware that the planet we live on is the home of Satan, the devil and his demons. Scary thought but true.

Satan's Global Agenda

Appointed demons oversee nations and cause chaos and separation between its populous, this is done by the demons controlling the mind of the unsaved leaders, their pawns and using every conceivable method of law and political correctness to forge their evil ambitions into law or actions of disturbance. Once a government is taken over by power-crazed leaders who abuse their power with ambitions of global destruction, and other power struggles within the country these leaders feed from demonic sources. Heads of Satan's spiritual army oversee those countries political movements. In Daniel 10:12-13 this passage tells of an angelic messenger sent from God to deliver a message to Daniel but a demonic spirit blocked his way. This demonic spirit kept God's angelic messenger from delivering the message and this spirit called a prince, a prince of the kingdom of Persia who was manipulating demon spirits who was manipulating human pawns within Persia's government at that time to do Satan's will.

As the stage in being set for a new world order of business on the planet Satan has a great part in that preparation, of course behind the scenes as he watches events unfold globally. The hot spots in this country and around the world Satan and his angel demons are involved in their political treachery with no letting up. There is a demonic hatred for the human race and it operates through the devils pawns that will change the world through cultures, societies, political and economical meandering.

A World Wide Dualistic Conspiracy

"To understand what is unfolding on this earth is indeed a monstrous conspiracy so great, so grave, so meticulously planned and so near completion…and the vast majority of the people are wholly ignorant of it, and on such weighty matters concerning the loss of liberty and freedom of life and death, both physical and spiritual, ignorance is not bliss." — Ian Welsh

The conspiracy is two-fold. It is first, unobtrusively orchestrated within the kingdom of Satan. He has the ability to convince, influence, and tempt humans to do his work, by doing his will. His exertion is shown in the world's unrest, in national unrest, in family unrest and in individual's unrest. Turbulence in international relationships, instability throughout the world will be sitting the stage for his definitive entrance as the answer to the world's problems. The conspiracy is from the spiritual realm and the physical realm is involved. It will be achieved by demons, demonic activities, and human manipulation by spiritual forces. These forces of evil have infiltrated minds of very intelligent people that will continue to make this country a godless society.

Satan remains in the background, behind the scenes manipulating worldly events by using and moving his human pawns in positions that will create unrest in worldly affairs. They can be in governmental relations, in human relations, in civil, in human rights, in theology, in history, in fighting the real meaning of our Constitution and in any area that will create difficulty in people, and create chaos and create a division among us.

Satan's kingdom has a fine-tuned futuristic plan that includes continuing relentless pressure from the sin nature to keep the lost, lost and what is hidden, hidden. Satan's kingdom is a kingdom where only the wicked live, where the demonic influences build their schemes, plan their strategy, and use wicked tactics against the human population.

The futuristic plan includes that of a world ruler, not ruling Satan's spiritual kingdom but ruling the physical world. This ruler, the world will embraced with open arms mainly because of the so near ruin of the world's economy and financial institutions and with worldwide terroristic violence and his promises to bring solutions to the world problems and peace to the world especially to Israel.

Known throughout the world is the unrest of Israel and their enemies that want them removed from the face of the earth. This will be one of the new world's focal point and that threat is escalating just as there is relentless pressure from the sin nature escalating with wars rising in the world.

There is an invisible war going on in the spirit world and those who are non-believers are hopelessly left with no discernment for survival. The war is between the spirit of Satan, which is an anti-Christ spirit and with all his demon spirits against God and his holy angels and, they spar within our realm affecting our destiny.

His Strategy

Satan's strategy is to ruin man, breaking down his will, breaking up his families, building up walls, by doing so, he creates a separated population of the nations, they have less morals and more immorality. He creates weakened imbalanced individuals, he creates them in government positions, in families, in relationships, they work for him in governments of nations, in this whole world order. He is the prince of this world and worldly system he operates in the spirit realm controlling and manipulating the minds of man to achieve what he determines his. The minds of the human race are his pawns. His strategy has numerous facets working together to achieve his goal which is to control this planet and its inhabitants as himself in the physical realm and he well accomplish this soon.

The Spiritual and Human Conspiracy

His pawns at every minute of every day are working toward achieving his purpose, his goal. He is pushing toward a one-world leader, which will govern a one-world government, one-world currency and economic system. How will a spiritual leader that has his own kingdom strategize and become a physical leader governing this planet? He will do it through humans and one particular human.

His human pawns that are influenced by demonic forces to create a passage to usher in this satanic antichrist and are even now they are setting the stage for his entrance. He is using human pawns, the movers and shakers internationality in governments, in courts, financial institutions. He will use who ever else he can in this world to cause global chaos. From worldly financial and economic collapse, through greed, fraud, wasteful spending, and bonus's that are ridiculous and they have no shame, causing havoc in our court system to divide the people. His demonic forces can cause famine, natural disasters, they can cause sickness and disease, you can read this in the book of Job, and they will do what ever it takes for Satan to become the physical human authority over the world's inhabitants.

Creating a worldwide diversion from the spirit life, he uses a conglomerate of intellectual minds, individuals in many occupations, for instance television and radio shows that sweep large audiences, they can lead many astray. He will use law firms, individuals in local, state, national, and international governments, and even implementing these diversions worldly with means to draw attention to matters that create legal separation in the populace. While diversions are occupying the courts, time, people, and money these diversions are also holding the lost captive by feeding them lies that they believe to be true and worth the fight. These intellectual minds have the ability to sway and influence millions in ways that seem right but are lies from Satan's toolbox, his demented mind.

For instance, abortion let us look at it from Satan's mind. In 1973, abortion was made legal and this was done by Satan's pawns in government, law firms, judges and courts. These individuals were persuaded by intellectual minds that the fetus was not a person. However, with-in eight-weeks of development the fetus was recognizable as a human. Of course, Satan and his demons were behind all of the persuading of the human minds. Satan knows that fetuses would become people and these people would have potential to become Christian children of God, who Satan hates, which would mean to him that he, lost more sinners from his twisted diabolical sin nature. Satan was behind the whole abortion concept (the diversion) from the beginning to the end, implanting it and even the law being passed, thanks to his pawns, his attorneys, his doctors, his organizations that benefit from the body parts and his judges in the Supreme Court. So, murder and destroy them before they are born by calling the defenseless child something else than a developing human being in its mothers womb. Now he does not have to deal with that potential praying Christian, let the mother deal with her loss and continue living her promiscuous ways. Are you pro-life or pro-choice?

It is the same with any of his agendas. He works his demons in the minds of the pawns to achieve his goals; Look at gay marriage, the same is true. Governments are involved, law firms are involved, courts and judges are involved individuals who firmly believe they want to marry someone of the same sex. What is Satan thinking? He uses wealthy gay activist that significantly influences state Supreme Court legislatures. He is causing chaos where there need not be any, but he has put it in the minds of sinners that sex and marriage with the same gender is desirable and worth fighting for. This is blinding the minds of these people and keeping them captive in the sin nature where all this takes place. All that are involved in this matter are persuaded that they are right, and they have rights even if it means redefining marriage from one woman and one man. Their mind is so pre-occupied with this issue, (the diversion) because Satan has introduced this desire in them that God and Jesus Christ do not enter their mind, there is no room for them, because their thoughts are not wholesome thoughts. These come from traveling the wide path of life, the sin nature. In the sin nature, God and Jesus are not in the equation of the sinner's activities, because minds are bent toward ungodly situations that cause chaos and create a speedy passage into the depths of darkness for all involved.

The minds of sinners are so corrupted with demonic influence that they feel that they have rights as any other human. If children are brought into a same sex relationship, their minds will forever be confused, saddened, and ashamed as maturity sets in. Does Satan care, no, just as long as everyone stays in the perimeters of sin nature. Lost, blinded and confused and traveling the speedy passage further into darkness.

The conspiracy involves nations that are promoting wars; their leaders are following this spiritually designed strategy from darkness as their minds are directed into fearless military tactics, developing weaponry of devastating proportions of the earth, creating tensions with nations that the palm of their hand is inches from the button.

Militant factions with relentless advancements of destruction for those that are in their way and have no use for will be exterminated. Demons put in these leaders minds a grip of profound hatred towards their enemies. They are creating a worldwide satanic movement, a conspiracy staging a strategic move of deception to deceive the world.

How would the demon world do this, by their human counter-parts, through the godless people, whose wills and minds that are corrupted with satanic lies and thrive on conspiracies, and are hyper-vigilant.

Satan orchestrates and maneuvers his demonic agents throughout the world and gets involved in governments, in political arenas, in law making sessions, in cultures and in family matters.

Besides the inhabitants of the earth, the earth itself will feel Satan's wrath as we draw closer to that event. He will increase in terror, terror throughout the world will spread like a deadly infection, he will push chaos and confusion to its limits; he is the one behind it all and he is the one now causing the increase in prejudices in the world. He has turned nation against nation, religion against religion, he will cause a world financial collapse, he will instigate the rise of the tribulation, he will ramp-up the heat of his terror on the population of this planet with his fury, call it global warming, and the whole earth will feel an increase of satanic activities in the last days. His fury and his intense hatred to do us harm will be repeatedly exercised especially towards the end of his reign. Earth will not be a fun place to be. Satan can create situations in glocalization (See Appendix), entangling governments with diplomacy that can get out of hand very quickly and turn to wars devastating the people on earth.

Rankings of demons

Satan's kingdom is a well-organized army with different levels of demonic authority. Demons rank as follows, principalities, powers, rulers, and spiritual wickedness. Think of them as Generals, Lieutenant Generals, Major Generals, and Brigadier Generals.

Principalities indicate that there are political demons. That there are sovereign demonic princes over certain proveniences, countries on the earth, these are high in rank and they may have charge of specific cities and are evil rulers. Powers are authorities of the unseen world.

Rulers are of the darkness of this world, as spiritual world rulers. Spiritual wickedness in high places is wicked spiritual beings in the heavenly places. Satan is the prince of the air. These are his soldiers, his army of demonic angels that carry out his commands on the human species. The kingdom of Satan consist of our air, known as the first heaven, the earth, and all within as he personally roams the earth seeking authoritative figures that he himself will influence, devour that soul and bring that victim into subjection to his mentality of evil thinking. The answer to demon warfare in the mind, demon influence, and demon possession is Jesus Christ. Christian counseling is recommended, not counseling from the secular realm but counseling grounded in the word of God.

> "The devil is a better theologian than any of us and is a devil still."
> –A.W. Tozer

The Kingdom of God

> "*But seek ye first the kingdom of God, and his righteousness.*"
> — Matthew 6:33a

The whole picture of the Kingdom of God is not just heaven and his throne and the entire goings on in heaven, nor is it just the vastness of the universe as far as the mightiest telescope can see, or this wonderful earth and the vegetation life that feeds man, but also man himself.

Unlike Satan's kingdom, God's Kingdom is everlasting, eternal. Nothing or no one, no man made god from a man-made religion will remove Him. No god, no lord and no king of earth will have an eternal rule above God. The Kingdom of God is the entire sphere of God's rule including the kingdom of Satan and man. The external and material world of man is relating to the present expression of the Kingdom of God, our earthly resources are God given but the Christian conduct is an expression of God's Kingdom. *"For the Kingdom of God is not a matter of what we eat or drink, but of living a life of goodness and peace and joy in the Holy Spirit. If you serve Christ with this attitude, you will please God, and others will approve of you, too"* (Rom. 14:17,18 [NLT]). The Christian represents the Kingdom of God to the world through our actions.

All human life is eternal, heaven and hell are eternal, and these are abodes for eternal beings. Although hell is, eternal it will not be a continuation of Satan's now kingdom. When he is sent there, his kingdom here will be disbanded and he will remain confined, incarcerated, in his own surrounding, he will not have rule there, he will be in torment for eternity, as well as the demons and the stubborn and rebellious sinners who refused to repent and accept Jesus, the Christ.

The Kingdom of God is at hand, this is saying the Kingdom of God is in the midst of you; it is in the heart of the believer, God reigns internally in the believer. Potential believers he awaits, this is what the Bible says about sinners. *"Do you not know that the unrighteous will not inherit the kingdom of God? Do not be deceived. Neither fornicators, nor idolaters, nor adulterers, nor homosexuals, nor sodomites, nor thieves, nor covetous, nor drunkards, nor revilers, nor extortioners will inherit the kingdom of God"* (1st Cor. 6:9,10). If you are not in the Kingdom of God then you are in the kingdom of Satan and *willingly* being in the kingdom of Satan you choose the wrong path for your life's journey and you are deceiving yourself, as the scripture said;

"Do not be deceived." Deception is outside of the Kingdom of God where the sinner lives.

"For indeed, the kingdom of God is within you." Luke 17:21b

PART IV

TRILOGY OF MAN

Chapter 9

❦

"Slightly lower than the angels" is a whole lot better than slightly higher than apes. Let's get the order straight. God, angelic beings, man, animals, and vegetables. — Stuart Briscoe

MAN

Man is inseparable from eternity, there is no separation whatsoever between his identity now and his eternal identity other than his physical body. His spirit and soul will continue through the ages to come. Man has a decision to make in life to where he wants to spend eternity being in an eternal conscious state. The fact of now knowing of heaven and hell a well thought-out decision can be made. It is not a hard decision to make you know what lies before you, do you want life or death. Ignoring the decision, by design you have sealed your fate. Not wanting to know what you are facing is foolishness; you can experience a freedom, discernment from all unrighteousness.

Through our spirit we were made to commune with God. That spirit in man would in turn put soul and body into subjection through obedience to God. The supernatural power flowing from God would enter into the spirit of man and empower man to serve God. The human has a spirit, a soul, and the body of flesh this makes man, a very special creature; our lives are a gift of the Creator of the universe. Some cannot wrap their thoughts around this. God created man with a purpose to serve, glorify, honor, and worship Him.

Being a resident of planet earth, we are in a dimension of incompleteness, again by design of the sin nature, our inheritance, and in that incompleteness; we live our lives against the laws of God. We live a negative life style developed from the sin nature that is against God's approach to life. Man lives blindly not knowing what he is doing, why he is doing it and where he is going, operating his life with no spiritual knowledge, he lives beneath his intended capacity because he lacks spiritual knowledge and without that knowledge, spiritual matters are foolish to him, which is the exact opposite of which he should be. The worldly life that he lives again by design is serving 'self" this is the natural state of man not the spiritual/physical state. *The man without the Spirit does not accept the things that come from the Spirit of God, for they are foolishness to him, and he cannot understand them, because they are spiritually discerned"* (1st Cor. 2:14 NIV).

The natural man is clueless of what God's best is for him. However, in our created formation, God imparted a spirit and through this spirit He gives inspirations, He gives knowledge, understanding, direction, guidance, and He gives us the truth of life. *"But it is the spirit in a man, the breath of the Almighty, that gives him understanding"* (Job 32:8 NIV). It is our spirit, that God lives through us and if our spirit is not born again, it is dead to sin and being dead to sin, Satan has access to that deadness. That deadness is the void within us that Satan attempts to fill with filth. In the book of James 2:26a *"Without the spirit the body is dead*, the mind does not function in reality, the Lord is telling us that our natural physical life on earth is incomplete without his Spirit in us, God's Spirit, which brings our spirit to life. Without our spirit brought to life our natural whole being is dead toward him and now that deadness that emptiness succumbs to evil, again by design. By design, is meant that in the sin nature man's spirit is not living; it is dead toward spiritual matters. The nature of the sin nature is incompleteness, there is no whole meaning of life, it continues in revolving circles spiraling downward gaining momentum guiding man into a way of thinking that makes sense to him but the end is destruction. By design is a choice, to live in incompleteness, a willingness to shun truth to where there is freedom.

The mind without God is an open cesspool for the devil. In this corrupted, murky contaminated environment, he plants seeds of doubt, seeds of unbelief, seeds of evil, of wickedness, seeds of sexual perversion, seeds of confusion, fear, depression, discouragement, and all forms of lust that transform into thoughts in the human mind. When he takes stealth possession of the mind, he does all he can to keep that mind occupied with any thing that keeps the mind from looking toward God, keeping that mind from wanting to read the Bible, keeping that mind, that person from wanting to go to church and knowing what is truth. He makes activities happen for individuals to experience, those secrets they have within them that know one knows about. He keeps the function of the sinner dulled to spiritual things. He keeps the individual physically happy, through the lust of the flesh, the lust of the eyes, which the eyes of man are never satisfied and the pride of life and he keeps that individual lost, he keeps that individual in unbelief, and he keeps confusion in the forefront of man's life until that person's soul is severed from the body.

Our journey through the sin nature provides a misleading process for our mental faculties, established by our conformity to the repetitious ways of the world. Our every day living in meaningless matters, our every day living in selfish-ambitions, our every day living with the wrong motives, our every day living in confusion, our every day living in pleasures, living in extremities, living in deceit, living in denial, our journey is living in unrighteousness and within this conformity, we treat ourselves with blind favoritism. The provisions of the sin nature, the sinful elements that blind us and holds us captive in that void of our mind does not let us know our true selves, our spiritual side.

We are not humans on a spiritual journey, we are spiritual beings on a temporal human journey, as we mentioned, but ultimately we will remain spiritual beings on an eternal spiritual journey and this, is the way we should see our selves. The human journey centers on the physical-fleshly-elements, material elements, of gain, covetousness and we live in a 'get-all-you-can' attitude world, living for self. The spiritual journey is living for Christ and with a 'give-all-we-can' attitude, denying self, sharing the gospel, winning souls, and sharing God's love.

The natural journey is through the wide gate and down the broad way of life and experiences everything in life that the sin nature offers, but the human's spiritual/physical life is not found down this path.

The mind that is with God, Satan's strategy takes a different approach, because we live the spiritual/physical life with discernment and we can recognize his tactics, but still his approach is covert, with the mature Christian, the Spirit of God undermines his approach. He wants to keep the believer from church, from worshiping God, from fellowshipping, from reading the bible, from giving their testimony, from witnessing, to leading the Christian into sin and disobedience.

You are a spiritual being. We are told we are of the dust of the earth, but, we also have another dimension about us, the body is the material part of us, the dust but we also have an immaterial part. *"Then the* LORD *God formed the man from the dust of the ground"*, (our material components.) *"He breathed the breath of life into the man's nostrils, and the man became a living person"* (Gen. 2:7 NLT). While the man was either lying there or standing there facing God like a mannequin, an anatomical structure, body, until God *"breathed the breath of life into man's nostrils, and man became a living being,"* some translations say a *"living soul"* our immaterial components. The breath of life is our spirit our soul. We are spiritual/physical beings, when breath leaves our bodies, our material matter, our **spirit** and **soul**, our immaterial spiritual matter, return to God from whence they came, we are now separated from the material life and enter into the new life of the spirit world.

Spirit, Soul, and Body

There are three separate identities of man, his spirit, his soul, and his body. It was said in Chapter 1 that we are spiritual-beings on a human journey. The spirit and soul and their attributes are the immaterial part of man that concerns life, action, and emotion the intrinsic balance of man's being.

The Spirit

The spirit is that part of man that communicates with God, where we worship and show reverence. Our spirit is in spiritual union with our conscience, our will, our moral character, your spirit is the real you, the spirit is the center of man, with the born again experience the Holy Spirit becomes the center of man's being. Adam communicated with God through his spirit. God supernaturally empowers man with his Spirit to have communion with Him, this is the born again experience, empowered with His Spirit.

Without man's spirit alive in him, his entire person, his nature is under the constant attack of the sin nature and his soul becomes darkened with deceit. God thinks of the natural man as being dead, spiritually dead because his spirit is immersed in darkness. Even man's body is dead to spiritual matters, because it is worldly. His spirit is not alive in him and he lives to please his physical desires.

Without man's spirit alive through the Holy Spirit he is considered dead. Man's spirit is known as the hidden-man, the hidden-man of the heart, the hidden-man is the real you. When the Spirit speaks of the heart, it is speaking of the spirit.

We do not see the invisible part of man, when we see man we see a body that has a soul and a spirit. That soul receives spiritual nourishment from either the sin nature or the divine nature and whichever one the individual feeds from it is shown in his speech, his thoughts, his actions, his whole being will live either for one or for the other. When the Spirit is absent from the heart, a life with superficial concerns rule the heart. A false love is expressed, because truth is not known, the lack of truth is a lack of the knowledge of true love where true love resides.

The Soul

The soul is our living being, the man himself, person or individual, the soul is, self, it is life, it is our person, our appetites, physical and mental come from our soul, our desires, emotions, personality and passions. With our soul, we relate to ourselves, our personality, our character, we relate to society, we relate to other people. We develop in the world, in life, by the soulish decisions we have made for the previsions for the flesh. The soul and the spirit are associated with the mind, the will, feelings, with faculties of thoughts, actions, emotions, conscience, intelligence, personality and conceived as an immaterial entity. This unit is susceptible to happiness or misery. The soul is an immortal being designed for everlasting life which differs from the body and it will not decay at death. The soul and spirit depart from the body of a person at death.

The Body

The outer compartment, which is our body, our house, someone called the body, our space suit that we are wearing while we are here on earth, I heard it called a tent, what ever you want to call the body it is a temporary dwelling place for us. We are in this house for a short while and then we must leave, we do not have a choice we will be evacuated.

The body houses your whole being, your soul, all that is within and spirit. When our bodies die off, we will still exist. While we are here, we are human beings, when the body dies and goes to the grave we will become spiritual beings, eternal spiritual beings, as the Lord, and the angels. We will not be angels or any other spiritual creature we will be ourselves. We will live in the spiritual world, the spirit realm when we leave our physical body.

By the nature of the world, by us being human we think with a carnal mind, we naturally think and live with a carnal soul. While living in carnality the human spirit has no knowledge of God and with no knowledge of God, the Spirit cannot emit the things of God to our spirit. The natural man, cannot receive the things of God.

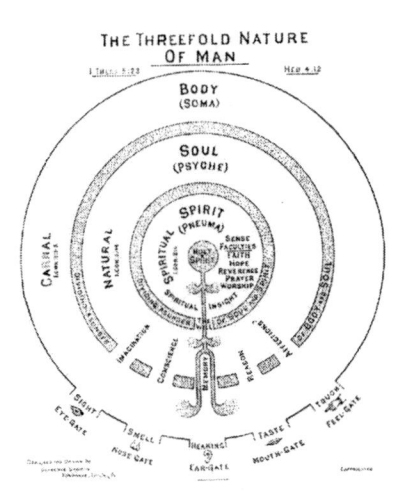

This illustration by the late Rev. Clarence Larkin (See Appendix) depicts man's complete being, spirit, soul and body. The outer circle represents the **body** of man, the middle circle for the **soul** of man, and the inner circle represents the **spirit** of man. The **body,** shown touching the material world and through the five gates senses of sight, smell, hearing, taste, and touch, reach the soul.

The **soul** is not involved in wanting to know God; it is only through the **spirit** that God's known. The gates to the **soul** are imagination, conscience, emotions, memory, our ability to reason and rationalize and the affections, and feelings. This is where our enemy camps.

Our intellect, our mind, our heart, our soul, our spirit are imperceptible, and cannot be spiritually separated. Only God can separate the soul and spirit. Your soul is your life, while living in the sin nature and taught all its erroneous teachings there are no spiritual truth. It desensitizes the human soul, the conscience, the emotions, by injecting increasing amounts of negative thoughts, lies, satanic and false doctrines that will lead to bondage and establish in the mind false imaginations, false philosophies about life and against God. This is why they say the battlefield is in the mind. In the mind, your thoughts are governed by the sin nature, through carnal thinking and you are decoding or processing thoughts of the flesh, of the world, of the pride of life and are stuck in this bondage by you opening up strongholds to the enemy that are controlling your mind and by controlling your mind he can control you.

What are some strongholds? A huge one for the devil is compulsiveness, because an irrational psychological force, the sin nature, drives the irresistible carnal thinker, because he knows no better. Another favorite of the devil's is oppressiveness, with imposing fears, worries, bitterness, resentment, uncontrollable lust, pornography, all sexual perversion, phobias, and negative criticisms, the enemy can destroy families, relationships, businesses even the individual. The soul is the living you, your body houses your soul, your soul is the real you.

The **soul** carries our consciousness, our intellect, our imagination, our breath etc., and the **spirit**, the heart, the mind, our existence. Since the **spirit** is dead in man, the **soul** is in bondage, held down with shackles of sin penetrating the deepest parts of man, here is the key to all man's dilemmas, man is weak even though he thinks he is strong, spiritually speaking. He is weak in his knowledge, in his consciences, in his discernment, his understanding, and he is weak in wisdom this is the cause of the nature of sin he lives in, thus man leans on his own understanding. The mind being weak in these areas leaves the mind bait for the allurements of the worlds system and what ever captures the mind captures the man.

The gate to the **spirit** is through our **will**; the **spirit** receives God's Spirit as you can see here God's Spirit lives within man's spirit as scripture teaches us. Our **spirit** is our life force; the spirit of man represents him as a living being. The spiritual faculties of the spirit are faith, hope, reverence, prayer and worship, fellowshipping and our ability to commune with the God of the universe. This is man living a spiritual/physical life, not with the will of man but with the will of God.

This illustration shows man as a complete being, living within God's divine nature. Living in the sin nature, the **will** stays intact but the **spirit** is missing, it is spiritually dead and without the **spirit** there is a cavity, a void, within the **soul** of man, where the **spirit** should be, and this void is now filled with the spirit of the world and not the Spirit of God as should be. Satanic and demonic influence enters man through these gates, they enter through the senses, and direct demonic activity for the bodies appetites. Our senses are a target for demonic attacks of the desires or cravings of the flesh.

They enter our **soul** through our mind and take control of, and seize our **will** and with demonic activity penetrate the **soul's** appetites. The world speaks many languages, but all men in all languages speak with a carnal mind, void of Godly spirituality.

Before the great fall of man this illustration was man's spiritual condition, man's spirit was in a *willing* communion with God with an open communication between them. When sin *willfully* entered man, his **will** sealed the gateway to his **spirit** and man's spirit sealed off from Godly communication. Without his spirit man is not a spiritual creature, he is a **carnal** a **natural** creature, worldly, with a body and a soul. His spirit shut off from him, and his spirit shut off from God because of the enormous might of the stubborn will under the influence of the *willful* sin. This leaves man in a condition called lost, his spirit is lost, here is the void and with his spirit void in him his condition is, darkness, no illumination from heaven, no clarity in spiritual matters, and no communion with his Creator. Being in a lost state, the **spirit of error** fills the mind with erroneous evolutionary types of beliefs, beliefs that direct mans gullible incomplete being to a **self**-absorbent style of life. Man is in an incomplete state, and will remain so until his death and die a sinner or, until he is *willing* to accept Jesus as his Savior and be converted and let, Gods will replace his. Without a conversion, man cannot understand spiritual matters, mans will obstructs the Spirit's entrance to his spirit.

The will must be surrendered for the Holy Spirit to enter the unsaved person. If the strong willed person continues with his strong, stubborn "*will*" and continues to deny the truth, continues to not relinquish his rebellious attitude, continues to live under the dominance of the **"spirit of error"** and continues living a life of meaningless adventures in a world that is saturated with evil, that person will perish. Perish into an eternal life in hell, shared with other regretful, sorrowful rebellious stubborn sinners, all because of a prideful heart.

Our **will**, which gives us a sense of **self**, is very strong in the sin nature of unrighteousness and because of a stubborn **will** and **pride**; this stops us wanting God entering our heart. Remember the **will** is the "gatekeeper." The **will** guards the entrance of the **spirit**, the **heart**, and the only way the Holy Spirit can enter is by us *willfully* surrendering our **will**, dissolving the stubbornness and pride and humbling ourselves in repentance and confession of our sins and then our will yields to, "His will."

We are self-deceived, because the spirit is dead and defiled, depraved and doomed into slavery, we are enslaved captives, enchained by the world, through the flesh and the devil and the world. The mind is blinded by sin and the heart, is ruined by sin and the will now under control of evil is bound by sin. This is achieved by being independent from God *willingly*, being in disobedience and rebellion. The will is in bondage.

We are the wounded, the by-products, and inheritance of a nature that we did not ask for, a life that we did not choose. We entered life bound and gagged, lost and blinded and not able to see what happened or why life is like it is.

We have three enemies in this world. The world is one with its system of enticing networking's that will lead the lost down a path of further darkness. It is not meant the world itself but the people of the world, the manmade infrastructure, of the world, its establishments, its originations, its governments, its principles, its cultures, its people, its institutions, etc...

The second is the devil. With his army of angelic demons, which they are working overtime to ensnare the human soul, bring it to a closure and drag it into the abyss. It is a very evil manipulating kingdom that sits upon the whole world keenly watching the souls of man for the opportunity to enter and take over the soul. We are not fully aware of the power of this malevolency and unaware of its presence among us and in the human mind. Its evil effects and influences will bring man to do what it desires and man does just that.

The third is ourselves; we are selfish-greedy-people with desires beyond our means. We will go after what we want no matter who gets hurt. We do not have to go back to study the atrocities throughout history to compare that evil of today, just look at today and compare it with itself. In recent headlines thought out the word, greed has taken over the mind of the corrupt that lead this country and world into near financial and economical bankruptcy.

The Conscience

The confrontations we experience on our life's journey have a profound consciousness in our soul of perception and awareness through our conscience. Our conscience was given to us as moral insight. Dr. Charles Stanley said; "Think of the conscience as the voice of God in our souls, divinely implanted convicting us to act morally."

Living in the sin nature we have been conformed to the world systems, which programs us with misinformed information, which feeds our mind and our conscience with these errors, and we build faith and beliefs on something we know nothing about. Through our beliefs, we experience a worldly knowledge, and at the same time an ignorance of spiritual Godly principles.

You can listen to your conscience or ignore it, by ignoring it your conscience will be seared, it can get like scar tissue, it will not sense right or wrong and that is a matter you do not want to happen, for you will be your own enemy. Habitually sinning you can dull your conscience until you cannot even hear it, this is a seared conscience. Our conscience is a gift to protect us. If your conscience is not hardened because of the worldly life surrounding you, when you do something wrong, your conscience will convict you of that wrong. Sin will hinder your life from knowing God. If your conscience is hard then it will not convict you of your wrong doings. Our conscience is to give us a moral sense of right and wrong, our conscience is to protect us, is the bottom line (See Appendix).

The Imagination

The imagination is a device where demonic activity flourishes, they grow steady and strong in negative growth patterns creating and devising schemes, transcending to the mind that will conjure up evil thoughts and then evil acts, and evil works. As long as the mind of the individual is open to them and the individual *willingly* chooses to live a life without biblical knowledge and is open to the worldly system, then demonic activity is surely bound to take place, because the individual has opened the door to them by rejecting the truth. Without God, the mind is a cesspool, an open drain for filth to enter, for evil thoughts to manifest into devilish acts by the imagination flirting with dangerous devilish influences.

The nature in which we live, our minds are wayward, we are lead astray, we are lead into corruption by corruption. The kingdom of Satan creates social diversions, political and economical diversions, they create conflicts in the religious systems and in nationalities and cultures. They do their best to fill our needs of spiritual meaning with false religions, which he made, occultism, eastern mysticism or any supernatural phenomena to divert us from what is really ours.

When they enter the imagination, all of sudden, mischievous strategies are conjured up, devious plots are devised, and demons are behind it all. Our minds are the battleground for spiritual warfare; our thoughts influenced with demonic trickery that causes superstition, phobias, suspicion, irrational thoughts, imagination gimmicks that will lead one to sadistic acts on their journey. They will cultivate in your mind by working off your character and personality.

Once they have a stronghold they waste no time influencing and bombarding the mind with satanic thoughts, subtle thoughts controlling the attitude, personality and behaviors of individuals and take them out of character and into a dark corner in their mind away from reality. These satanic features change attitudes, personalities and behaviors and lead to deeds of extremely darkness. They open up the floodgates for provisions for the flesh; demons are behind missing and exploited children in this world, filling the minds of the perpetrators with imagery of pornographic filthy perversions.

Our Heart

The eyes see what the heart loves. If the heart loves God and is single in this devotion, then the eyes will see God whether others see Him or not. – Warren Wiersbe

When the Bible speaks of the heart, it is not referring to the physical internal organ that is our lifeline, pumping five liters of blood and circulating that blood to every part of our body, pumping sixty million gallons of blood in a lifetime through one hundred thousand miles of blood vessels precisely arranged to reach every cell. As wonderful as that is, the heart the Bible speaks of is our mind, our spirit. In Luke 5:22 Jesus asks the Pharisees who were plotting against him, He ask, *"Why are you thinking these things in your hearts"* He could of said why are you thinking these things in your minds.

The heart is the mind, the heart and the mind are the spirit, the heart, and the mind and the spirit are one, they are the seat of our understanding. Our heart is our inner most being, it is the center of our spirit life. It is the accommodation of gathering of our intellect, our personality, our consciousness, our emotions, and our imagination and yes, also our will. God made sure that we do not come with him by intelligence but rather a humble *willing* heart. Only a person with a redeemed heart can live in proper fellowship with God because after conversion, the law of God is written in their hearts (Heb. 8:10b [NIV]).

For the unbeliever, their natural nature of their heart is away from God; their *"heart is the most deceitful of all things and desperately wicked"* (Jer. 17:9a [NLT]). *"Out of the heart proceed evil thoughts, adulteries, fornications, thefts, false witness, blasphemies"* (Matt. 15:19) and all other sins that we commit. War comes from the human heart, family tensions and problems come from the human heart; rebellion comes from the degenerate heart, but at conversion the heart changes, the behavior changes.

Evil originates in the heart; an evil heart and attitude motivates the sinner. Sin comes out of the heart of people, thus defiling them. In the book of Mark 7:21-23 this passage is telling us this; *"For from within, out of the heart of men, proceed evil thoughts, sexual immorality, theft, murder, adultery, greed, malice, deceit, lewdness, envy, slander, arrogance and folly. All these evils come from inside and make a man 'unclean.'"* Evil thoughts are evil schemes, and the heart being the mind and the mind being the thought process, the seat of passions are bound up in the will, with the desire, and the determination to disobey and sin, by following the dictates of their evil hearts and in doing so, they went backward and not frontward.

The natural heart is a carnal heart, and the carnal mind is where demons hide and rummage around the corridors of the psyche, our consciousness to know what spiritual buttons to push that will open doors of temptation to sin. This passage is from Psalms 10:7 NLT, *"Their mouths are full of cursing, lies, and threats. Trouble and evil are on the tips of their tongues."* It is very easy and very natural for the carnal heart to speak with a perverse tongue. The carnal man's heart determines his speech and his speech is filled with poison and his speech reveals it.

Growing in the world's ways from childhood leaves nothing spiritually desired from the young, except foolishness, as Proverbs 22:15 says, *"Foolishness is bound up in the heart of a child; The rod of correction* (physical discipline) *will drive it far from him."* It is sad enough to see families breaking up, but to see families with children breaking up is the devil's dream. That foolishness grows into ignorance of conduct, of moral standards, and the conscience starts callusing and without discipline, the child grows into a troubled youth entering society. Coming to an age where the child can control his will, age of reasoning, but he does not, his mind will grow full of darkness, dull his spiritual understanding and wander far from the life God gives because of the ignorance, the *willful* closed mind, hardens, as does the will.

An insensitivity towards absolute truth and moral right and wrong flourishes and spreads like poison, living a life of doing greedy and wicked things. Their speech grows full of yelling; speaking with filthy mouths with malice, fornication runs in their blood, covetousness and foolish talking speaking vain empty words.

In the natural it is hard to understand the hatred in the hearts of man, it is a reality, and results are massacres, scenes of terrible atrocities, severe abusive situations, violence and murder from the extremist with no remorse.

In the book of Ecclesiastes 9:3 New International Version this passage is telling us that the hearts of men are full of evil, and accounts for the evil that is happening in the world. *"This is the evil in everything that happens under the sun: The same destiny overtakes all. The hearts of men, moreover, are full of evil and there is madness in their hearts while they live, and afterward they join the dead."* They join the dead at the second death if repentance does not enter their heart.

Just as you can identify a tree by its fruit, so you can identify people by their actions of their heart. The heart tells who you really are, and what family you show allegiance to and your personality shows your temperament. Proverbs 4:23 New Living Translation, *"Guard your heart above all else, for it determines the course of your life."* Here are some of the heart's attributes. Heart's are fickle (Hos. 10:2 [NLT]), the unbeliever's heart has become hard towards the truth because darkness fills their mind, they wander far from God (Eph. 4:18 [NLT]). The heart becomes filled with arrogance and the spirit hardened with pride (Dan. 5:20 [NIV]). It is the heart that plots evil things (Ps. 140:2 [NIV]). It is the heart that turns man away from God, because Satan fills their heart with his doctrine (Acts 5:3), the heart is sly and crafty (Prov. 7:10) our spiritual heart is stubborn and rebellious (Jer. 5:23 [NIV]), and those living with perverse hearts are an abomination to the Lord (Prov. 11:20). Man is so foolish, he does not know that God knows all things about him, (Ps. 139:1 [NLT]), he knows the secrets of every heart (Ps. 44:21 [NLT]), he knows the thoughts of man and that the are futile (Ps. 94:11), he knows man's actions and imaginations and intentions (Isa. 66:18 [NLT]). God does not see man as man sees man, because man sees the outward appearance, God looks at the heart and knows man's thoughts (Rev. 2:23). Man pleases man to justify his actions in the eyes of man, but this is detestable to God, for God knows his heart (Luke 16:15 [NIV]). I said all of that to say all of this, what matters in life, is in the heart; the heart is either hot or cold.

What you believe, the way you act, the way you talk, your personality and character all come from the heart and determines the course of your journey, the course of your life. The harder the heart and colder the heart, the further away from answering the knock of the calling of the Lord. The heart of man can turn like a cold stone away from God by rejecting him, by hatred, bitterness, un-forgiveness, resentment, blaspheme develops in the heart, these speed the hardening.

Your heart, your spirit is the center of your being. It is the core of your spirituality and your deepest of motivations. Your spirit, your soul, your heart is the real you.

We hold convictions in our hearts that we emphatically believe to be truth to our being. Whatever our beliefs, they are personal and special, religions who worship animals, religions that worship idols, religions that worship people, people who blow themselves up and kill others all to the glory and will of their god, and believe their actions to be advantageous and justifiable to their entrance into heaven. They are very sincere in their convictions but they are sincerely wrong. Millions immediately will awaken after their physical death in the presence of dreadful horror to their surprise wishing they never entered through the wide gate of the status-quo, the wide gate of destruction, where they themselves will perish. They will perish by their own stubborn rebellious lost will, their hard foolish heart.

In our worldly hearts, we have filled it with the garbage of the sin nature of what it has to offer, we must clean out this trash, to allow the Spirit to work in us. Whatever the condition of your heart, will determine your future, your eternal future. We must guard our heart from the worthlessness of the world, which are contrary to God's ways.

"This is the evil in everything that happens under the sun: The same destiny overtakes all. The hearts of men, moreover, are full of evil and there is madness in their hearts while they live, and afterward they join the dead" Ecclesiastes 9:3 New International Version. It said, "there is madness in their hearts," there is madness in their minds. Think, think, think stop and think of all the evil in this world and some of it is close to home, you have heard enough of the senseless madness in our society; this is why man does what he does.

Chapter 10

They Infiltrate Our Mind

If we could see demons in bodily form, they would be as ravenous beast with sounds like mighty roaring insatiable beastly lions on the path of cruelty with violent voracious devouring hatred. Swirling around us in the spirit realm are these fierce demon spirits waiting for the right opportunity to devour a human soul. In the movie "Raiders of the Lost Ark" by Steven Spielberg, at the latter part of the movie he depicted evil spirits swirling around and tormenting humans, a small glimpse of the fieriness of spiritual terrorism, they are with us. You cannot see television airwaves, radio airwaves, you cannot see microwaves, you cannot see the source of power for cell phones, you cannot see gravity but you know these are out there and they are working.

They can bring a barrage of angry insults; they will creep into depression of the mind with obsession and do all they can to control and influence the individual at these weaknesses.

Through this cleverly infiltration of the mind, they can convince the sinner to kill to commit murder even to kill their own children. This is all to frequent today in our mixed-up crazed society, those who have committed such horrible crimes, their friends or relatives say that those doing the killing were not in their right mind, and agreeably so. They were not in their right mind and did not have control of themselves because the dark nature ruled by the devil is at the helm of the sinner's mind. Some of the murderers themselves believed that Satan was inside their mind. Some of those who have harmed their children believed "they were doing their children well by saving them from hell." Another said, "the killing happened because she wanted to give her child to God," a deceptive satanic twist. Think, really think, you know right off these are troubled minds. Anyone who kills children by whatever means, or molest them or both has something going terribly wrong on inside, now you know what that is. These horrible acts are a good sign for the public, the unbeliever to recognize without spiritual discernment that these minds are possessed or heavily influenced by demons. Do not shake this knowledge off it is not to be forgotten, you must realize that we are under spiritual attack our minds are being toiled with, manipulated by invisible forces of the spirit realm an enemy that want you dead and forgotten.

Demons primary safe haven is the human mind; here a demon finds rest as he torments the soul he has inhabited. They are safe here from anyone of our physical world unless; a human in the name of Jesus approaches them, and then their celestial knees bang together. Satan lays his cross hairs on the human soul, attacks our five senses gaining sensual influence over our bodies because the flesh is a weak vessel and he subdues our mind with his schemes.

They can cause psychotic disorders, dissociative amnesia, to where the individual is doing things he does not know he is doing them or even why, he does not know the nature or the quality of his actions and on top of that, he does not know his wrongfulness of his actions. Functions from childhood on where the sin nature develops in the soul demons can have a powerful psychological influence throughout our lives.

Demons do not change the genes or neurons in the brain they just stop the individuals from thinking in reality by blocking thoughts with their conduct, or darken condition. They lay a maze of twisted paths in front of us laden with sensual temptations and temptations of the world that our lives can go in many directions. When we talk about darkness, we are talking about demons and when we talk about demons, we are talking about darkness. The realm demons live advantageously to their conduct and their conduct operates from the darkness of the spirit world. When they enter a human mind they bring with them their natural condition, their natural condition is sin, sin comes from darkness and darkness and sin is anything away from God, and the depths of wicked sin are the blackest of darkness.

Think of demons as the most vicious diabolical invisible spirits who are spiritual beings, spiritual people, infected, with deadly, sinful devouring viruses with the most wickedness degree of evil, which, have the capability of penetrating your mind without your knowledge. The **only** antidote is Jesus. They can cause intermittent explosive behaviors, this disorder usually others are victims too. They have an anti-social personality disorder a behavior that also can turn violent. Tantrums in children carry over into adulthood. They can affect us physically, which will affect our sexuality, our health, they can affect us psychologically, affecting our mental processing, keeping us from knowing God, they can affect us spiritually, keep us from knowing the truth, they can and will assault us in all aspects of our lives.

Today mental illness is increasing, our minds are the battleground for spiritual warfare; our thoughts influenced with demonic trickery that causes superstitions, suspicions, extreme paranoia's, irrational imagination, devilish gimmickries of persuasion and deception and add the element of disparagement. Demons will develop in the mind by working off the character and personality; they will overlap their own character and bring serious confusion to the mind.

The battle is in the mind, some call it a "cosmic battle" there is no fiction in this eternal life, and it is strictly spiritual, supernaturally charged by the Spirit of Truth or the spirit of lies.

When satanic forces attack your mind, they also attack your identity, your self-image, personality, character, and it infiltrates the soul, they work on 'self' image in all of us. They will build and build, re-construct and build even more self-image that they can work in; they will move in feelings, emotions, the intellect, and ego, they will give individuals puffed up fullest egomaniacal pride that they will control. They will either lift individuals up or tear individuals down into a deep disparity and then take over their thinking that will lead them into a life with actions of demonic influence behind their actions. They will take you through a lifetime of identity crises because of 'self-image,' of depression, leading you into a life of mistaking your own identity not knowing who you really are and not knowing your full potential, your purpose and meaning of life. The sin nature in which we live, our minds are inherently wayward, our minds are lead astray, they are lead by us bending toward corruption.

The mind is the entrance into our soul in which Satan will use humans to execute his deeds of evil on this planet. Deeds of harming others, destroying one another through any means he can get a human soul to perform satanic acts. He injects into the human mind his thoughts, that are nothing but satanic, you may think that they are your thoughts and that is what he wants you to think.

What goes through our mind in a day's time like images, emotions, impressions, feelings, even sounds and sights from our five senses constantly keeps our mind busy with information that is overwhelming. All these and more are meant to divert our attention away for spiritual matters, godly matters, matters of our tomorrows, matters of today, and matters of truth.

Oppressive schemes, tactics, manipulations, strategies of the spiritual forces of the invisible world that surrounds us, besiege our minds. They can dominate our own foolish thoughts.

We get evil images, visions, dreams, impressions, feelings, emotions, suggestions; these all enter through the sense realm and sway to our natural realm. Our thoughts governed by our observations in education, associations, our listening to others and so on and our will, will control our course of thinking.

Being in darkness, we are not in our own mind-set, we are susceptible to evil influences from the sin nature. Darkness creates deadness; deadness creates dullness in our understanding by living the ways of world that have programmed us. Our thinking is in character of a darkened world, but listen to what 1st Corinthians 15:34 New International Version says; *"Come back to your senses as you ought, and stop sinning; for there are some who are ignorant of God-I say this in your shame."* The New King James Version says, *"Awake to righteous, and do not sin; for some do not have the knowledge of God. I speak this to your shame."* If we think of the things we have done, if we watch the things being done, we should realize that evil is within us, this should be enough to want to stop sinning, and turn and face the truth; this will awake your sense of reality. Whether we are aware of it or not, a spiritual battle is going on, a battle for our minds. You have heard, wake up and smell the coffee or wake up and smell the roses, well, wake up and realize that sin is all around you and is destroying every thing and every one around you. Shake off that ignorance.

Satan has the power to transmit evil attitudes and thoughts in our minds while he tries to persuade us to do evil. With discernment, we will notice struggles in our own minds where good and evil thoughts and attitudes battle for dominance to shape our behavior. With ignorance, there is no discernment. This is a tactic of the devil to bombard our minds with worldly junk and create an information crisis so that we do not know what to think or believe. The unbeliever is unable to intercept the transmission of evil from the devil because of no spiritual discernment for lack of spiritual knowledge and for the absence of the Spirit. Those of us with the Spirit we have a new mind and a sound mind. In 2nd Timothy 1:7 *"For God has not given us a spirit of fear, but of power and of love and of a sound mind,"* a sound mind is a disciplined mind, awakened from the blindness of darkness and come to the light. The light of the gospel is the truth of Christ.

The god of this age has blinded the minds of unbelievers, so that they cannot see the light of the gospel of the glory of Christ, who is the image of God" (2nd Cor. 4:4 NIV). Those familiar with this passage recognize demonic influence through discernment and the obvious life styles of the unbelievers, and recognize the schemes and tactics of demonic activity within the sin nature that is rapidly degenerating and deteriorating this world. When you know the truth, you can discern the error.

Our minds are the target of relentless seductive schemes with efforts to shape our minds to the worldly system of untruth through a void filled with spiritual inheritance and a conscience that does not work well; we are primed for demonic activity. Every sinner, every lost person, every unbeliever is a prisoner of their mind, held captive by the dark forces of this world.

The sinners profile from the sin nature is less humility and more ignorance. In ignorance, we are tempted, encouraged, influenced to sin. Our human nature has a natural tendency to sin through temptation and we sin through the world, through the flesh and through the devil and we will be tempted in our spirit, our soul, and our body, hence our mind, our will, our emotions and in this state our character shows pride and ego, our character is assassinated.

Metaphorically, our minds have two doors, two paths, two gates, two ways, to travel through, one opens to darkness, this is through the wide gate, where sin and unrighteousness reigns, and the other opens to light, the narrow path to God and eternal life, the highway to heaven.

Out of our mind

Going back to the garden, having "free-will" is a privilege that keeps us from being puppets. Satan used the human's senses and entered into their minds, by reasoning, imagining, enticing them into sin. In Genesis 3.6 Eve saw that the tree was good for food, (taste, feeding the flesh, the fleshly appetite, the lust of the flesh) and she saw that is was pleasant to the eyes, (the lust of the eye's) and was desired to make one wise, (feeding pride). Our will is a measure of freedom, it is a gift, it is up to you of what degree, and what direction you will go in life, and whether the will, will stay corrupted or not. Compromises, corrupts reasoning, our false emotions, even by our flesh, and there are corruptions by false gods of the world through the sin nature.

In the natural man, the unsaved man, the unbeliever, the mind is the playground of satanic activity. To differentiate between an unseen, unknown, and supernatural malevolent force in the mind for the unbeliever is not possible. The characteristics of the unknown remain unknown to the unsaved because they are supernaturally superior to human beings. Remember the unsaved live in the physical realm not in the spiritual/physical realm where spiritual discernment is exercised in physical and spiritual matters. Assumptions are as close as the professionals can come in their corporeal perspicacity or diagnosis of spiritual matters.

For some lost souls that have sought after professional help, believe what the professional is telling them. Delving into the spiritual mind is a study of the invisible unknown. Demons are insurgents and resurgent's and do not turn away when confronted with man's way of dealing with their involvement in the human mind because the carnal mind does not know what they are dealing with, psychiatrist can not recognize demon activity in a mind. Medications are prescribed for these types of mental illnesses. Medication will do nothing to the demonic influence except make that demon happy that this person now incarcerated in his own mind and still under the influence of the snickering demon.

Your mind is the devil's command post. Once in the mind demons are unseen navigational devices directing the sinner's life down the broad road of deception and self-destruction. The terrible things that are happening in our nation, in this crazed world do you think this evil came from comic books or cartoons? These atrocities are developed in minds that have been open to satanic oppression or possession. A door was open to them, they got a foothold and developed a stronghold and rule that individual. That door could have been anger, violence, bitterness, un-forgiveness, hatred, prejudice, malice, jealousy, envy, even a simple misunderstanding, and they will attack when we are weak, emotionally; they will use self-pity, to turn your life up side down, filled with chaos and confusion. They will attack when we are strong emotionally, self-centered, and with a puffed up ego, prideful, and arrogant. They can twist thinking, implant anger in minds, where that anger gets out of control, the individual thinks he can justify his anger whether towards God, toward anyone, toward religion, toward the government, toward freedom, toward good, toward evil; but his resentment is selfish acts against others. They want to act through your mind and if you let them, they will lead you into bizarre actions that will hurt you and others. They will reduce your life to shambles.

The sin nature contributes to mental illnesses; demon influence definitely rearranges our thinking to where the carnal mind cannot and does not differentiate the presence of deeper darkness. Just as alcohol changes the thinking and thoughts of the user, as do demonic activity. It is the same with the drugs and chemicals that so many are hooked on alter the brains thinking. Why would anyone want alcohol, drugs, and chemicals altering their brain chemistry to a deteriorating degree of unconsciousness or beyond, no consciousness? By the way, these and any mind-altering substance that is self-inflected are tools of Satan. Demons maneuver around the corridors of our mind between our will, our conscience, our sub-conscience, our intellect, our reasoning, our thinking, our thoughts, and plant these thoughts of getting a high, they plant schemes, mental plots and tactics against the outside world while leaving an undetectable trail of the presence of darkness.

Living normally, what we think is normal is the devil's discretion, he can lead us into sinning just by letting you feel that you are right in your judgments.

For instance, homosexuality and lesbianism, their individual and group campaigns against homophobia because if their beliefs, their feelings, their emotions, their passions for equality is a prescription for demonic influence. Demons are in what we are interested in, they will instigate attitudes of prejudice in our culture, in social issues and moral values, life styles in general, family, relationships, manners, some have a sense of entitlement, religion, work ethics, culture issues, like a defiant counterculture, with equal rights. With those allurements comes self-centeredness, selfishness, self-will, self-deceptiveness, pride, very prideful towards accomplishments. Living a life of deceptiveness and deceitfulness, sexual perverseness, all forms of lust and this evil mentality brings on doubts, depression, manic-depressiveness, destruction, creates chaos, confusion, it can bring on sickness and disease, it goes deeper into self-delusion, self-deceptiveness, all forms of fear, forms of fantasy, or unreality. Mix in there stubbornness, rebellion, soon comes discouragement, mood disorders, mental disorders, metabolic disorders, psychosomatic disorders, psychosis, bizarre psychotic behaviors, anxiety, depression, sadness, loneliness, despair, being withdrawn, feelings of hopelessness, self-destruction which leads further down the darkest path of no-return, suicide. These are some of the destructive ways the spirit of darkness works in the human mind that is occupying this world and leading us astray. All these and other evil forces injected into the human soul by the wrong motives in life through the sin-nature. Wrong motives come from pride, lack of spiritual knowledge, being self-oriented, being egomaniacal. A good definition of ego I once heard is, **e**xcluding **G**od **o**ut, ego. A person can manifest a combination of these emotions. They are of the demonic life straight from the pit of hell. These forms of emotions are evil spirits ready to attack at the first sigh of weakness in a human mind.

Our country is deeply divided, we do not have to go out of the country to find enemies, they are within our boarders. There are extreme enemies with irrational thoughts and beliefs that are no different then the extremist in the Middle East, just different tactics and the source is the same, the realm of darkness. These forces will molest your soul, your will, your heart, your mind, they molest your conscience, your imagination, they inject evil fantasies and take over your personality, your character, your attitude to do and to be what they are spiritually persuading your whole being to be and do. For example, in recent years think about what has been in the news, concerning homegrown terrorist, Timothy J. McVeigh, the Oklahoma bombing, which killed 168 innocent individuals and considered the deadliest act of terrorism within the United States. The mastermind of this cowardly act had an accomplice and possibly others and their motive was in retaliation for the Waco siege and others by the government.

Remember the Unabomber, a twisted domestic terrorist, this man was a Harvard graduate, received a Masters degree and a PhD from the University of Michigan and was an assistant professor of mathematics. He wrote what is known as the Industrial Society and Its Future commonly called The Unabomber Manifesto. The mind of this man was against the industrialized revolution thinking it is harming the human race and a radical reform or even revolutionary change in the social structure is necessary. He murdered his victims by sending letter bombs through the mail. He killed three people and wounded twenty-eight. Intelligence is not the couplet; intelligence is a gift, the couplet is the *willingness* to crawl further into darkness. "*You educate a man like this and you have an evil genius.*" –Adrian Rogers

Anthrax, beginning on Sept 18, 2001, letters containing anthrax bacteria were mailed to several news media offices and two U.S. Senators. Five people died, and seventeen others fell ill.

Look at the high profile assassinations in our time, President John Kennedy in 1963, Martin Luther King in 1968, Robert F. Kennedy also in 1968 these shooters and mass murders could of also been victims of character assassin, with bullying, razing and any other defamations of character that build up in the mind of hate, rage of all sorts. There is no doubt they were demonic influenced.

There is shooting every day in this country and around the world of innocent lives. Who, is really behind pulling that trigger?

Serial killers; Jack the Ripper, over one hundred years ago this infamous serial killer from London that killed prostitutes. Jeffrey Dahmer was a serial killer; he murdered seventeen people and preformed gruesome acts of cannibalism, rape, torture on his victims whom were all males. The Boston Strangler, Albert DeSalvo, murdered thirteen females. Ted Bunday, he murdered young women, lured them with his good looks and charm. It is quoted that *"he was soulless but intelligent."* He murdered thirty-six people and they do not know how many more. BTK killer, bind, torture, and kill, his name, Dennis Rader. He murdered six people both male and female. Angelo Buono Jr. known as the "Hillside Killer" he murdered nine females and dumped their nude bodies over Los Angeles-area hillsides. The "Lone wolf" homegrown terrorists usually are unconnected by network or without leaders but have similar violent vengeances from histories of troubled past. They harbor feelings that ferment to anguish, torment and distress boiling over into murderous rampages. They act from beliefs of extremism. Like 'white-supremacist,' those who believe in dangerous racism have no qualms of committing criminal acts to further their perceived causes and all the while behind the scenes are satanic influences nagging hatred at these individuals and lead them down the path of demonic possession to commit these horrific acts. The Fort Hood shooter was he also a victim, a victim of a satanic assault. Anti-abortion extremists who threaten to attack clinics and the killing of doctors, who are abortionist, are domestic terrorist. Suicide bombers are the extreme desensitized to reality, and their mind is no longer theirs. The cruel and mean people in this world, who perform gruesome and barbaric acts towards the defenseless, are themselves victims of demonic activity because they opened the doors to evil participation. Terrorist do cowardly acts and are cowards themselves. When caught, how many of them admit to their deeds of darkness, they want attorneys, plead innocent and drag their case through the courts.

Demons target our physical or psychological weaknesses. You know what your physical weakness are, if you desire fleshly appetites, sexual and sensual contact with the opposite sex or even the same sex demons will make a way for these interests and desires to come into your life. If you are a chronic liar demons will give you subjects that will listen to and believe you. They will strike up interest within you, like an uncontrollable urge to want to be a pyromaniac; if you are a compulsive person, they will make sure your life is filled with irresistible interest. If you have an inner urge to hurt someone, if you have prejudice in you, demons will provide the means and the someone. No matter whom you are, no matter what the circumstances no matter what the situation is they are there to tempt you to commit sins beyond what you think you are capable of committing.

The mind of a child while still forming in puberty, adolescent, is a target for demonic influence; they waste no time in reaching for the young mind to sway toward the wide-gate of life, which leads to destruction. Implanted in the heart of the child are such characteristics as, selfishness, hatred, lying, resentfulness, inappropriate actions, inappropriate language, inappropriate behavior, despitefulness, being defiant, disobedient and rebellious characteristics. Darkness infiltrates the weak and the spiritually blind. The worse thing parents can do to their children is to keep them out of a God preaching, God-fearing church.

When demonic spirits enter a human, the humans are noticeably out of character; their actions are the ways of darkness. Demon spirits entangle themselves in the human mind and set up a point of operation in that individual.

While we are in the sin nature we are not in our right minds, there is no clarity of truth. When a demon or demons take possession of one's mind, that mind will think things that are out of character for that individual. Now that person will commit and carry out crimes that are demonically influenced and demonic by nature. How can we be in our right mind when we are not fully developed, only two-thirds complete, we lack the most important element, our spirit. Our spirit absorbed by God's Spirit that brings spiritual knowledge and brings a renewing of our minds.

Demons will destroy the human mind to where the person will not be able to think for themselves to get themselves out of deep domestic and worldly dilemmas. Letting your sinful nature control your mind leads to death, but letting the Spirit control your mind leads to life and peace, should there be any thought here on which way to go, let us see, life or death, there is no comparison. Satan will come with evil's undiluted power to deceive sinners who have refused the truth, refused Jesus Christ that could have saved them. No one is exempt from demon influence, they destroy and consume with devious and shrewd thoughts.

As a virus enters a computer it spreads, it will corrupt files, documents, damaging the integrity of saved and stored data etc... As a virus enters a human body, it multiplies, spreads throughout the body, it can complicate, compromise the immune system, and sickness sets in. When a demon enters a human body, it enters the mind; it spreads throughout the soul probing for weaknesses of the mind, instilling beliefs that appeal to the individual's personality and character such as evolution, secularism, agnosticism, and atheism dragging along their attractive interest of theory that is poisoning the mind. It seeks out the weaknesses of the flesh; appealing to that individual, leading that person into filthy fleshly sins, it searches the emotions, instilling fear, rebellion, stubbornness, anger, pride, hard-heartedness, changing moods and attitudes, entering the imagination, setting up fantasies that take action that usually hurts others.

When an individual lives in the sin nature, he is not in mental reality, and when demonic activity sets a stronghold in an individual, the individual loses his identity he does not know why he does what he does. Demonic activity impresses pleasing issues on our minds; they fixate on our desires firmly, frequently, and with forceful repetition to keep us occupied and preoccupied and away from the truth, this is their objective and our minds are subject to them.

Mistaken Identity

Everyone who is lost, who is not saved, in some way has an identity crises some are aware of an inner crises, but of a different sort. Let us look at homosexuality, abortion, transsexuals, and transvestites. You are going to read and understand how Satan works in these issues. Homosexuality is one of the most difficult issues individuals, families and churches face today, is a deeply troublesome issue. The gay and lesbian Task Force is up against the law with legislation and court rulings with their strident rallies and the committed couples, they want "equal-rights" and for some it is not politics but personal that they be recognized as equal citizens. They feel that religion based bigotry and prejudice has a lot of weight pushing against them. Popular culture tells us it is simply an alternative way to live. Mainstream media promotes it as genetic and unchangeable, the pro-gay movement works overtime to politicize the education system, alter biblical truth regarding sexual behavior, and redefine the meaning of marriage and family.

Abortion has similarities. The panels of judges, politicians, doctors and nurses, lawyers, and those who plan parenthood (Satan's pawns) have also been persuaded by demonic spirits that the unborn is not a living soul, and proceed with infanticide, the gruesome procedure of ending a defenseless, helpless precious life sending it into the arms of their loving God. These lost, unsaved individuals making these decisions are numb to the thought of mistaking the identity of the unborn child not as a living being. God will not have mercy on their souls at judgment, but he will, if they repent of this very dark sin and stop their sinning. This sinister act is child abuse of the worst kind.

Transsexuals feel they are trapped in the wrong body. They go through a life of confusion, to say the least. They feel they were dealt the wrong cards that something in their genetic make-up was twisted, short-circuited someway in the birthing process that leaves them asking, who am I and undergo treatment to change his or her anatomical gender. Homosexuals are similar. They also have awareness that something is not right on the inside. They go through a big part of their life trying to find, that right, trying to find who they are. They feel they were born to be gay, just as the transsexual feels he was born to be of another gender, they become fanatical. This mistaken-identity is from the devil and his cohorts. They enter the mind with twisted persuasions relentlessly pushing these issues beyond the individual's capacity to seek out the truth and they succumb to vicious lies. Demonic spirits characterizing these traits enter the mind and with convincing thoughts of persuasion, these human souls go through life fighting for a mistaken identity that they will die for and that is exactly what Satan wants, he wants them dead without them ever knowing the truth. Transvestites are those who adopt the dress and often the behavior of the opposite sex, this dark influence works on the physical and mental facilities of the individuals when these kind of issues surface Satan injects diversions so that, everyone misses the critical point. Diversions such as the laws, legislation, court rulings, rallies, throw in there bigotry and prejudice with their own issues and the Bible. The education system is a division, as is biblical truth regarding sexual behavior and the defining meaning of marriage and family. Christian beliefs are spiritual and scripturally sound and God will not honor gay marriages. God is not a bigot he is the Creator of the human race, man has intervened Gods teaching on sexuality, with their influence of sexual perversion, and behind it all, is the snickering demons destroying lives.

The critical point is these groups do not realize that God does love them and wishes they turn from their wicked ways and to his Son who will set them free form these false and damming and damaging beliefs and gain the knowledge that they may know they are wrong. He does love them because he created them and they are spiritually part of him but he will not close his eyes to these matters, he will not overlook, he will not excuse these behaviors.

There is the same satanic principle with secularist, evolutionist, atheists; humanist, etc., diversions are thrown into the mix so the critical point does not surface, so that the sinner may swim around in his sin until he drowns.

These issues here are taking over the mind by a sinful nature driven by the devil and his skillful militia of mind assassin spirits. Look at some leaders of nations that do and have done atrocities beyond your comprehension. Everywhere and anywhere look at the evil in this world, where do you think it really comes from? The mentality of the writers of some dark blockbuster movies, the horror movies, is sin nature driven, possibility demonically driven. Those who create videos and video games of murdering, raping, shooting up drugs, sadistic activities and so on are demonic driven, these individuals (Satan's pawns) do not go to a God preaching, God fearing church if they go to church at all.

The enemy is a master of taking lives; he will go to any means to bring the human race that thirst for worldly affairs to his water trough that they may ingest his poisonous nature filled with destructive, corruptive, deceptive, insidious ways of living. Satanic forces invade the mind that can take control of that mind and lead it into self-destruction.

Satan, the master deceiver with his tactics, deceives generations after generations and they are held in delusion, by diversions of darkness in thinking about everything in life but committing their lives to Christ, who died for them. The last thing that Satan wants you to think about is believing in Jesus Christ, being a believer, because then you would have eternal life in heaven, the inheritance of immortality, life ever lasting and you would turn to be a foe of his. The mind is in delusion, under bondage, in captivity, incarcerated by the sin nature, and our minds are fogged over by a spirit of untruth, the spirit of error, thoughts and actions from the sin nature defuse God's work in your life.

What comes to your mind, what goes through your mind, what comes out of your mind can transform your mind, to good or evil.

Attitudes

Our personality, our intellect, our senses, our ability to reasoning, our will, our imagination, our soul, our spirit, our life, our breath, all of our inner faculties are an inner woven bundle of wonderful complexities. Even so, the enemy will take satanic advantage of any of our faculties he can penetrate to lead us to sin, but our spirit, if not cold-hearted will convict us when we sin, without the spirit, no or little conviction.

Demon activity in the mind uses many tactics on us, they impress upon us what they know are our weaknesses; they fix something firmly on our mind through frequent and some time with forceful repetition. You have heard the statement that someone said; he/she needs an attitude adjustment. So what are they saying, the attitude of the person must of made some out of the ordinary, derogatory, out of character comments that were inappropriate and possibly with a dark side to it. Once demon activity finds a home, they will be expressed in personalities, characters, and attitudes and actions through that soul. Some have attitudes that are so obvious with a detrimental slant that they are viewed as trouble, political, and religious extremist, for an example, they are violent, extremely obnoxious, and anti-Semitic with malice and hostility. White supremacist, black supremacist, racist, the Nazis proclaimed supremacy over other ethnic and nationalities of what they believed to be of an inferior religious heritage, genocide became their answer. These are sadistic attitudes performing sadistic actions; you can say demons are attitudes.

Behaviors

While implanting desires for our hidden fleshly appetites of lust, they bombard our minds with evil thoughts, dark schemes, hideous actions and our behaviors turn violent, filled with evil with no remorse for others, performing sadistic behaviors acting out grisly murders, workplace violence, and actions with furious attitudes.

The human's behavior reflects which path of life that they journey, the nature in which they live. They will be known by their respective actions, life-styles, their vocabulary, their beliefs, everything about them and their allegiance to their life style. Their lies can be persuasive and damaging. We who discern must test them, must question them, must know them and obviously shown by their beliefs, their reflective behavior and their actions reveal their nature. Humans are recognized as spirits in the Bible. *"Dear friends, do not believe every spirit, but test the spirits to see whether they are from God, because many false prophets have gone out into the world"* (1st John 4:1 NIV). Here the Bible is talking about false prophets, false teachers, false preachers who today teach false religions, these spirits are humans, these humans are spirits.

A function of the mind is a function of the heart, where we can reason with our heart. In addition, a function of the heart is a function of the intellect. You can find an interesting scripture relating to this in Mark 2:6, these scribes *'reasoned in their hearts.'* The heart is the scriptures way of saying, your mind, your spirit"the inner-self".

Our carnal minds are a complicated mass of confusion because our lives and our beliefs are complicated and confused, let God in and he will make all the necessary changes in your heart, strengthen the whole mess out, and reveal the truth to you.

You have read how the five senses affect your thoughts and actions in the sin nature and with a negative attitude; these are contrary to God's word and have grave consequences.

Thoughts

So how does a carnal mind think? Thoughts come from three sources. We have our own thoughts, we hear thoughts of the world, meaning what you read, what you watch on television, hear on the radio, what you hear from your friends are thoughts, the educational systems, from acquaintances, thoughts through your every day walk through society, our worldly environment, cultures, etc. and we hear thoughts through Satan. For the believer we can add another, there are thoughts from God through the Holy Spirit. Therefore, for the unbeliever there are our own thoughts, thoughts from the world, and thoughts from Satan.

We have two choices what we can do with thoughts. We can accept them or we can reject them. If one does not have discernment, or does not know truth, he will probably act on these thoughts. There is a point in a thought moment that can be accepted or rejected. The mind of the unbeliever is wide open, remember the wide road, open-mindedness, and in this condition the unbeliever is susceptible to receiving thoughts straight from the pits of hell where demons are waiting to bombard the unbeliever with thoughts of deception. With no discernment, the unbeliever will easily believe what is not true; with no spiritual, Godly truth in them, they will remain living in untruth, defending what they believe, and believing lies until the unbeliever dies, this is sad but true.

Satan's playground is the human mind; he dumps thoughts of ungodly garbage right into our minds, he will work through inquisitive minds, thoughts of curiosity, and tempting imaginations. Thoughts will affect every part of your life, your family's life, your work life, and your social life. Thoughts from the human nature, are thoughts through of the sinful nature, this is the carnal way of thinking.

The carnal mind is under constant surveillance from the dark spirit realm and the slyness of satanic forces maneuvers throughout the facilities of the mind implanting irrational, illogical, unreasonable, ridiculously difficult to deal with, hot-tempered, and without much common sense attitudes.

What are satanic thoughts that are being used in the worldly system, and being used in our every day life? They are thoughts of pride, prideful thoughts turn into prideful acts and someone else will feel their repercussions, thoughts of greed, thoughts of unkindness, thoughts of perversion, all evil thoughts, of untruth, which are filled with lies and deceitful actions.

I heard a preacher say, "Thoughts lead us into either positive or negative action. The right words produce the right thoughts, which produce the right action, which produce good results." The wrong words produce the wrong thoughts, which produce the wrong action, which produce wrong results. The bullying in schools that start at a very young age can create great harm to its victims. The old saying, "Sticks and stones may break my bones, but words can never hurt me." That is untrue. Words can give us hope and encouragement, or they can break our spirit to discouragement. The victim can grow much older carrying around this hurt, holding grudges and can fester for years, smoldering into hated, not a good thing.

If we let devilish thoughts come into us and act on them instead of rejecting them, which we should give no place to the devil, (Eph. 4:27), this is giving the devil a foothold in you mind. *Willingly* letting these evil thoughts surface, the devil will tempt man to do evil through his manipulating and scheming ways that are tantalizing to the flesh to say the least. Look at the thoughts of illicit sexual behavior, sexual spirit demons will enter that person with such intense force and lead them into activities that can change minds, break up families, ruin individuals, create a sexual addiction that will turn lives up side down.

He has the spiritual power to get into the mind and manipulate the character of an individual and change the direction of his journey; he will lead you down the path to the valley of the shadow of death as he did in the garden as he instigated man to sin. He enticed man with the thought of having more; deserving more, through knowing more and it was all designed to strip their loyalty from God by the act of disobedience. They gave him a foothold by listening to him, believing him, exchanging dialogue with him as that foothold increased to a stronghold then he convinced them to disobey their Creator by their action.

He does the same thing today. The difference between then and now is that in the garden they lived in righteousness, in the divine nature. Today because of the great sin, we live in the sin nature of unrighteousness. It is easy to sin, sin is covered over with cotton candy, it is appealing and the consequences are not considered.

The thought of fraud, embezzlement, corruption, thoughts of lying, cheating, stealing are implanted in the carnal mind and sin evolves into webs of deceit, and now destruction is only a matter of time. Satan can mislead our thoughts; he can mislead our purposes, and our intentions.

Today it is as easy or easier for man to be encouraged to sin, sinning is the way of the world, the world spins in sin, sin is the kingdom of darkness, the kingdom of the air is Satan's and all who are unbelievers are under the rule of this disobedient one, the devil (Eph. 2:2).

People in high positions in our time have succumbed to temptations that lead them into disgrace, they were weak, they did not use self-control over their *will*, where the enemy camps, or over their flesh. Sin threw them into a life of shame, dishonor, humiliation, and literally drug the families through scandals that will last through their life and even longer, because people do not forget.

You have heard people convicted of some horrific crime and some time doing their questioning, they said they heard voices well as much as we would think that they are wrong they are right. In the spirit realm, thoughts are voices whether they are your own inner voice, thoughts from the world or from the devil or our Creator. No matter what image you have of yourself the forces of evil can use it for their purpose, they will use you through your thought process.

If an unsaved person rejects Jesus Christ, rejects God and his word he stays in the physical realm not the spiritual/physical realm and blindly wanders around in the sin nature. Being in the physical realm, man, will yield to the fleshly nature of sensuality, of the sin nature, which is yielding to the spirit of error, here you have reached your lowest low. The reason is when the body dies the spirit faces judgment and the second death, eternal damnation is in place. The nature of the sin nature controls your thinking and your life style, the way you think and the way you act. You live in biblical untruth. Sin originates in the carnal mind bursting through the wide gates down the dark corridors of the sinful-inundated sin nature gathering sinful thoughts on the way to perpetrate with sinful desires.

The believer on the other hand when the body dies faces rewards and eternal life in heaven, he is judged but not for sinning. Is this really worth taking a chance of losing? When one makes a losing choice like this, he is making the decision with his intellect not his spirit, not his heart. He is *willingly* deciding where to spend eternity.

"No one can know a person's thoughts except that person's own spirit, and no one can know God's thoughts except God's own Spirit." 1st Corinthians 2:11 NLT

Self

What is self? 1. The identity, character, or essential qualities of any person or thing 2. one's own person as distinct from all others 3. one's own welfare, interest, of advantage; selfishness [obsessed with self] (See Appendix). Within your soul and the development of your character, you have an opinion of your self, who am I, a sense of your self, an opinion of your self, your self-worth, your self-esteem, your image, your personality, self is your ego.

Self is selfish, it is self-endeavored, it is self-centered, and self can be self-indulgent, self- absorbed, self-willed, and self-righteous, self can be self-deceptive and self-defeating. There are many aspects to self, and to this person life is all about me, and his two best friends, myself and I, the three of them, me myself and I are totally lost and out of control. Self is immersed in the sin nature basking in its own glory.

Ego is to fulfill the interest of self, personal self-beliefs, personal devotional practices; self is in love with it-self, with an obsession for individual betterment. How many times a day do you say the word I, how about me, my, myself, you have quit an image of yourself, do you not, with all your self reflective acts and all these personal pronouns you are sitting on the throne of your life. When self is on the throne of your life, your eyes are fixed on you; your interest is within self, and the affairs of this world. Your back is towards God, when your back is towards God, you cannot see what you are looking away from. Now you are surrounded with worldly circumstances, situations, temptations that fit your character and personality and you are riding high on ego. This type of living we are hiding ourselves from God, at least we think we are by turning our back on Him, we do not let him in, not even in a figment of our imagination, because we are the self-*willed* unbeliever.

There is a sense of detachment, deterrents, retaliatory action, through a self-absorbed selfish-life style with irresponsible behavior, in an unfulfilled life. We let our imaginations rule us, (as Satan feeds the imagination) now we have the wrong motives and are governed by them and self. We are controlled by our own selfish sinful desires down the paths in the sin nature. By denying yourself the truth, self, is your worst enemy. You choose not to believe so your self, is rejecting the truth. The way the Bible tells us to find our real life, is by denying your 'self' for the Truths sake. To find the real you, you must refuse your own claims upon yourself, and by yielding to the claims of Christ's lordship over your life.

Jesus told his disciples, "*For whoever wants to save his life* (hang on to the life you now live) *will lose it, but whoever loses his life for me* (give up this sin-filled selfish life) *will find it*"

(Matt. 16:25 ^{NIV}). You are promised to find your real life, the real you, who you are, what you are intended to be, to know your purpose in life. Can you deny your self, to find your, self; this is all God is interested in, deny self, to find the real you. It is a straightforward question demanding a straightforward answer. Your self-will is holding you back from knowing what truth is, holding you back from knowing who you are and about your purpose in life. The natural man must deny his own self-centeredness, his self-ambitions, his selfish impulses, his self-will. God is after your old self, your life style because it is controlled by your *will* in carnality, in the sin nature, the natural self, this is what we come into the world with, a selfish life style within, and holds you back from the truth. Your self is on the line here, how are you going to answer this, and what do you feel about Jesus Christ? Do you believe that Jesus Christ is the Son of God? Do you believe He is the only way to salvation? Do you believe He came in the flesh, and He died for your sins? Do you believe He rose from the dead? Do you believe he is alive today? Do you believe He is the savior of the world? A simple yes, or no.

It may not seem like much to you but it is the pivotal point of your life, it is like a secret, a mystery locked up inside of you and you hold the key to reveal your spiritual consciousness and it is done by denying 'self' to have control over your will, here is the meaning of self-control. Grab your will by the throat, drag it to the cross, and nail it there. You must overcome your 'self,' your carnal spirit that has rule over you, if you do not overcome, overrule; you are like an open sore where bacteria can enter and overcome you. The Bible uses this analogy; *"A person without self-control is like a city with broken-down walls"* (Prov. 25:28 ^{NLT}). An unfortified city will succumb, submit to outside, external influences and be overcome itself. Listening to outside influences we become deadened to God and our spiritually broken down and overtaken. Pat Robertson in his book The Ten Offenses wrote, *"we as a nation are becoming numb to the voices of God and conscience." "We have fallen under the spell of the self." "In other words, the self is God."*

"Every one of us is our own deity." He goes to say, *"This is the idea that is taking hold in America today."* To become sensitive to our inner-spirit we must overcome our *'will'*, our stubborn will power, our old 'self' *"and to put on the new self, created to be like God in true righteousness and holiness"* (Eph. 4:24 ᴺᴵⱽ). *"Don't lie to each other, for you have stripped off your old sinful nature* (got rid of self, overcome the power of the will) *and all its wicked deeds. Put on your new nature,* (the new self, your new spirit) *and be renewed as you learn to know your Creator and become like him"* (Col. 3:9,10 ᴺᴵⱽ). *"Those who belong to Christ Jesus have nailed the passions and desires of their sinful nature to his cross and crucified them there"* (Gal. 5:24 ᴺᴸᵀ). It is a good thing when a man exercise self-restraint to control and rule his spirit,." *"And he who rules his spirit than he who takes a city"* (Prov. 16:32b). Look at self as an separate inner entity, look at it as a wild beast corralled only within the nature it has ever known, wanting to run free with no restrictions and its will is fierce in doing and getting what it wants. The void within is filled with a self-spirit and is taking you for a ride places you should not go, in your mind and body. Self is saturated with the sin nature and with a very strong self-will and to break it, one must ask an outside source, God. If you are not an over-comer of self, then you have been over-come by self.

Selfish-ambitions, self-serving objectives, selfish-gratifications and lust of the eyes includes sinful cravings, activated by what is seen, by envy, material stuff, status positions, the pride of life, arrogance, egomaniacal living, living the fast life, high society, a desire to be important, flaunt what you have, live for yourselves, self is fueled with pride, and humanistic-tendencies.

The worldly person's journey moves forward by what they see, and without God, life is all about them, about self, a self-loving, self-righteous, self-centered life. The spiritual person's journey is all about God and their life filled with the knowledge of their God.

Chapter 11

This World

"For everything in the world – the cravings of sinful man, the lust of his eyes and the boasting of what he has and does – comes not from the Father but from the world." 1st John 2:16 NIV

The Worldly System

The planet provides for us our every physical need, its resources feed us, gives us drink, shelters us, keeps us warm, shares us with its beauty, but it does nothing for our spiritual need except, re-direct us. The world houses over 6.7 billion people and its resources keep us all. On this planet is a dark spirit with its own resources, it also feeds us, gives us drink, shelters us in its darkness, and keeps us captive by its allurements, and within this darkness is an universal insurgency against God. Its intention is to immerse you in sin and can achieve this through you *willingly*, living in the sin nature. Within the sin nature, all of the devils evil characteristics develop naturally in the human soul, a product of our inheritance, the unrighteousness we are born-into, hence, moral and spiritual corruption in this world.

The world that we journey through is not a pristine world, it is not nirvana, it is not a utopia, it is a world contaminated with deep dark sin, and the world is ruled by the devil himself, this is his domicile. When you start realizing this and put it all together, it will all make sense to you, why there is so much evil, and how man plays his role, in the destruction of his brother, it is all done through the sadistic darkness of the sin nature.

The world's system is set up to bombard our minds with so much useless information from junk mail to television commercials, that the mind processes these every minute and hour of the day, every day, turning into weeks and months and years keeping the mind occupied from Godly interest.

The world is full of terrorism, hatred, fear, un-forgiveness, bigotry, because we listen to theories telling us man was an accident, a product of evolution and not that he is a created being. Why would man live like he has a God to answer to when he can live and do what he pleases and believes there is no Creator that will judge him. This is a tactic of Satan to where he brings to the forefront of mans thinking; issues that man can be persuaded to believe and live a lie. The carnal man of the world is such a pathetic specimen of the human race and he has no clue who his spiritual father is, he is a child of the devil. Those that are friends of the world, those that enjoy its sinful pleasures have made themselves an enemy to God, you make the choice, and if it is the wrong choice, you will, suffer the consequences.

The carnal mind is a descendant of the sin nature and developed from its evil spiritual volition. The carnal mind IS NOT of the human's true capacity of thinking. It is controlled, influenced by the nature of darkness of the spirit world. So of course, those that are not in their right mind, but are of the carnal mind cannot imagine that evil rules this planet, and devours the soul of man. Remember within the sin nature the world lies in deception. The nature of darkness does not blind man's intelligence, it blinds man's common sense, man's spirituality, man's spiritual knowledge, his morality, man's moral decency, it keeps man from knowing what is truth and keeps man bound in his own selfish ways under the control of his self-will. It blinds man's feelings of love, of what the meaning of true love is.

The demons of this world instigate the evil in the world. They help guide humans to commit evil, wicked atrocities. These spiritual rulers have access to your soul, to your thinking, to your carnal thought process of life, your carnal mind. They live in the sin nature and the sin nature is of the world, and you are of the world. They work covertly through our cultures, conforming us to darkness in our social involvement and development; they affect our ways of thinking, acting, our personal interest, our skills, and arts. For instance, have you taken a good look at television programs, the movies, videos, concerts, the whole entertainment industry, even magazines, and computers, all the viewing media? People are scantly dressed, dialogue is vulgar, and the messages they transmit are impure and in disgrace and our young soak it all up. What they are saying to us is, look at me, I am a sinner I am of the sin nature, I am a unbeliever, I do not believe in the Lord, so I'll live the way I want. I make a lot of money doing this, thank you very much, I believe in being free, natural and doing what I want.

The sin nature will dictate and program ideas, customs, religions, our morals, our laws, and capabilities, habits, our thoughts and patterns of behaviors. Institutions, technologies, occupational and professional skills and handed down by generations through spiritual cultural heritage, which the worlds cultures are an increasingly dominating our behavior. We do live in the belly of the beast.

"Those of the world are like dead fish floating down stream"
— Unknown

These worldly philosophies accommodate all who want to live their lives away from the truth. These baseless philosophies are filled with presumptuous theories that invade the mind of the foolish and hold them captive in these ridiculous deceptions. They hold them captive because their *wells* are weak in the sin nature but strengthened with lies. They *willfully* refuse to believe the truth.

The unbelievers grew up reading the wrong books, believing the wrong people, doing and living these wrong philosophies. Their philosophy is that they are their own god; *self* of the unbeliever is their god. *"This wisdom does not descend from above, but is earthly, sensual, demonic"* (Jas. 3:15). To the Christian, God, is the God of their life.

The world's system is full of godless values with secular ideologies, empty philosophies that are anti-god, anti-truth, anti-Christ anti-family that are fed from the darkness of the sin nature. These ideologies and philosophies are tactics, and strategies of the satanic forces of the dark world that ensnared this world's system, holds the sinner in a blind stopper, and literally keeps him from knowing anything truly spiritually. Being carnal is having a spirit of conformity to worldly affairs. People make unbelievable errors in judgment and they engage in sinful acts that hold them hostage in their conformity because we live in a world with corrupted views.

You do have a choice, choosing to live within the worldly system is *willfully* remaining in the sin nature, staying within the sin nature many paths of iniquities open up to you and can lead to extreme immorality. The attitudes, theories, philosophies, beliefs, passions, all the addictions, and habits, evil imaginations, all the worldly religions and false gospels, assumptions and belief systems are of the world, which is the devil's recreational area. Do you think you have a chance of finding real-truth when you live in a world filled with lies? You do have a choice to make a change.

The world is full of sin, deceit, unbelief, discouragement, nervous apprehensions; the feeling of unworthiness scans the mind of the allusive sinner. Allurements and enticements capture the sinner's worldly passionate desires, and evil cravings. Lust of the flesh is provoking perverse fleshly behavior, sexual involvement, sexual thoughts and sexual activity found its way into the minds of our young and they are expressing themselves without regret or shame. The young are targeted with craving of the flesh and with the lust of the eyes and the pride of life. Cultures today are driven with a humanistic involvement putting self-first and expressing great individualism.

We are brought up in a world saturated with sin, and that sin is a condition and that condition is repetitive, hypnotic in nature if you will, we weave in and out of this wide-road of deception. The world's ways will persuade you; indoctrinate you, fill your mind with sensuality, immoral thoughts, and a lust pattern arises inside. The worldly system is full of deception, division and destruction; it is a society without God and it is meant to keep you away from God, away from the Word of God, if you read the Word, you will not understand the Word. The world is an accumulation of sins and evil that are fighting against God's best for your life, the world is marred by sin. Shakespeare was right, "*we live in a weary world.*"

The allurements of the world are for every human traveling the broad way of life, from his physical weaknesses to his distorted beliefs arranged in an impressive and structured way to entice and increase their effectiveness. The feeble-minded human, no matter how intelligent is victim to the enemies prey.

The philosophies of the world are hostile to God; the works of the world are evil. Go back to the founding of the United States of America, just a few hundred years and you will find we were founded, as a Christian nation, and look where we are at today. This worldly system is hostile towards God, the spirit of the world hates Jesus (John 7:7 [NIV]). The world system is a calculated plan designed by the devil himself that hold the inhabitants of he sin nature hostile toward God. This world system hates Jesus, because Jesus testifies that what is in the world, what the world does is evil, and unrighteous. Through God's Word as Jesus lived, there is a standard of right and wrong and this is against the world's ways. Those whom are conformed to the world are called "*adulterous people*" because they are for the world, they love the world, they are friends of the world and the Bible says they are bent of hatred toward

God. *"You adulterers! Don't you realize that friendship with the world makes you an enemy of God? I say it again: If you want to be a friend of the world, you make yourself an enemy of God"* (Jas. 4:4 NLT).

A deadly corrupt system rules our society. The nature of our society is dangerously short-fused, and the greediest of all are the prideful, the self-centered victims of darkness. In them, there is not a clue of what is truth; their minds are polluted with unbelief, deception, and self-deception. Their lives exalted in disobedience, rebellion, and believing lies in the sin nature of unrighteousness.

We live in a nervous society, a stressed society, a world full of chaos, because the world is in a fallen state, meaning because sin entered the world through the great sin and the earth was cursed, and because the earth was cursed, we live in the sin nature. Therefore, the entire planet is a sinful, nervous and stressed out world and if you pay close attention, it is escalating. The nature of the world is sin, the devil can and does deceive the entire inhabitance of the planet.

What we must know is that we live on Satan's turf; this earth is Satan's home. He is not the adversary of the unsaved; he is their master, but he wants the saved, he wants the saved back in his kingdom. Satan's spirit is an antichrist spirit, which operates in the sin nature and his domain is planet earth. Remember he has authority of the earth, in the spiritual realm, which is his kingdom. Earth is temporally his; he rules here, he is the prince of this world; he is within the structure of the world, and in every nation. If you are a citizen of this world, a satanic authority binds your mind from knowing what is the truth because of your unbelief, your unbelief in the gospel. All the societies of the world's system are godless societies, people without God in their lives and those are the ones who are under the control of the devil, the evil one, but he does not have God's children any longer. *"We know that we are children of God, and that the whole world is under the control of the evil one"* (1st John 5:19 NIV).

Living in the world, as a sinner the missing vital ingredient remains missing, the heart remains filled with the world and all it has to offer. Those of the world do not see, do not know what is happening to them, they do not see or feel the destruction that is coming upon them. The alcoholic does not see his liver going bad; the smoker does not see the disease by carcinogens deteriorating his lungs, when a criminal is caught, immediately the consequences will slap him into reality.

Pollutions of the world, it's philosophies, it's cultures and it's systems of entanglements, include books, films, movies, documentaries, the news media, false religions, even our universities, the secular educational system all geared toward the philosophies of untruth, pollute the mind with sadistic activities that are appealing to the viewer, to the thinker, to the lost. They are disguised in many ways, and are appealing ways.

The nature of the world is to defile man, its design is to lead man astray, it is designed to create in man an ignorance of himself, of God and of Jesus and lead man into a selfish exploration of himself and to befriend the worldly system that will feed all his desires.

The worldly system and evil spirits produces human-automatons; programmed through this world's system and governed by our physical needs and wants rather than spiritual consciousness and awareness, and we become slaves of Satan.

There are preset devices called personalities, attitudes, moods, imaginations that automatically respond to pre-programmed directives for our physical, emotional, psychological needs, desires, and appetites in the sin nature. The individual who blatantly commits adultery, with the 'never-getting-caught attitude' the individual who commits murders, with the 'never-getting-caught attitude' the individual who commits fraudulent deals, contracts, programs etc. with the 'never-getting-caught attitude' are responding naturally within the sin nature they live in. The individuals who lie, cheat, steal, destroys, with no shame, with no remorse, unless they do get caught commit these crimes, these sins because they live in a nature that is governed by the devil himself. They are in the world and they are of the world.

All crimes, and all sins are of the sin nature, and those who are of the world naturally respond to its, ways. Remember the devil rules this world and you had better believe he has put-in-place a system that controls human souls to do his will without their knowledge, of what they are doing. They are narcissist naturally, they are programmed to respond to temptation and behave in a clever sinful manner under the radar with the attitude of 'never-getting-caught.'

The evil that is in the world done by humans have an evil nature saturating their soul with demonic influences penetrating their mind with deeds of darkness and man *willingly* does what he should not, there is anarchy in this world.

The World's Wisdom

"For the wisdom of this world is foolishness in God's sight. As it is written:" "He catches the wise in their craftiness." 1st Corinthians 3:19 NIV

One of the easiest things to do today is to get in debt. Credit cards are a financial tool, a great illustration that Satan uses as a hook and abuses all that he can with it. Even though credit cards are of the world system, the devil uses many devices and institutions to damage individuals, families, businesses anything and anyway he can. People do not realize that the kingdom of darkness rules this world.

Here is some of what you will see in the world by traveling the broad way of life. "I will do it my way," "eat, drink and be merry," "evolution," life came from a rock that we came from nothing, to a glob of living protoplasm, wherever they think that came from. The world says that "abortion" is the right choice, murdering babies in the womb, infanticide they encourage. "Homosexuality," "gay-rights, equality," if they marry, they will never be married in God's eyes, "your religion is inferior, ours is superior." The extremities in the world have created chaos; have created terrorism that is shaking the world. This thinking comes from the sin nature deeply rooted in manmade religions, and from the pits of hell, and if you do not believe that or consider that, then the devil has successfully done his work in you.

These tendencies have gradually entered the mind through a process of learning from the paths they take and with companions who live in darkness and travel the wide road of thought that liberates these individuals with selfish, self-centered admirations. They cheapen life and the individuals who believe these things, are in their own little world. However, the little world they live in is the sin nature, and controlled by the master of mind manipulation, Satan himself.

As the dichotomy unfolded to the civilizations of the planet, countries throughout the world and throughout the ages who were Christian hecklers, the unbelievers from ancient times who vehemently rejected the word of God, drove Christianity out, and replaced it with manmade religions that served them to fit their beliefs and passions. These ancient manmade religions throughout the world brought division between Christianity and them. Countries, nationalities, individuals of the world shun the truth of God's word, believe lies of man, and so surface the current madness in ancient lands of the outer most ends of the world.

The world is not a world in peace, religious fanatics, extremist with a twisted ideology have a hatred for other religions, for counties with freedoms of democracy that their country does not have. They are ruled by extremist who have committed their lives to destruction and the destruction of others and this they believe is right, but all the while their carnal minds is under spiritual hypnosis. The world believes you cannot find peace until you find all the pieces, but the truth is you will not find peace until you find the Prince of Peace, Jesus.

When thinking of worldly matters it is in relation with the flesh, with the devil, earthly, and sensual contamination and is not wise. Some use worldly knowledge to be cleverly evil, sensual and devilish and not wisdom from God. Our world is only part of actual reality; the two spiritual kingdoms are at constant conflict with one another with their agenda hinging on your choice of living within their gates.

The roads through life are paved with appealing temptations that steer you into the oncoming paths of hungry demon possession that will consume you, ingest you and turn you into immoral sinners. If your interest is greed, material possessions, hording, making money, either literally or figuratively, so much money you can not spend it all, these all controlled by 'self' of the sin nature. If you have an obsession with sex, which constitutes hyper-sexuality, as cougar's, nymphomaniacs, cradle robbers, which some may say are caused by over active libido, or psychological disorders but behind it all is the deep dark nature in which you travel under the constant surveillance of demon possession or demon influence.

Demons will work together in achieving their agenda of what confronts you; they will use everything for their advantage. They will lead you into many ways of acquiring money. Defrauding and embezzlement, robbing, gambling, cheating on taxes, and not claiming taxes, not claiming income, stealing, and whatever interest there is for the all mighty-dollar.

They will bend and twist the path in front of the traveler where exits will appear diverting the individual down the path of appealing perverse temptations, appealing perverse sexuality. They know human physiology, they know what is appealing to you, and they know by observation what devious path to set before you. They are a constant threat to the sanity of man and a constant threat to his destiny.

People want rights, what they think are their rights, what they believe are their rights, what they want to be their rights, what the sin nature tells them are their rights. The gays, abortionist, evolutionist can choose their life style, what they feel is right in their heart, in their soul; in their cavity, their empty void, is where these thoughts are forming. This is a beaten path off the wide road of life, the radical thinking of the unsaved. God gives ever person the freedom to choose their path of life, the wide road or the narrow road. Choosing the wrong path, thinking the wrong way, living the wrong way, one will be accountable for his life style and will bring consequences for their actions. This truth is the unbeliever wants to reject any type of judgment, he does not want to answer to anyone, he puts this thought out of his mind, and eternal judgment is not in his vocabulary he does not believe in it.

The world and its ways are spreading the wrong message

"We have not received the spirit of the world but the Spirit who is from God, that we may understand what God has freely given us." 1st Corinthians 2:12 NIV

Everything of the world is temporary, its wealth, its wisdom, and its mystifying philosophies, its power; the world offers temporary gratification but God's kingdom offers eternal joy! *"For the world offers only a craving for physical pleasure, a craving for everything we see, and pride in our achievements and possessions. These are not from the Father, but are from this world." "And this world is fading away, along with everything that people crave. But anyone who does what pleases God will live forever"* (1st John 2:16a, 17 NLT).

The spirit of the world, the wisdom of the world, the world's system, its philosophies, its worldviews are in the movies, in television, radio, all Medias, magazines, books, novels and educational, worldly religions, cultures, in our educational systems, in our universities, in our economic system, in our work place, in our government and the governments throughout the world. From the small town local governments to our capitals, its values, and life-styles, the spirit of the world is opposed to God.

The world does not have a problem with an unknown god out there somewhere because the false religions have their own god or gods that they worship. The world's problem is with the name Jesus Christ their Creator. Jesus the God man is not accepted in societies; in cultures, it will start fights, break up families, and start wars. The name of Jesus is not allowed in some countries, in some churches, is not allowed spoken in some families, in some religions, his name is not considered important to some and just by mentioning his name, preaching and teaching about Jesus, one can be prosecuted and even face death. Why?

The answer is those human pawns that work though satanic and demonic influences are doing the will of Satan who has penetrated their mind with worldly beliefs with their carnal thinking, through the wide gate. They do not live the spiritual/physical life, only the physical, with their carnal mind. Behind the scenes are demonic spiritual forces influencing the situations and circumstances on earth.

God has made a way to overcome the ways of this evil world, because the ways of this world, if man continues in them, will literally destroy him. God does not want to see anyone perish, he gives all men the same way to overcome this world, that is through His Son, Jesus, and through Jesus, you will have victory over this world through your faith in God. 1st John 5:4, 5 says this,"*for everyone born of God overcomes the world.*" "*This is the victory that has overcome the world, even our faith.*" "*Who is it that overcomes the world? Only he who believes that Jesus is the Son of God.*"

How we choose to live our lives while in the world, we will reap its effects. There is only the wide road, which we become slaves to unrighteousness and the narrow road of life, being slaves to obedience, to righteousness. The way of many, that is lost, the way of the natural, the way of the sin nature, and the way of disobedience, the way of the unrighteous, the way of Satan, or the way of righteousness. The way you choose to live, you become slaves to, with all of its doctrines, all that it has to offer. Romans 6:16 [NIV] "*Don't you know that when you offer yourselves to someone to obey him as slaves, you are slaves to the one whom you obey—whether you are slaves to sin, which leads to death, or to obedience, which leads to righteousness?* We are slaves to the devil or we are slaves to God, the Creator of the universe, the choice is yours.

The devil is the *"god of this age"* the ruler of a world system that is sadistically opposed to Christ.

Chapter 12

Living in the Spirit Realm

Here you will find our soul, this is where the spirit man lives, and this is where the spirit of the two natures resides, which are:

- The divine nature, God's safe haven for the believers while we are on the planet, here is where we experience the spiritual/physical life given to us through the new supernatural birth, the born again miracle, born of God.
- The sin nature, the nature of the world where the unbeliever resides until his call to judgment, he lives the mere physical life, given to him through natural birth.
- The spirit population of the earth, I believe is greater than the human.
- Demons can be blamed for dangerous and destructive moods of our nature and for sickness, pestilence, death, possession, nightmares and others.
- There are three classes of spirits;

Satanic, Worldly, and Human

There was the invisible Spirit of God and the Word of God that brought all this into being. The invisible was here before the visible. The invisible world will out-last the visible world, *"So we fix our eyes not on what is seen, but on what is unseen. For what is seen is temporary, but what is unseen is eternal"* (2nd Cor. 4:18. NIV).

Things, seen, are temporary and things that not seen are eternal. What is not seen is more real than what is seen. Faith is the evidence that there is an unseen world out there, *"Faith is the confidence that what we hope for will actually happen; it gives us assurance about things we cannot see." "By faith we understand that the entire universe was formed at God's command, that what we now see did not come from anything that can be seen,"* (Heb. 11:1, 3 NLT). The visible formed out of the invisible, which is that the invisible was here before the visible, before there was anything.

Darkness Revealed

"to open their eyes, so they may turn from darkness to the light and from the power of Satan to God. Then they will receive forgiveness for their sins and be given a place among God's people, who are set apart by faith in me." – Jesus

Here is the realm of darkness, the home of the kingdom of Satan, his satanic demons, all the forces of evil, and the sin nature. Here is where our carnal mind roams and stumbles around the wide-path of life, trying to feel our way and find our way through life with no light.

What is darkness, it is mentioned numerous times in the Bible, "rulers of darkness," "kingdom of darkness," "powers of darkness," "chains of darkness," "works of darkness," "walk in darkness," "full of darkness," "covered with darkness," "physical darkness," moral and spiritual darkness, characteristic to moral and spiritual depravity, metaphorically bending toward evil. Within the human soul, darkness is a condition, an evil condition synonymous to the sin nature. Darkness is spiritual, home of our enemies; its mighty forces are satanic and demonic and mean nothing but malicious harm. The land of darkness covers the earth and is to cause physical, mental, moral impairment, destruction, damnation, and deterioration of the human soul with blindness to the human spirit. Nothing good comes from it.

Darkness is a metaphor for a lost condition. Satan and his militia of demons brought darkness with them when cast to earth. Darkness of the sin nature, integrates us, Satin's condition is dark, his nature is sinful our condition is dark and our nature is the sin nature. Satan rules the sin nature, meant to keep us preoccupied with the world system. The world system is anything outside of Christ. The cultures throughout the world, the world's religions, and our beliefs are covered with this condition called darkness. This dark condition affects our soul and spirit. Within this darkness are snares, tactics, schemes and devices used by Satan to capture and hold us in the sin nature that we will by our own omission surrender to the world's ways because of the pleasures, because of the freedom that comes with it. That freedom from the dark sin nature that we live in allows us to do what we want without answering to a higher power, but does not allow us to do what we should do and this dark freedom comes with a great price.

In darkness is denial of the absolute truth, in denial there is ignorance, in ignorance there is a lack of knowledge, with lack of knowledge there is damnation. With the lack of knowledge and ignorance, we seek answers in all the wrong places, in false religions, affairs, adultery, drugs, alcohol, gambling, sexual perversion, possessions, material wealth, money, power, personal power, and power in authority, physical and controlling power.

A writer wrote, "*Darkness is a religious state where unbelievers exist, where there is spiritual ignorance with its attending immorality and misery.*" Because of this satanic driven condition, the human soul has no idea what is going on, they cannot see, understand or comprehend that they are held captive in an evil condition under an ominous evil ruler.

If you can believe and have faith is Jesus, God wants to take you from that lost condition. That you may have forgiveness for your sins, and turn you from the power of Satan's darkness to God's light, that you may be sanctified by that faith, and that your eyes may be open and that you may receive his inheritance. In the book of Acts 26:18 Jesus said, *"to open their eyes, in order to turn them from darkness to light, and from the power of Satan to God, that they may receive forgiveness of sins and an inheritance among those who are sanctified by faith in Me."*

In darkness, the devil has power in your sins, our sins give the devil a foothold and he over takes that foothold like night over takes the day. In darkness, there is no clue that there is more to life no clue who you are; and no clue truth is hidden.

It dulls your mind to spiritual things. When you drive by a church, you do not care one iota what is going on in there that you do not think about the mysterious supernatural virgin birth of Christ, the crucifixion of him nailed to a wooden cross that was carved from a tree that he planted. nor the spilling of his precious holy blood, nor the burial and resurrection of Jesus as being the savoir of the world. These thoughts are held back from you by covering your mind with a fog of darkness called sin letting you think of other so called spiritual matters, ESP, clairvoyance, fortunetelling that are false, if you think of spiritual matters at all. The carnal mind is directed to our physical desires not our spiritual needs. Have you ever wondered why you have not thought of these things, I doubt it?

We can be very easily driven to dissatisfaction with ourselves, we do not want to be what God created us to be, we want to be what we want to be. We create false lives out of dissatisfaction of our real selves. Some loose themselves in television programs, soap operas, movies, sports, having an unshakable quest for power, higher status, a "I am better than you attitude." People get obsessive with a mate, with the digital networking systems, lost in their computers, all the digital equipment; they give their God given talent and ability to the devil instead of glorifying God with it.

Deception

Everything about you they target, they want your personality bent toward hatred, prejudice, shrewdness, toward the worlds networking system of counterfeit ways, fraudulent deception of their misguided understandings, reasoning, thoughts, and using man's intelligence for self, for evil for that dark system. In doing so, they build an egomaniacal structure within the mind, the soul of the sinner; this is the price of being an unbeliever.

Through friends, family, reading material, advertisements, television, music, movies, and entertainment in all categories are powerful mediums that can and do have mighty influences that are beneficial or deadly to us. They can affect our thinking expand our understanding and knowledge in either a positive or negative way. Our minds are stimulated with increasing excitement and challenge of life itself. Emotionally, we benefit immensely from the outside nurturing influences that contribute enormously to our personal and spiritual underdevelopment. These are the children of the devil and live a life of disobedience toward God.

Some tactics the devil use in deception

You think irrational, which with the carnal mind is understandable, then you will show irrational behavior, the way you think controls the way you live and the way you live will show how you relate to others, noticeably that is, righteous or unrighteous. Your thoughts will influence your decisions and your decisions will turn into actions, and your actions will tell your beliefs, and your beliefs will ultimately reveal your character. Whatever is done, what ever is said, shows where your allegiance lay.

The mind of the sinner is deceived, bombarded with mental and physical activity that keeps the mind pre-occupied so that the negative thoughts are around the truth but never being able to understand it. The heart is filled with facades; people appear to be something that they are not especially when that appearance is false or meant to deceive. Veneer finishes is upon the hearts of the sinner, their feelings, their love, their caring, are superficial, cold and calculated. We can be lead by peer pressure, a dark culture, traditions; at times personalities become increasingly twisted and perverted.

Deception and discouragement are powerful tools that the devil uses on us to totally throw us off balance in our thinking and keep us bound in darkness. Satan's tactics are introduced to those living in unrighteousness because in darkness there is no spiritual knowledge that the sinner does not understand what he does not know.

Satan's greatest deceptions involve convincing a person that happiness and fulfillment is found only by success, revenge, money, material possessions, and satisfying selfish-desires. We are enticed to sacrifice future blessing in favor of feeding present desires.

Discouragement, envy, bitterness; opens the door for demons, they will fill your head with all kinds of negative thoughts. With this type of mental distress, the satanic forces can and do oppress the weak and take extreme advantage with that deceptive oppression. The oppressed have no comfort, full of anxiety, stress, fears and the oppressors have great power and does not let up and their victims are helpless (Eccles. 4:1 NLT). They get inside you and convince you that you are different, that you are someone that the outsiders do not know, that you are meant to be different than what you are.

Through darkness, demons engulf and saturate the nature of sin and it penetrates the human race living in that nature with corrupt, evil ways. Satan does not hesitate, he does not waste time, he does not over look an opportunity, his crosshairs are on the soul of man and in a nanosecond, he can be in you like a maggot on a carcass devouring you from the inside out. Let us go back to the garden for a moment, first off, the devil lied to the humans, and they fell for his tactical persuasive and skillful means to their end. This action was the end of these humans as for living a righteous life. This couple had children and these children were taught of the evil deception among them. Just as it is today, people who hear the gospel have a choice to accept it or reject it as it was with their children. There children grew up hearing about God and the way to live in a life of obedience, unfortunately one of the two brothers would not accept what was taught them and yielded to his own ways of doing things. The story is about Cain and Abel I am sure you've heard of the story, but I am also sure you've heard the rest of the story. Abel believed and lived his life in respect and obedience to what his parents have taught him but his brother bent on doing evil by not giving as he should, yielding to the self-life and became corrupted with the darkness of the now sin nature brought into existence by his parents. Now what is happening behind the scenes in the spirit realm is Satan is watching ever move of these two brothers and seeing who is the weaker and the one bending away from righteousness and toward unrighteousness, his fangs are out and ready to seize upon. You know the story; Cain killed Abel, but why, was it just because of an offering? This is what happened and this is how it works today, the same way. As Cain, grew toward his self-life and rejected instruction that was taught him, this disobedient action developed into deeper sin in his mind, from selfishness. His parents went through this, he should have known better. As he yielded toward his way of thinking into disobedience and rebellion Satan entered him because this gave Satan an open door to enter, the open door was disobedience and rebellion to instruction, to truth, to authority through a self-life these are evil acts. Satan could not enter Abel because his mind focused on obedience, truth, and this keeps Satan away. Obedience is a resistance to the enemy. The mighty scripture is proven, "*Resist the devil and he will flee from you*" (Jas. 4:7b). Cain rejected the truth; he rejected obedience, and in rebellion killed his bother. Before the killing, in the disobedient and rebellious thought process, Satan entered Cain's mind and Cain became under the control of the devil, the devil had him. Read this passage in 1 John 3:12, *"Do not be like Cain, who belonged to the evil one and murdered his brother. And why did he murder him? Because his own actions were evil and his brother's were righteous."* Satan entered through the doors of disobedience and rebellion and found a foothold. His crosshairs magnified with a zoom lens today watching every move, listening to every word, concentrating on our actions waiting for the weakest moment to enter and devour us, as a roaring lion.

Laziness is a tool of the devil, for he knows the lazy person is a procrastinator and a procrastinator has a lot of idle time on his hands for the devil to do his work creating another pawn. Resting and relaxing is one thing after a days work or spending quality time with the children or family, but hours on a computer of those social networking sites minding everyone's business and them knowing yours, he is behind that. The computer is another tool the devil uses to hook the sinner and turn that sinner toward allurements with intense interest of the sinner's weakness. Wasting time is stumbling into Satan's box of tricks, and he will use illusions of interest to lure the sinner.

Fear is a huge emotional tactic that Satan uses. It can bring on anxiety, thinking negative thoughts bringing on more fear. It can close your world into a self-efficient world, at the most, and separate you from the rest of the world and hold you in fear.

The devil deceives us into thinking that the way to happiness lies in continually seeking self-satisfaction and gratification. We fail to recognize that this very thing is what ultimately leads to crime and untold human suffering, and, lead to the great fall of man. Satan knows, by holding you captive in sin, it will have negative eternal consequences.

Satan will attack you in a particular way in your life where you are weak, where you have a weakness, an interest a desire. What is your weakness? Drugs, alcohol, smoking, over eating, gluttony, sex, sexual orientation, stealing, conniving, fraudulent matters, cheating, gossiping, vulgarity, adultery, he will over whelm you with temptations, plunging you into depths of worldly pleasure and fleshly desires taking you places where you did not want to go. He is our personal enemy. Again, he will produce strongholds in the mind, he will never give up, if you conquer one, he will generate another, even several at a time, if you conquer those, which is unlikely without the Lord, he will produce more. He will never stop; he does not want to lose an unsaved soul. Anger will create an opening for him; he loves those who get angry.

Strongholds will very quickly develop into emotional struggles and inner turmoil for some, for others they may develop into habits of fleshly pleasure. They can affect your friends and family, your coworker, your social life, anything to work against God. Satanic strongholds gain entrance with your permission, just as Jesus will have entrance with your permission. In Ephesians, 4:27 *"Neither give place to the devil."* Giving a place in your life to the devil, he will make a home their and devise an environment within those conditions that you choose to take place in your life. If you choose to live a life without God then you choose to be a child of Satan, now you have given him position to operate in your life with his authority.

He calls evil good, and good evil, and sinning for you will bring you freedom. He is the author of all lies. He corrupts our reasoning's; he can overwhelm us with a prideful heart, cause malice, and envy to rise up in us and to entice us to do evil to others. When you live a life of darkness, this is his domain; by you dabbling in sin, you have given him ground to set up camp. Satan loves those who lie, lying can be traced back to him because he is the father of lies *(John 8:44)*, being a liar is being just like the devil, living in any sin, in being as the devil, Satan's kingdom is built on lies. He loves a human who lives in dishonesty.

He will interject fear, worry, anxiety into you where an emotional cloud of confusion and fear that will deter your focus and concentration which can be very harmful. Harmful in the sense that these can stress you out, and we all know that stress is very harmful to the body and the mind.

Satan is trying and has been trying to tear apart the marriage amendments by trying to pass same-sex marriage amendment modification. To abolish the sanctity of marriage of one woman and one man by indoctrination of same-sex marriage of those in the homosexual lifestyle is playing right into the hands and devious mind of Satan. Who wants to destroy families, wreck marriages, confuse children to where they will follow him into a lifestyle from the depth of darkness. Redefining marriage will crumble that sanctity and their twisted strategic campaign will draw the hearts and minds of their alike and lead them into a lifestyle that will be severely judged.

Intimidation is a tool of the devil, used between husband and wife, between parents and child, between schools, between children, between adults used in many areas of life, domination is used in these matters. Violent temperaments are evil darts Satan shoots at us that sets our souls on fire. Evil desires, blasphemous thoughts rise from within.

The further you get away from God the more you get into destructive living. The more malice you have, the more deceitfulness, more hypocritical, you are full of envy and evil speaking. This is for lack of knowledge of the gospel of truth, which is hidden from those who are perishing, the unbelievers (2nd Cor. 4:3 ^{NLT}).

He fills the spiritual-airwaves with filth with perverse lips, and dark violence seemingly intriguing and desirable to minds of all ages to where they would be enticed to participate. The devil's work is done on earth through the weakness of man who is Satan's pawns because man has become hardened through deception of the doctrines of the devil towards God, (Heb. 3:13).

Another trick of the devil is 'spiritism' God forbids this. It sends the unbeliever in a spiritual profession of foretelling, mediums, crystal-ball gazing, using Ouija boards, ESP and the like; these influences open up a floodgate of demonic spirits that will control the mind and thoughts of the lost. This opens wide the way of their territory.

These are part of his tactics, abortion, perverse opposite-sex marriage, accepting and promoting homosexuality, to pervert television and movie content. Corroding of cultures and moving into a self-enduring welfare, of me first. He puts into minds the indifference of the value of the human life. Satan does not work in puny attempts to deceive the mind of humans he works on a huge scale unprotected by man from his inferior kingdom.

They come after our emotions, our intellect, our social status, our physical being. They will use whatever means it takes to accomplish their agenda. They have no use for the human but to make pawns, use them, and then destroy them.

Deceptive Tools

His pawns have turned themselves over to him by remaining in the sin nature and refusing the grace of God. Demonic influence subtly works in the unbelievers mind and shows in his actions, his speech, his beliefs, his demeanor, personality and character.

Some of the devils most used tools, malice, and hatred, holding grudges is huge, making mountains out of molehills, envy, jealousy, sensuality, deceitfulness, and discouragement. Discouragement is one of Satan's most successful and powerful tools used on humans. With discouragement, he can pry open and get inside a conscience and implant distress, depression, and so on. Antagonism, hatred develops when anyone wants to impose superiority over another and makes demands from the other, this can create poisonous hatred; inject mocking, ridicule, pain, and opposition.

His pawns are filled with sinister schemes devised with hypocrisy speaking kindness coming from their lips but filled with evil in their hearts thriving with endeavors of wickedness. Satan has human agents in all our concerns of life, wherever there is a human there is a demon.

Satan preys on our emotional weaknesses and discouragement, we can lose vigor, energy, emotionally we can lose touch with reality, don't want to be involved, mentally we do not feel needed, do not feel loved, everyone needs someone even if that someone is God, who is waiting.

Homosexuality is a human invention encouraged by the devil to lead man down the spiral-path to destruction. In Matthew 19:4b-6 And He (Jesus) answered and said to them, *"Have you not read that He who made them at the beginning 'made them male and female,' and said, 'For this reason a man shall leave his father and mother and be joined to his wife, and the two shall become one flesh'? So then, they are no longer two but one flesh. Therefore what God has joined together, let not man separate."* The unbelieving sinner does not want to hear this; they do not want biblical pressure, they do not need oppression from an area they do not believe in.

Satan knows if he can break up the families of America, the Christian woven fabric of this country will come unraveled and chaos will prevail. He is doing just that today. They say one out of two marriages fail, what is that doing to our country. It is having great effects on the children in those broken marriages. Children have no father figure, there is no fatherly responsibility, there is no fatherly protection, there is no fatherly leadership, no family unity, no church and Sunday school as a family unit, and these children go astray. In church is where they will learn good morals and what is right and wrong.

Satan works behind the scenes always, he is a sneak and he will implant devilish schemes in the minds of fathers. He will tempt them with adultery, he can bring someone into the father's life in an innocent fashion and it can develop into an adulterous affair. Satan can lead a weak minded man in alcoholism, into drugs, into gambling, where he can squander their savings away, he can promote self-ambitions always working, never home, a father can be pre-occupied with selfish-interest, self-happiness, he can be turned into nothing but a stubborn, mean, selfish-man.

These lost, lonely children now depend on their mother, who now has to live both parts of parenthood and it will be overwhelming, working two-jobs, getting behind with bills, collectors at her door, on the phone, receiving mail from them and even getting threats. In the mean time the children are heading in the wrong direction, they are heading so far off track. The male children can get into drugs, selling and buying, alcoholism, stealing anything that his peers lead him. The female children can do the same as the boys and they can be lead into promiscuity that will damage their life, and all this at very young ages.

Satan has weapons of mass destruction to achieve his purpose on this planet, and breaking up families is a huge tool he uses to dismantle righteousness. Destroying families are one of his main targets, the more dysfunctional families he can make, the more chance he has of controlling broken down individuals. The more the individual is broken the easier it is for him to lead them into deeper darkness. He knows the broken family members are unlikely to become saved, or church going people, the chances are they will hit the bars and the kids will hit the streets, where drugs, prostitution, alcohol will make these kids think they will be happier, what ever the case may be, Satan has the upper hand in leading these individuals into sin. Satan also uses some types of music as a tool to capture the young and older individuals and hold them in delusion and away from the truth. He also targets individuals with puffed-up personalities that he knows so well, because pride already rules in these individuals now he can maneuver them into circumstances and situations to do his devilish work. There is nothing and nowhere that he is not involved in, he never stops his quest to destroy, he has penetrated every part of our societies and our cultures, his manipulations, distortions and abnormal thinking and teachings he uses on man.

Demons will use the flesh for temptation, the sins of this world, they will stalk you, they will harass you through their pawns, they will bring aggravation into your life also through others, and they will churn-up irritations in you that will bring out a defensive mechanism and with all your irritability strike out at others with an uncontrolled viciousness.

Darkness arose out of sin and before sin, there was light, and in that light, man lived and man was sinless. In this short sentence are two dispensations, the dispensation of Innocence, and the dispensation of Conscience. Before man's conscience know sin, he know God, man did not know evil, he did not know sin, he lived in innocence, man lived in purity, he was innocent of everything. Light refers to God, to innocence, it refers to understanding, and light refers to purity. When sin entered the world, light was gone, God was gone, purity was gone, the innocence was gone, now conscience raised its head, and showed them what sin they just committed, the rebellious sin of disobedience, just as Satan did when he sinned as Lucifer. This changed everything for man, there was no reversing this action and we are the inheritances of that devilish scheme.

Satan knows man very well; he knows that man now lives in depravity of spirituality. He knows the more you get into destructive, deceptive behavior, lying, criminal activities, fits of anger, killings, murders, abortion, stealing, deceptive living, homosexuality, all sexual immorality etc. the more its satisfies the flesh and the more it satisfies the flesh the more he can excite you with these evils. You do not really know that these activities are damning your soul; you do not have the spiritual discernment to know that these are morally wrong.

Of the lesser degree, you can feel deep inside that lying is a wrong thing to do, that it does carry deceptiveness along with it, with a host of other two-face blatant cowardly acts, but you still lie. Stealing also, you know is wrong; it can harm you and many people in many ways. However, do you stop and think that homosexuality is wrong, some do, and others want to change laws to make it right. Think, just think about what you believe, this sin is a physical desire with the physical behavior that is contrary to why man was made but is bent toward the liberal perspective of being accepted by social tolerance.

Demons know as long as your eyes are off Jesus Christ they can make your life ineffectual.

There are some on the left that believe homosexuality is a gift from God, this act of *willful* sinning and its severity is beyond the comprehension of the sinner in addition, isolation is the antithesis of what is needed. We should be open about ourselves and at the same time be *willing* to understand what is behind openness.

God does not hate homosexuals; on the contrary, God loves them because they are a part of this miracle called life. God loves the individual but hates the sin, the act of homosexuality. It is not what he designed man for; Satan designed this physical desire as another strategy to keep the human race at ends with one another. To the participating individuals it is a casual, natural thing to do, but is frowned upon by society.

To those who have lived in the closet for a time and those who are still there have heard the Biblical statements regarding homosexuality, the Bible plainly states that if a man lies with another man this is an act of abomination, Leviticus 18:22 this is a detestable act; they shall surely be put to death, 20:13. This cannot be taken lightly, the deceptiveness is there and to see it, spiritual discernment is needed. When one *willfully* chooses to disregard the warning of God, refuses the forgiveness of God, refuses the blood sacrifice of Christ God's Son, they are putting themselves in grave danger. God knows their heart, and if they choose their sinful acts over righteous acts, then he is through with them. Look what it says in the book of Romans.

Romans 1:26, 27 says, *"For this reason God gave them over to degrading passions; for their women exchange the natural function for that which is unnatural, and in the same way also the men abandoned the natural function of the woman and burned in their desire toward one another, men with men committing indecent acts and receiving in their own persons the due penalty of their error."* Due penalty of their error, this is not an insignificant punishment my friend.

Deception is a key tool that the devil uses against us and we are unaware of his devices. You have the ability to think for yourself, you have the ability to know right from wrong; you have the right to reject truth, but remember there is a penalty a server penalty. The more you sin, the more you *willfully* sin the more your conscience is seared, hardened. The Bible says, that, "such teachings come from hypocritical liars, whose consciences have been seared as with a hot iron.

"Don't you realize that those who do wrong will not inherit the Kingdom of God? Don't fool yourselves. Those who indulge in sexual sin, or who worship idols, or commit adultery, or are male prostitutes, or practice homosexuality, or are thieves, or greedy people, or drunkards, or are abusive, or cheat people — none of these will inherit the Kingdom of God." (1st Cor. 6:9, 10 NLT).

Satan's best defense against knowledge is to keep you from knowing what truth is, to keep you from wanting to know if there truly is absolute truth. In the sin nature, this is natural by the alluring elements of the world's system. The more one conforms to the world's system the further away that one is from the truth, the further away one is from the truth the measure of ignorance increases and continuing captivity is certain.

Darkness is a sanctuary for satanic activity, and anyone who *willingly* wants to remain there is subject to its deeds of evil. The devil tells lies about God, he promotes a Christ-less society and a Christ-less Christianity and is recruiting unbelievers for his cause.

Satan comes when you are tired, confused, lazy, and lonely, secluded, depressed, he works in deluding his victims. A delusion that Satan throws in our path is he distorts reality. He also throws in cravings and desires that the flesh is weak over. Satan naturalizes the individual he re-directs their thinking away from spiritual matters into pleasures of sin.

Satan is after our young children. There are terrible things going on now in our public schools. Authorities of public schools have let books come into classrooms teaching that homosexuality is acceptable and accepted in society. He infiltrates our universities, colleges, and recruits students and through atheistic propaganda teaches God is despicable, and disputable with intellectual intimidation. As these students spill over into society with their argumentative debates with their collisions and conflicts and their random-mutation beliefs have attacked God's people. Here you can see Satan's pawns of different ages and different vocations doing his work, to promote individualism, because individualism streams from humanism, which is a tool of Satan to deceive millions and millions of individuals throughout the ages. When Satan has entered a person's soul, he has the capability to take that soul captive, take that persons *will* into captivity and make that person do the will of Satan. There is a passage in 2nd Timothy 2:26 [NIV] that the writer is referring to sinners, the lost that have been taken captive in their minds, *"and that they will come to their senses and escape from the trap of the devil, who has taken them captive to do his will."* If individuals willingly stay in darkness because they love their evil deeds, Jesus says this to them; *"You belong to your father, the devil, and you want to carry out your father's desire. He was a murderer from the beginning, not holding to the truth, for there is no truth in him. When he lies, he speaks his native language, for he is a liar and the father of lies"* (John 8:44 [NIV]).

Who are these misguided bewildered Pawns

Misguided pawns are volunteers from the sin dumpster with the mind-set of unrighteousness and who the devil uses to covertly thwart citizens of the human race in attempts to recruit more pawns that they will join them in their cause, these menacing pawns are at all levels in humanity. More and more unrighteousness is surfacing in the halls of justice, in the fields of humanity, on the shelves of literature, on the streets of societies in the forms of culture. Pawns are strategically positioned in areas of life that they will bring opposing views into the debatable arena and will fight for the cause that they volunteered for, whether it is abortion, gun laws, capital punishment, human rights, free speech, religious rights, civil rights etc. They are there for the sole purpose of undermining Gods and the Christian principles in areas of life that will protect the human race from the advancement of evil this is their cause.

Groups of pawns have taken prayer out of our school, they have taken the Ten Commandants out of public areas, and they want to remove at Christmas the manger from public places. They want to remove God from the pledge of Allegiance, they want to remove "In God We Trust" from our money, and this will most likely lead us into a cashless society.

There is a cosmic battle going on in the spirit realm between the kingdom of God and the kingdom of Satan and this fight is for your soul. There is coming a time on the planet that the only people who will be here are the pawns, and the battle is to recruit as many as possible.

Wicked spirits are moving with great force in this country and in the world, every day we see the evil that is taking place. When you see the news and hear or read about a person that slaughtered another, or a person disembodied someone, these acts are satanic and perpetrated by the devil's pawns. How anyone can forget the horrific killings that have taken place of soldiers, civilians, captives in the Middle East, the beheading, torture beyond our comprehension. These came right out of the mind of Satan, as it did on 9/11, the pawns that are severely misguided.

The evil tyrants of countries, or those that are hiding in countries, like little rats that send their mice out to do their dirty work, rule with brainwashing techniques and cruelty and power of unjust authority that hate our freedom and our democracy.

The Two Simile Gates

"Enter ye in at the strait gate: for wide is the gate, and broad is the way, that leadeth to destruction, and many there be which go in thereat: Because strait is the gate, and narrow is the way, which leadeth unto life, and few there be that find it." Matthew 7:13,14 KJV

The gates are of the spirit realm where our mind travels and our soul lives, the wide gate is a broad way to travel, a wide-open path. This inference tells the path is wide so that all those traveling have as much freedom as possible, are not crowded with restrictions and they have enough room for all their baggage, and their personal closets. This path of life is our inheritance, it is a way of thinking, and it is traveled by most of the inhabitance of earth. All is welcome, any belief is welcome, there are absolutely no restrictions, but what is kept unknown to the traveler is that the end of this path awaits, destruction, devastation, which will shock the traveler into the real world of reality with the gates closed behind him.

They enter through the wide gate by the millions, those entering through the strait gate by single-file, one by one.

Through the straight gate the narrow path, it also is open to everyone, but there are restrictions only one belief is required, this narrow passage leads to eternal life. To enter through the narrow gate is to accept Jesus Christ as your personal savior.

The inheritance of the wide gate is of the natural realm, the sin nature where the kingdom of Satan rules and the sinner is under a spiritual hypnotic state traveling down twisted paths that are intentionally laid before him to cause him to lose his way, and to keep him lost. This is the passage where sin abounds, it is a passage of error, of untruth, rebellion, disobedience, rejection of Jesus, these are mans natural weapons against God. This broad way is the home of the children of disobedience where judgment will fall on these unbelievers. *"For this ye know, that no whoremonger, nor unclean person, nor covetous man, who is an idolater, hath any inheritance in the kingdom of Christ and of God." "Let no man deceive you with vain words: for because of these things cometh the wrath of God upon the children of disobedience." "Be not ye therefore partakers with them"* (Eph. 5:5-7 ᴷᴶⱽ). We are warned not to partake with the unbelievers for their lives are approaching the wrath of God. Those who love the world's ways cannot enter through the narrow gate. It is only done by a rigid denial of self and leaving all your sins outside the narrow gate.

The narrow gate is of the supernatural realm where the kingdom of God rules, where the saved regenerated sinner travels a narrow path. This is the path of the spiritual/physical man. This is the passage of truth, of obedience, of righteousness and godly living through the acceptance of Jesus, who is the gate, the "door" (John 10:9) entering the passage that leads to God and eternal life.

These ways to live our lives reference to two classes of people, the saved and the unsaved, the righteous the unrighteous, the believers, and the unbelievers. For the unbelievers they are sure that what they believe is the way they prefer to live their lives and this seems right to them, but they are receiving this message from the dark corridors of the sin nature where their father the devil strategizes their paths and their lives are heading for destruction. In Proverbs 14:12 the bible says, *"There is a way that seems right to a man, But its end is the way of death."* For those who travel the narrow path of life, Proverbs 15:24 says, *"The way of life winds upward for the wise that he may turn away from hell below."* The way the unbeliever lives and believes is because he is of the sin nature, the world, and the sin nature and the world are ruled by the devil. Do they recognize that they do wicked evil, do they know they practice deceptive lies, do they recognize the filthy language, do they recognize their erroneous ways, do they recognize they are lost, do they know who is leading them in this arrogant way?

The Comparison

The secularist on the wide road are show-offs, they show-off their material stuff, their cars, homes, their bodies, their intellect, their wealth, their luxury, their stuff. The wide road is paved with pride.

The narrow path is paved with love. A Christian wants to show his spirit of God's love, his love for the Lord, his peacefulness, his gentleness, his own love for the world, his joy through Jesus and they are prosecuted for it. This narrow way of thinking goes against the dominant thinking of those of the world.

What the Lord looks at are our motives and character of our heart they carry a tremendous amount of personal insight into our being. Our character is shown or obvious to the outside world but they have no idea what motives we have hidden under our mask. The way of good and the way of evil, the way of right and the way of wrong, the way of righteousness or unrighteousness, the way of truth or untruth.

Through the wide gate lay many paths of allurements, temptations, sin of iniquity. Sexual immorality, impurity and debauchery, idolatry and witchcraft; hatred, discord, jealousy, fits of rage, selfish ambitions, envy, drunkenness, orgies, and the like. There are false religions with twisted idolatries. A warning to those who live these life styles, they will not inherit the kingdom of God (Gal. 5:19, 20, 21 NIV).

Through the narrow gate lays a strait way with no alternative paths. This way of life the Holy Spirit works in the believer, the Christian producing love, joy, peace, patience, kindness, goodness, faithfulness, gentleness, and self-control (Gal. 5:22,23 NLT).

This is what God says about the believer; *"Those who lead blameless lives and do what is right, speaking the truth from sincere hearts." "Those who refuse to gossip or harm their neighbors or speak evil of their friends." "Those who despise flagrant sinners, and honor the faithful followers of the* LORD, *and keep their promises even when it hurts." "Those who lend money without charging interest, and who cannot be bribed to lie about the innocent"*. *"Such people will stand firm forever,"* (Ps. 15:2-5 NLT).

I read this comparison about the sinner traveling the wide path of life. "They prefer sin, to holiness, indulging the lusts of the flesh to walking according to the scriptures, self to Christ, the world to God." This author is right it is as the Lord Jesus declared-"*Men loved darkness rather than light, because their deeds were evil*" (John 3:19) "men refuse to deny self, abandon their idols, and submit to Christ as Lord; and without this, none can take the first step toward Heaven!" (See Appendix).

The wide path represents darkness and the narrow path is God's Light, one leads to death one to life, "*Then Jesus spoke to them again, saying, "I am the light of the world, He who follows Me shall not walk in darkness, but have the light of life*" (John 8:12). It is simply this, the paths of life are separated by sin, either path we take our hearts are empowered with good or evil, truth or lies.

> *"Let those who are wise understand these things.*
> *Let those with discernment listen carefully.*
> *The paths of the LORD are true and right."*
>
> Hosea 14:9 NLT

The wide gate leads to many detrimental paths, it also hinders our spiritual grow and maturity and labels us as sinners bound with several negatives attached to our soul.

Blindness

"*Satan, who is the god of this world, has blinded the minds of those who don't believe. They are unable to see the glorious light of the Good News. They don't understand this message about the glory of Christ, who is the exact likeness of God.*" — 2nd Cor. 4:4 NLT

Traveling through the wide gate, we inherit many spiritual handicaps. The meaning of being blind is referring to the mind that cannot understand spiritual matters, our minds-eye, our minds understanding cannot see, you are spiritually blind, asleep, fully deceived all from the lack of spiritual knowledge because of sin. Anything that takes your mind off

God is an attraction that leads to endangerment; in addition, they cannot see what their sin is because of their blindness.

Blindness, darkness, keeps the sinner from moving from the kingdom of Satan to the kingdom of God, from ignorance to understanding. There is no good thing being spiritually blind even though it is a temporary state of blindness. It was temporary for the saved and it is temporary for the *willful* sinner, because as a sinner enters through the valley of death, he is no longer blind, no longer a skeptic, no longer an unbeliever, no longer an atheist, or evolutionist, or humanist but still a sinner. Now he can see the truth, all that he rejected is now factual in is eyes, the sinner no longer can close his mind. The sinner will realize that through his earthly life he called himself an unbeliever is now a firm believer, sadly, it is now too late.

Ignorance

Ignorance keeps you from the truth, ignorance is shallow it has no room for moral, ethical and spiritual precepts ignorance is a *willful* state. Ignorance comes with your *willfulness* to remain a sinner, to be a rebellious, depraved, confused, lost soul. The *willful* sinner puts the truth out of his own life; he does not find the truth because he does not want the truth. *"They are darkened in their understanding and separated from the life of God because of the ignorance that is in them due to the hardening of their hearts"* (Eph. 4:18 [NIV]). We are born in ignorance to spiritual matters and educated by the world's systems, our intellect is consumed with 'self' and the outside world is our playground leaving our hearts hardened towards the life of God. Ignorance of spiritual knowledge is an unintelligent thing to have. Lord Bertrand Russell said it this way, "Men are born ignorant, not stupid. They are made stupid by education." Educating ourselves in the world's system with the world's philosophies leaves us blind to the truth; we *willingly* turn from the truth.

Captive, enslaved

"And that they may come to their senses and escape the snare of the devil, having been taken captive by him to do his will" (2nd Tim. 2:26).

Born in the sin nature we are sinners, being sinners, we live in darkness, and living in darkness, we are subject to the snares, the trickery of the devil. Being of this state, he takes us captive, by the blindness that is in our heart, in our mind by our ignorance and by our *willful* lack of knowledge.

You have a choice, spiritual sight or spiritual blindness. The result of spiritual sight is life; the result of spiritual blindness is doom.

Satan has the capability when he has entered a person's soul, to take that soul captive by possession, take that person's *will* into captivity and make that person to do his will.

There are demonic spirits working in the world, they are of an antichrist spirit with their main intention is drawing us away from Jesus, by giving us a world full of fantasy and lies. They pollute our minds; pervert our will, diverting us from redemption by holding us captive behind the walls of darkness.

The kingdom of darkness's quest is to capture and hold the world's population in bondage by lies, by deception, by allurements of the world's system, (Rev. 12:9). Captive and bondage are the terms used for us to see how we are incarcerated by sin. Bitterness and jealously are sins and hold a tight grip on the sinner, they are consumed with these. *"For I can see that you are full of bitter jealousy and are held captive by sin"* (Acts 8:23 NLT).

Dead because of sin
Eph 2:1

Sin separates us from God, from the truth, from the true facts of life and leaves us in a spiritually dead, spiritually depraved state of comprehension. We are not able to grasp, we are unreceptive to the supernatural effects that sin holds us in, we do not understand the deadly seize it has on us. *"Do you not know that to whom you present yourselves slaves to obey, you are that one's slaves whom you obey, whether of sin leading to death, or of obedience leading to righteousness?"* (Rom. 6:16). Being of the sin nature we are slaves to the sin nature, in reality, we are slaves to the devil and the devil leads to death. Sin lies to us and the more we sin the more strength it has in our lives and the more strength it has the more we sin and the more we sin the more dark and rebellious we become. Here we become a slave to sin.

Those who live this type of life are brazen they are impatient, they are blasphemous, and they are rooted in the baseless philosophy of evolution, that is not factual and is secular humanistic. They strike out continually to Christians, to God, to his word and his principles, and try relentlessly to remove any Christian beliefs from public viewing; the liberals are tolerant of different views and standards of behavior in others with their tolerance or open-mindedness except where the name of Jesus is expressed.

Sin is the act of *willful* disobedience toward God, and sinning brings results affecting not only our relationship with God, but also our relationship with others. Intrinsically sins have emotional, spiritual dominion over the sinner and the results are disobedience to God. Disobedience to God is living against God's will for your life and against the laws of God.

Lost

Lost is an acronym of living without direction aimlessly roaming through life like a leaf driven by the winds and at the end gathered and discarded with the others. Lost is living in a nature so dark it has no spiritual illumination.

A lost person does not know they are lost; they cannot put their mind around that concept. The hymnal, 'Amazing Grace' explains it. The words of the first verse are; "Amazing Grace how sweet the sound, that sav'd a wretch like me! I once was lost, but now am found, was blind, but now I see." The words, 'I was lost, but now am found' is not speaking of being lost in the middle of the ocean in a ship with no directional device, or being lost in a far country with no familiarity and no companions. No, it means that the individual was spiritually lost with no knowledge of God or his savior, with no hope of tomorrow. The words, 'was blind, but now I see' is not speaking of not having eyesight and through an operation or some mystical medication, now I can see. No, he is saying that he was spiritually blind to the things of God. He was spiritually blind to the knowledge of the truth, because of sin, because of lack of knowledge, but through God's amazing grace he was found and he was saved, and his spirit was converted. He was born again and this conversion lifted the blinders from his cold earthly heart, and given a new spirit and a new heart and he was able to see the things of God. If the lost person knew about being found, they would understand about being lost.

Being lost is having that void, a vacuum and the missing link is God and the truth. This void creates restlessness in us and there will be no rest until God is found. The fact that He loves us does not determine our eternal destiny; we are still separated from Him in our lost condition.

If you are an unbeliever, you are lost, and if you die lost, you will remain spiritually lost through eternity, but take heed, Jesus came to seek and save the lost (Luke 19:10 NIV).

Scripture makes it clear that there is only one way to eternal life: by trusting in Jesus Christ as Savior (Acts 4:12). Weigh the evidence, and then make a wise decision to follow Him.

Death

Death is fascinating, because this is where the Christians have no fear, they will pass from death to life. Here is where the new resurrected body joins the spirit life, they left the spiritual/physical life behind and are now living the glorious eternal spiritual life.

When death occurs, there is no second chance, there is no re-incarnation and no purgatory, there is no coming back as a fruit fly, and there is no seventy-two virgins waiting with open arms, there is no asking for forgiveness.

When the Christian dies, there will be rest, but when the sinner dies, there will be unrest, torment, suffering, the curiosity that spread through their minds has just now ended, and everything has now become absolute truth, so unfortunate for them. Some think when the human dies, then there will be rest, this is not true. This sadness surely could have been prevented.

When a sinner dies, his life ends with a soul filled with untruth and a bankrupt spirit. The sinner will perish because of what he refused to know, because he chose to live in the sin nature with ignorance, which is deeply rooted in the sinner's soul. Perishing does not mean, evaporating, decaying, vanishing into nowhere, it means eternal separation with the five-senses intact and the consciousness of it all and never able to inter into a paradise made for us, never. When the lost person dies from *willfully* being attached to the world, he will be counted a sinner as he goes down to the grave, deepening his journey to Hades. His wonders will be known from the darkness of the grave.

Those who *willfully* remain in the sin nature, they will automatically go to Hades at their death because they are automatically against God because they rejected his Son. Those are unbelievers, the cowardly, the abominable, and those who corrupt others. The murderers, sexually immoral, sorcerers; those who practice witchcraft, idolaters, and all liars, these God says <u>will not</u> enter heaven. Their fate is the fiery lake of burning sulfur, and tormented forever. All this is below the cross at Calvary, which represents the only way, the only hope for salvation.

This life is but for a moment, then we must proceed and prepare to the next life, as a cicada leaves its shell behind it moves to a newer life so we must follow this natural expected departure. Death is our wage for being sinners, "*For the wages of sin is death,"* and death is also our enemy, it is our last enemy, unless you choose to remain a sinner. *"The last enemy to be destroyed is death,"* (1st Cor. 15:26). Every one of us has a pre-determined amount of days on this planet. We are one breath away from death.

"Death is but a passage. It is not a house, it is only a vestibule. The grave has a door on its inner side." – Alexander MacLaren

Your Choice

The knowledge you carry around with you whether spiritual or worldly is where it will be decided what you would do with your knowledge. With the knowledge, you have or the lack of knowledge you have of Jesus Christ as your central subject your decision will be made through your will. Look at it this way. Here you will decide whether you will respond to the voice of the Spirit of truth or to the spirit of error leaving you either living in the divine nature or the sin nature. The decision is made in the soulish realm through the freedom of will. You truly do have a choice, and the wrong choice will be fatal.

If you sincerely want to know the truth it takes a *willful* decision you must make, and that decision will enter you through the straight gate, where truth will be revealed unto you and a continuous decision to walk on the narrow path, to retain the narrow way of thinking, the godly way of thinking. We are sinners by birth we remain sinners by choice. God has given us the freedom to choose between two separate paths of life, two different life styles the choice is yours, but God says this about it, *"Today I have given you the choice between life and death, between blessings and curses. Now I call on heaven and earth to witness the choice you make. Oh, that you would choose life, so that you and your descendants might live!* (Deut. 30:19 NLT). The choice you make to either stay in the sin nature, which has other consequences; or choose the Lord, here you see that your family may be blessed with your right decision. You have a choice to choose between life and death, which do you choose?

Unbelievers, come out of darkness, surrender your *will* let His light shine in you, answer that knock that calls to you and open the door to truth.

Judgment

"And I tell you this, you must give an account on judgment day for every idle word you speak. Every carless word, all your thoughts, all your words, everything you have every done will be at the judgment. And you will be condemned by your own words." "For he will bring our darkest secrets to light and will reveal our private motives. Then God will give to each one whatever praise is due." (Matt. 12:36 – 1st Cor. 4:5b NLT)

The heart is the center of your character, your being, of your personality, of your whole person your heart reveals who you are and your heart is God's concern. Your daily walk in life, your deeds, and your actions reveals your soul, that are determined in the heart and the motives are formed in the heart. God will judge according to truth and deeds. "Deeds give unarguable, unquestionable, irrefutable, incontestable, undeniable proof of what is in the heart." God sees us as though we are translucent, in the sense that he sees through to the invisible part of man, not, our inner organs, vessels, nerves but the heart, soul and spirit. He sees the secret things of man's mind, he knows the heart of man how deceitfully wicked it is and how weak is his *will* toward him is, he knows our motives, our thoughts, our intentions. He intently scrutinizes our lives. There is nothing hidden from God, absolutely no excuses (Heb 4:12, 13 NLT).

A Holy God will demand payment for disobedience. God hates sin, he hates a proud look because these are self-motivators and what is taking place is you are hiding from your true self. The day is coming when God will judge man's secrets, his secret life (Rom. 2:16 ᴺᴸᵀ). *"For God will bring every deed into judgment, including every hidden thing, whether it is good or evil"* (Eccles. 12:14 ᴺᴵⱽ). "But because you are stubborn and refuse to turn from your sin, (your unrepentant heart) you are storing up terrible punishment for yourself. For a day of anger is coming when God's righteous judgment will be revealed" (Rom. 2:5 ᴺᴸᵀ). The Lord's light penetrates the human spirit, exposing every hidden motive (Prov. 20:27 ᴺᴸᵀ).

"Of how much worse punishment, do you suppose, will he be thought worthy who has trampled the Son of God underfoot, counted the blood of the covenant by which he was sanctified a common thing, and insulted the Spirit of grace? What a fearful thing to *willfully* ignore God how much more will be their punishment. God says, *"vengeance is Mine, I will repay,"* *"It is a fearful thing to fall into the hands of the living God"* (Heb. 10:29, 30, 31).

Judgment is for the unsaved church member that has religion but do not have the Lord Jesus Christ in their heart. Religion does not save anyone. The things of unrighteousness come from the children on disobedience, and we know that God's judgment is based against those who do such things, and *"to carry out the sentence written against them"* (Ps. 149:9a NIV).

We all have an appointment with judgment, this is the standard that you will be judged by, that you neglected and rejected His Son, you neglected and rejected the truth, and you *willingly* turned away from it all. You were caught up in the worldly affairs and you let the culture determine your eternal destiny, the content that is in the books will reveal the sinners' moral state when opened at judgment.

You may not be a Christian and you may have never given your life to the Lord. Jesus Christ is, inescapable, He is unavoidable, one day you will meet Jesus and you will meet him as your judge. You may have ignored Him, you may have denied Him, you may have even cursed Him, but one day you will stand before Him.

Jesus is the judge; you will be kneeling in front of the one you rejected. His appearance will not be in a black robe as the judges that you are familiar with seeing on this planet. His appearance is described in Revelation 1:13-16, I suggest you read this passage; it is a fearful vision for the sinner.

"For if God did not spare angels when they sinned, but sent them to hell, putting them into gloomy dungeons to be held for judgment (2nd Pet. 2:4 [NIV]).

God will not judge the people of the earth, He has entrusted all judgment to His Son (John 5:22) who is the savior of this world. Have you rejected Him or have you accepted Him? We all shall stand before the judgment seat (Rom. 14:10c).

There is a countdown to judgment, a predestined appointment, you will be on time, there will be no delay, an unavoidable predestined appointment with the God of this universe, he prepared it before hand and it will happen. No one knows when his or her moment is up; your life has been predestined each unbeliever will stand before the judgment seat and give an account for their life.

Chapter 13

Reality

✥

"Reality is determined not by what scientists or anyone else says or believes but by what the evidence reveals to us" –Alan Hales

Reality and truth are synonymous. In the sin nature, we have developed a spirit of rebellion, a spirit of mythologies, a spirit of no absolutes through the spirit of error. This is because we are born blind, spiritually blind. You have heard that there are only two-things for sure; taxes and death are these absolute truths? O yes, you will forever pay taxes and your day of dying is approaching. These are etched in terrestrial and celestial stones. Uncle Sam will not leave you alone, and death, will not miss you. When you experience death, your spiritual blinders will be removed.

Both the sinner and the saved are in reality children of God, descendants of the Creator of the universe, all are created beings this means we have eternal life. God implanted eternal life in our seed at conception. God loves them both but has accepted the saved for his faith and repentance.

The sinner will live by the spirit of the worldly system. They know not the word of God, they live by what the sin nature dictates and their guide leads them down the path of deception, the wrong path of life and they will perish.

The reality of life is that you are going to die and your post-death experience hinges on one matter and one matter only and that is whether you accepted or rejected Jesus Christ as your personal savior, determines your destiny.

A God who created the universe and all that is within and most of all gave you the opportunity to know him and see him as he is, is not a God who would let you fade into eternity without a possible new eternal life, which is truly awaiting you.

By reading God's word we learn about God and His Son and gain knowledge and understanding of them and this is the truth that God wants us to have and it will remain with us forever (2nd John 2). This is why God wants the people of the earth to come to him, and to read his word, without his knowledge there is no truth and no mercy.

In the shadow of truth is the evil spirits of error gathering the feeble-minded, as clouds gather on the horizon, they are led into the world of darkness. If you don't expect truth then all other things can and will creep in your mind like Darwinism, atheism, humanism, secularism, evolution, and doubt, skepticism, and unbelief. *"I believe unarmed truth and unconditional love will have the final word in reality."* — Martin Luther King Jr.

The Bible

Enough cannot be said about the Bible, there is nothing like it on the planet and it will take you to reality. The Bible is primarily about Jesus and not about man; it is the precious thing where the mysteries of truth are revealed, the Bible is a book of life and death. The more we read the Bible the clearer life becomes, we gain knowledge of God's will in our lives we gain knowledge of the truth, the Bible is the voice of God. He speaks to us he shares himself with us. To the reader of the Bible, God is nearer to them, than without. A book can be written about the Bible but this is not our point here, but to share with you its eternal purpose. The Bible is our guide; it repeatedly urges us to know God, God wants us to know Him, it is our instruction manual through life, it cannot be overstated, read it. God's word reaches into the furthest secrets of man's mind and discerns man's thoughts, his intents and his motives. God's word helps you understand what God wants to do in your life (See Appendix).

God's Church

Not all churches are equal as not all religions are equal, the church of the living God should have New Testament characteristics. It should be a God fearing church, God's church preaches salvation through the blood of Christ, the Son of God, for he is the substitute, he is the sacrifice, for our sins by the shedding of his blood. A Holy God can only accept a Holy sacrifice for the sins of sinful man and that came from the spotless, blameless, the innocent Son of God. A holy deed by Jesus God accepted and that gave man through the confession and repentance of their sins to become God's children and welcomed into his eternal kingdom. It had to be a Holy sacrifice, God's churches preach this.

Jesus was manifested in the flesh for this purpose and so that we sinners would be saved from perishing. If this was not so then we would be doomed to the grave and Satan would do what he pleases. He would continue to rule the earth and continue eliminating human souls; it would be like this; man would be born, man would die, and they would go to hell. However, Jesus conquered Satan and death, and now Jesus offers paradise to those who believe in him.

God's churches on earth have altar calls, calling people who are seeking God to say the sinner's prayer. Altar calls do not need to be at the altar of the church, they can be in the pew or seat but in genuine sincerity, the sinner's heart is at the altar.

Having altar calls gives glory to the Lord, not the church, churches that do not have alter calls, who are they glorifying, are they concerned about lost souls for the Lord, are they interested in filling the pews, are they interested in larger congregations, larger collections? God must be given the glory.

Our Creator

Without the knowledge God wants us to have, nothing makes sense, but with the knowledge all things makes sense when we have faith and trust in him. We will not know everything because we cannot think like God, because we are humans and he is a spirit. He says, *"My thoughts are nothing like your thoughts," says the* LORD. *"And my ways are far beyond anything you could imagine* (Isa. 55:8 NLT). God is a spirit but God is the spirit of truth, *"the Spirit of truth, whom the world cannot receive, because it neither sees Him nor knows Him; but you know Him, for He dwells with you and will be in you"* (John 14:17), he desires a close and trusting relationship with you. This is done through his Son Jesus, his death on the cross and the shedding of his blood on your behalf.

The God of this universe is an absolute God; he is qualified, he is unlimited, he is not a God that sits on a throne hammering a gavel in His chambers judging humans when they sin, He is not judging at this time but he is recording our activities. He is a Holy God not stained with sin or corruption and neither will He live with evil man. *"You are not a God who takes pleasure in evil; with you the wicked cannot dwell"* (Ps. 5:4 NIV). Some try getting God's attention by doing "good-works" or doing what we think is a "good thing." They try going through the back door, but there is no back door, they try buying God's gifts by giving contributions, through philanthropy, but this is not the right way to get God's attention and this is not right with God (Acts 8:21 NLT).

We hide God, by the darkness in our heart and our sins; we are responsible for not knowing God, not Him. God is not jealous of you, he is jealous of what you worship, whom you worship, and says, *"Have no other gods before me."* Our God is above all gods. He is a God of love, of mercy, of patience, and of wrath.

The Ten Commandants reveal our Creator is a jealous God, and God himself throughout scripture says he is a jealous God. God is jealous against false idols. In Exodus 20:5 God is speaking of other gods, "*You shall not bow down to them or worship them; for I, the LORD your God, am a **jealous God**, punishing the children for the sin of the fathers to the third and fourth generation of those who hate me.*" It is not a good thing to hate God or not know him. For those who hate God they are hurting their children, and their children's children, to the third and forth generation. Pay attention you God haters do not take God's words of warning lightly. False idols creep into our lives and lead us away from godliness.

Our Creator's attributes derive from His three part Holy character, He is omniscient, all knowing, He is the almighty, all-powerful, omnipotent, and he is everywhere at all times omnipresent.

God has a hate list; there are seven sins that God hates, first is pride; pride is what started all evil. Those with prideful attitudes are his enemies; he hates a proud look, a proud attitude, one with haughty eyes. They are devious selfish people. He hates a lying tongue. A liar is a deceitful evil person, and God says liars will not go to heaven but to the burning lake of fire (Rev. 21:8). There is no such thing as a little white lie in God's heart a lie is a lie. To us a little white lie, what ever that is, may not be bad, bad is the word we use, but to God, it is evil, very evil because of its ramifications of its deceptiveness and deceitfulness. God also hates hands that shed innocent blood. Oh the wrath that will fall upon those who have killed murdered the innocent, the defenseless. God hates a heart that devises wicked plans. Those who premeditate and plot evil are wicked and will not escape judgment. Those who are swift in turning to do evil God hates. Their evil ways are against their Creator for He knows their evil deeds that others will suffer from. A false witness who speaks lies is covering evil and is making wrong seem right. In addition, God hates those who sow discord among brethren. Those who trash talk others, those who gossip, those who cause trouble, friction in families, are against God and he is against them. These seven can be found in the book of Proverbs 6:16-19.

God is a Holy God and he will not settle for an unholy, unsaved sinful prideful person to enter His kingdom. His Son sacrificed his life, his blood for our sins, and those who do not want their sins forgiven, those who do not want to accept His Son Jesus as their personal savior, and those who do not want to escape darkness that holds them captive by the power of Satan, and these will experience his wrath and will perish.

We all fall short of God's perfect holiness, and we being sinners He is unable to accept us in our fallen state, (Rom. 3:23). God desires an everlasting relationship with us, this is why Jesus came and died on the cross, and through the sacrifice of His Son God is working salvation is the midst of the earth and <u>all</u> are welcome to salvation. Can you think of any greater love than to give your Son for the sacrifice of the sins of the world? Would you give the life of your son for a crime that your neighbor committed? This was the ultimate expression of love. In 1st John 4:10 the Bible calls this the "propitiation for our sins." *"In this is love, not that we loved God, but that He loved us and sent His Son to be the propitiation for our sins."* Through this ultimate sacrifice, God will show us favor, if, we accept His Son and what He did for us. He wants to save us from evil, and this is the only way, through His Son Jesus' sacrificial blood. God's nature is Holy, righteous; our nature is sinful, unholy, and unrighteous. God made a prevision for us to enter heaven and he also gave us a choice. We could not enter as unholy, unrighteous sinners. We do not go to heaven to get cleansed or forgiven from our sins, we accept Jesus Christ for our forgiveness. We get forgiveness and cleansed while we are here on earth through the blood of God's Son. Why would a holy God let an unholy people into his righteous kingdom and contaminate it with a sinful people? he will not, but we are cleansed by the blood of Jesus that died in our place by accepting Christ as Savior.

God loves the human-race; he wishes all would realize that they are a product of his creation and that they belong to him.

The human race in its form is a degenerate race because of the great sin but we can regain our spiritual heritage by going to God in humility and in repentance. We are a lost people with no hope without God. All he is asking is for you to acknowledge him as your savior and creator. There are no other gods, mans imaginative-gods do not exist; there is no one above the truth living God of this universe.

Through God's Eyes

God does not see red or yellow, black and white people; he does not see race, our education level, and our social standings. What God sees are the results of the great fall that left the inhabitants of the earth divided into a dichotomy that is effectively leading man into oblivion, into nothingness. We are so focused on our own ambitions, greediness, and greatness that we totally cannot see what is to be seen and we cannot hear what is being said. The greatest sin of all in God's eyes is the rejection of His Son. *The Son is the radiance of God's glory and the exact representation of his being, sustaining all things by his powerful word. After he had provided purification for sins, he sat down at the right hand of the Majesty in heaven* (Heb. 1:3). For man to show indignation to Christ is appalling to God.

You are considered a spirit to God and he knows who is and who is not a believer, we the human race, are either believers or unbelievers, no other belief is possible in God's eyes. Your destiny hinges on what you believe about Jesus, your view of him is God's concern. This is how we know if a person is a believer or an unbeliever; the believer will have the spirit of God living in them. *"Every spirit that acknowledges that Jesus Christ has come in the flesh is from God," "If anyone acknowledges that Jesus is the Son of God, God lives in him and he in God"* (1st John 4:2b [NIV]). For this cause and only this cause are we given the entrance into heaven and the gift of eternal life.

God does not see us as nationalities, denominations, or religions, he sees us as righteous or unrighteous creatures, either believers or unbelievers, to God we are saved or not, we accepted His Son or not.

— **John 3:18 NIV** *Whoever believes in him* (God's only begotten Son) *is not condemned, but whoever does not believe stands condemned already because he has not believed in the name of God's one and only Son.*
— **John 3:36** *Whoever believes in the Son has eternal life, but whoever rejects the Son will not see life, for God's wrath remains on him.*

A personal God

God is not thought of as a personal God, he is thought of as a force, a power, an invisible essence out there somewhere. There are those who believe in a god and say god is in every thing, is all and in all. Some have concepts of re-incarnation, transmigration, you are what you are today, and in the next life, you will become something else, what a trap of the devil.

God wants us to know him, God wants so much for you to enter heaven to live in a place he has prepared for you. He wants to be your personal God. He wants you to see and feel the magnitude of his sacrifice through his Son that paid with his life and blood the price he paid to get you back from darkness from your sins. God is willing for you to spend eternity in heaven, with the condition that you accept Jesus as your personal savior.

Our Savior

Before Jesus, man was tumbling through life as tumbleweeds, directed by the winds with no life inside devoured by the scorching of the sun dying off with no passion to turn another way lost with no direction.

Jesus was manifested to save us from the evil in the world (1st John 3:5), to direct us to eternal life and he being the stimulant for us to turn to the right path of life, and in him, his sacrificial blood we have redemption, the forgiveness of sins (Col 1:14). Through the cross, God established a new covenant for those who place their trust in the Lord Jesus, His blood for your life (Luke 22:20). He agreed to forgive our sins, adopt us into His family, and watch over us. This salvation does not depend upon our good actions and deeds but upon our acceptance of the completed work of Jesus, who died in our place and because of our acceptance, salvation is our gift from God. (Eph. 2:8). Only Jesus can break that deadly moral virus called sin, which is the world's problems, there is no other provision for man. It is faith in the sacrificial death of Jesus Christ is the sole hope of salvation.

Christ is the nucleus, the heart of all life; he is the innermost figure of this life. He is the starting point of the next life, without Jesus, your life is a fruitless, meaningless, vain journey. God did not send Jesus into the world to condemn the world, or to judge the world but that through his Son the world might be saved (John 3:17)**,** to save those in the world that are lost (Matt. 18:11). We sinners have been given an opportunity to break out of, escape from the world of darkness and be released from the hold the devil has on our souls through God's Son. These two passages of scripture should penetrate your heart and open your heart to the reality of truth. *"Because God's children are human beings — made of flesh and blood — the Son also became flesh and blood. For only as a human being could he die, and only by dying, could he break the power of the devil, which had the power of death"* (Heb. 2:14 [NLT]). *"Just think how much more the blood of Christ will purify our consciences from sinful deeds so that we can worship the living God. For by the power of the eternal Spirit, Christ offered himself to God as a perfect sacrifice for our sins"* (Heb. 9:14 [NLT]). Jesus will restore life to your heart when you accept him.

People have searched for the fountain of youth, fountain of life; they have looked in the wrong places for Jesus is the fountain of life (Ps. 36:9 [NLT]). By rising from the dead, he took the power away from Satan, and by taking the power away from Satan, you are freed from darkness to light, from the kingdom of Satan to the kingdom of God. *"For Christ died (suffered) for sins once for all, the righteous for the unrighteous, to bring you to God. He was put to death in the body but made alive by the Spirit"* (1st Pet. 3:18 NIV), *"to open their eyes, in order to turn them from darkness to light, and from the power of Satan to God, that they may receive forgiveness of sins and an inheritance among those who are sanctified by faith in Me"* (Acts 26:18). God also sent His Spirit to live in us as proof of our salvation and to be ever-present with us. He is interested in every aspect of our lives and promises to hear our prayers.

"Seek the LORD while He may be found, Call upon Him while He is near" (Isa. 55:6). Jesus will save you if you let him.

Chapter 14

The Beauty of it all

Have you ever thought about why you do not think about heavenly things, if you have, the thought does not stay with you long, of course, this is a rhetorical question. Your mind is pre-occupied, conformed to worldly matters, work, family, hobbies, interest of your own, cars, girls, boys, school, grades, clothing, vacation, drugs, sex, parting, money, more money, texting, computing, and you can add another sheet to this list. The point is you do not take time to think on spiritual matters, not alone wanting to.

Your soul Christ died for that you may live. You are the only person on this planet who can keep you from the truth; you are the only person who can determine your destiny. You are snared with the words of thy own mouth, because of your beliefs.

You are a spirit on this planet and live in a body, without your body you remain a spirit and all spirits are the same as far as their composition goes. Everyone of us is equal, our spirit, our mind and heart, and the components within the soul, our intellect, our conscience, our imagination, emotions, feelings, our reasoning, our will etc.. When we die, we will be conscious of that fact that we are no longer on earth and because of where we are, we will be spiritually happy, contented, ecstatic or very sad spiritually sorrowful.

Those who do not go to heaven will not be tormented by demons and the devil. The demons and the devil will be tormented, but they will not torment.

In the spirit realm do not vision yourself with a body, vision yourself as a conscious identity, looking through your spiritual eyes into a new world before you, you will remain your own identity, you are now subject to your surroundings. Here you cannot refuse the truth of reality, reality is before you, there is no turning back, no other path to take on your extended spiritual journey, that critical choice you made on earth to either accept or reject Jesus Christ is now your life, you made that reservation or you did not. By the way, in the next life you will have a resurrected body.

You as a spirit on earth you remain spiritually the same; the only difference is that you have that physical body carrying you around while you are here. Separate from your body all your spiritual faculties remain subject to the spirit realm, as it will be when you pass through to the other side. Here, we are subject to those spiritual cohabiters on this planet, here; they have access to our spiritual faculties without our knowledge because we lack that knowledge because we *willfully* chose to. Therefore, energizing the unbeliever is satanic forces hidden within the sin nature that the world's system is subject to, all within the kingdom of darkness, where we live.

You have a will to choose what you want, but your will is in bondage to sin, in that dark state that condition that keeps you from knowing the truth. Nevertheless, light will break through and penetrate that darkness, through your will you must reach for the switch.

Examine yourself

Look intently into a mirror, a mirror does not lie, you are not looking for smeared mascara, broccoli in your teeth, or if your hair needs combed, look into your heart and ask yourself, what if, just what if what is being said here is truth? It is the difference between what you are and what you were meant to be. Be honest with yourself in the evaluation of yourselves. Do not think of yourselves as being better than whom you really are, our life is meaningless, vain and so full of pride without Jesus. The great reformer Martin Luther said, *"you are valuable because God loves you, He doesn't love you because you are valuable, you are valuable because he loves you."* Your worth is found in Jesus.

You are disguised to be normal, on the other hand what is normal in this sin inundated world. Is a so-called moral person normal, a caring person, a religious person, a self-sufficient having it all together person normal. We are disguised as humanist, evolutionist, secularist, atheists hypnotized by the philosophies and false teaching of this worldly system, do not waste your life in this sin sick world any longer it is ready to explode with all its religious factions. It is not easy coming to grips with your own ignorance, but if you feel that tugging at your heart, if you hear that knocking at the door of your heart, then expose yourself to God, before he exposes you. Take a long look a very long look at your short life.

A Haunting Question

"Do you really believe that what you believe is really real?" (See Appendix)

We are entangled in the world's philosophies that bombard us with constant lies, and being in a lost condition the people in the world gravitate toward what they feel is truth, what they feel is right what they are taught. The world's religions, and cultures have such a strong bond on their followers that they believe these religions and cultures are right. Do you really believe that what you believe is real?

The three most important decisions you will ever make

The most important decision you will ever make is will you accept Jesus Christ as your personal Savior. Your remaining journey in the physical will translate into your final destination, which hinges on this answer. The second is where you go to church. The wrong church will make you cold, will lead you astray, and will fill you with false doctrines not of salvation through the sacrificial blood of Jesus Christ. The third most important decision is whom you marry. Marrying one who is against your beliefs, against your steadfastness, against your values will also lead you astray and bring on difficulties that you cannot imagine.

Do you really want to know?

Do you really want to know the truth about life, do you really want to know there can be more to life than what you are living, do you want to know there is life after this; do you really want to know who you really are? Are you *willing* to move from your self-centered life to seek the life that Christ wants to reveal to you? Are you *willing* to know the truth? Do you really want to know there is a personal Savior, do you really want to know that the God of this universe loves you, do you really want to know that when you die you will have eternal life in heaven, God wants you to know these things and wants you to be with him in heaven. Do you want to know? Truth is only found in the Bible and through the Spirit of God.

He wants you to want to; if you really want to know, you must be *willing* to take the first step forward. That is all you have to do he will do the rest. If your heart is sincere, that is all that is needed.

You are not going to get out of your car until you release the seat belt, you will not get out of the world's grip until you release the sin nature in your life. It is holding you in the world and to denounce the world, you must believe that Jesus is the Son of God; it is that easy and that simple. Release the seat belt of the sin nature, the seat belt is the life of unrighteousness and get out of the world before it destroys you. Get out by believing in Jesus Christ and that he was raised from the dead, you believe through your faith and by believing through your faith, and trusting in Him you have overcome the grip the world has on you, now you are in the life of truth. *"For whatever is born of God overcomes the world. And this is the victory that has overcome the world – our faith." "Who is he who overcomes the world, but he who believes that Jesus is the Son of God?" "And this is the testimony: that God has given us eternal life, and this life is in His Son* (1st John 5:4, 5, 11, 13). He has given us eternal life, and this life is in His Son, this is God's promise you can know this.

Recognize that you are a sinner and sin separates us from God, with sin in your life you are in a different camp then God's people. Know that your journey is on the wrong path, it is heading for a collision with reality, and it is a path of evil deeds, eternity is racing towards you.

If you really want to know, forget about everything in your life, close it all out of your mind. All thoughts, all personal issues, your past, all philosophies, theories, your family, your friends, everything and focus on one thing only. Do I really want to know the truth about life? The truth at this moment is staring back at you; you are face to face with reality, no longer do you have to wonder, or be curious, you can stop all that right now, know reality, and know the truth about your life and the life to come. If you do not then you will foolishly perish but, if through genuine sincerity of a *willing* heart that you really want to know, then go to the door and open it, and let Jesus in, he is waiting on the other side. Jesus said in John 10:9a *"I am the door. If anyone enters by Me, he will be saved."* The New International Version says that Jesus is the gate. This is in reference to the narrow gate.

Come clothed in humility, come clothed as you are, a sinner with a broken lost heart but a hungry heart for the truth, as Jesus said, *"So I say to you, ask, and it will be given to you; seek, and you will find; knock, and it will be opened to you* (Luke 11:9). Sincerely ask and seek *"then you will know the truth, and the truth will set you free."* John 8:32 [NIV]. There is no other way to find the truth except through Jesus, this is by design of our Creator, we can only find the truth and go to God only through Jesus first, God's Son (John 14:6 ᴺᴵⱽ). If you want to prove there is a God, wake yourself up, you are here to prepare for eternity.

It is a simple step of faith, that is all that it is, but to those who are held captive, to those who are slaves to sin, those who are full of deception, those who are self-deceptive it would be like believing that is a beautiful horizon on the other side of thunderous dark clouds. No other way is possible; you must have faith that Jesus is his Son and believe that God rewards those who earnestly seek him. As it says is Hebrews 11:6 ᴺᴵⱽ, *"And without faith it is impossible to please God, because anyone who comes to him must believe that he exists and that he rewards those who earnestly seek him."* Invite Jesus into your heart, he comes where he is invited.

Are you willing?

A miracle is awaiting you, you just need to reach out and receive it. Reach deep inside and look at your heart, are you ready to conquer the darkness within and loosen the veil that blinds the mind to let God's light in that will set you free, are you *willing*? Are you *willing* to surrender self, pride, and ego and come to your Creator, are you willing? Are you *willing* to let go of the sinful world, its teaching and its erroneous ways and accept Jesus Christ as your personal savior who will save you from hell, save you from eternal consequences, are you *willing*? Are you *willing* to acknowledge that you are a sinner and need a Savior, if so, then say this prayer with a sincere heart.

THE SINNERS PRAYER

God in heaven, I know that I have sinned against you; I know that I am separated from you because of that sin; I know I am a sinner. Right now I want to respond to you and receive the gift that you are offering, I believe Jesus died in my place, shed his blood on the cross for me and I accept that offer of forgiveness for my sins. I ask you to come into my heart, take control, I submit to you, I give you my life right now, do with me what you will and make me the person you want me to be, I pray in Jesus name, Amen.

A Prayer for our Nation

Heavenly Father, we come before you today to ask your forgiveness and to seek your direction and guidance. We know Your Word says, 'Woe to those who call evil good,' but that is exactly what we have done. We have lost our spiritual equilibrium and reversed our values. We have <u>exploited the poor and called it the lottery</u>. We have <u>rewarded laziness and called it welfare</u>.. We have <u>killed our unborn and called it choice</u>. We have <u>shot abortionists and called it justifiable</u>. We have <u>neglected to discipline our children and called it building self esteem.</u> We have <u>abused power and called it politics</u>... We have <u>coveted our neighbor's possessions and called it ambition</u>.. We have <u>polluted the air with profanity and pornography and called it freedom of expression.</u> We have <u>ridiculed the time-honored values of our forefathers and called it enlightenment</u>. Search us, Oh God, and know our hearts today; cleanse us from every sin and Set us free. Amen!' (See Appendix)

Epilogue

Rebellion; When Lucifer rebelled, he rejected God's authority, he choose to go against God, sin entered the universe with an appalling event in heaven that separated heavenly host into an uneven number and the lesser were cast out of heaven. When man sinned, a dichotomy of natures arose on the planet and the population belongs to one nature or the other. With our birth into this world we are born in the sin nature, a nature that is a counterfeit nature, one that is a façade, a nature that is temporal, a nature that is contaminated with sin, an erroneous nature that holds man in spiritual limbo until his death. A nature that is ominous with many tentacles sucking us into many paths of life that we should not take, gradually insinuating its influence and control of our lives. This nature is of lesser moral values and a purpose that is thick with darkness, a nature that has a kingdom with a ruler who is bent on feeding you with erroneous teachings, ungodly values, actions, and philosophies; these are iniquities of the sin nature.

These two families, the believers and the unbelievers are at constant conflict with one another, as the world turns, as the ages pass, as your breath diminishes, are you going to continue to rebel, what will you choose?

Reality; the reality is, you are going to die, you can do nothing about that, but you can decide now while you are living where you want to spent eternity. Do not be deceived by all those false teachings and false beliefs that no one knows what is after this life, God's word tells us the truth. Life never ceases for the spirit and soul, after we leave this earth we soon face another life, that life is more of a reality, and everything experienced in that new life, is reality staring you in the face. Even though it is a new life for the sinner it will be a horribly sad new life, for the sinner will face judgment and his sentence is hell. *"And as it is appointed for men to die once, but after this the judgment"* (Heb. 9:27). The time is at hand, now is the time to prepare, not on your deathbed, you may not make it we are not promised tomorrow, we all get one chance to prepare for eternity, now is your chance. Our life is not only a journey; our life's journey is a story already told in the Bible, read it.

"Death is not a mystery of the beyond unknown, it is a passage of the known beyond." –The Author

Regeneration, born again; we are not saved by any good works that we do, we are not saved because we think we are good people, we are not saved because we are citizens of this planet, we are saved only by the mercy of God, according to God's mercy he saves us. If you are seeking the truth with a sincerely indisputable heart, God, the Creator of this universe will have mercy on you. He loves every person on the planet but we must take the first step, he will not reach down through the clouds and twist your arm to make you say uncle or give you a dinozzo, our hearts must be right. Three translations of Titus 3:5 says this, *"not by works of righteousness which we have done, but according to His mercy He saved us, through the washing of regeneration and renewing of the Holy Spirit,"* *"he saved us, not because of the righteous things we had done, but because of his mercy. He washed away our sins, giving us a new birth and new life through the Holy Spirit,"* [NLT] *"he saved us, not because of righteous things we had done, but because of his mercy. He saved us through the washing of rebirth and renewal by the Holy Spirit."* [NIV] The washing of rebirth is the cleansing of our sinful heart, life, and giving us a clean heart by the Holy Sprit.

Regeneration refers to the work of the Holy Spirit in the salvation experience that produces new life in the sinner who is now a believer. To express this concept, Jesus used the expression "born again." Regeneration is the work of God, through the Holy Spirit, of placing in one who has faith a new nature, a new heart. The Holy Spirit is the agent or divine worker of this regeneration.

Jesus; Christ is not Jesus' last name, Christ, means the anointed One, anointed by God (See Appendix).

The Christ of creation, the anointed One, God's Son came to earth for one purpose only and that was to save you from Satan, and he did that by breaking Satan's power by God raising Him from the dead. God loves you so much that if you were the only one person on the planet he would still send his Son to die for you, you are that valuable to Him. Jesus is the redeemer of our souls; by his precious blood such a costly sacrifice for your and my sins that he sacrificially stretched out his arms and died for us.

"Every spirit (person) *that confesses that Jesus Christ has come in the flesh is from God and every spirit* (person) *that does not confess Jesus Christ, is not from God,"* (1st John 4:2, 3). These are the unbelievers, the sinners of the world, that evolutionist, humanist, secularist, the atheists, the ones that debate with fire in their heart, these are the ones of the anti-Christ spirit that over takes the mind of the unbeliever, the unsaved. Simply put, these are the ones, "addicted to lust and allergic to God." –Eugene Peterson

Bible; reading the Bible we receive knowledge; reading and receiving knowledge penetrates our heart and leads us to salvation and saving our souls. When we read the word, we hear the word, hearing the word leads us to understanding the word. If when reading the Bible you do not feel convictions of your sins, then you are not hearing what the word is saying to you because the Bible is the only book that also reads you. We must have humility to come to God and to receive His word it takes a humble heart.

James 1:21 says, "*So get rid of all the filth and evil in your lives, and humbly accept the word God has planted in your hearts, for it has the power to save your souls.*" NLT

Execute the judgment of truth; those who are conformed to the world's system and have the wisdom of the world, those with intelligence, volition also have their own erroneous worldviews and like their sin, that separates them from God. Within these views, no absolute truth is determined, these individuals wear a mask of deception and disguised as scholars, teachers, lawmakers, professionals in all fields, and even though they believe, what they believe, God's absolute truth is a perceivable reality. Because God's word is truth and because of the conviction of God's word the Bible says that by telling you the truth I may become your enemy (Gal. 4:16), but I do not have a choice for the Bible also says to "*execute the judgment of truth*" (Zech. 8:16 KJV).

APPENDIX

∞

p. v How to Study the Bible; The best place to start is with the gospels, that is the books of Matthew, Mark, Luke and John. These books document the life of Jesus and help us to believe. Try to read about a chapter at a time and think it over carefully. It is good to read the Bible in a quiet place relatively free from distraction. You read it just like any other book, using your mind and thinking hard allowing it to speak to your heart. As you keep reading, you will find some things repeated. These are the things that God wants us to pay most attention to. Commands like love one another, forgive those who have hurt you and do not judge people. Read the Bible to grow in Jesus Christ and to live better. It is important to pray as you read the Bible. It does not have to be a long prayer, just something like "Dear God show me what this means and help me to understand."

p. 33 Staying in context of the verse in the Old Testament, "my people" are the Jews, Hebrews, the people of Israel and in today's life under the New Testament, people still are destroyed. In the Old Testament God is saying "my people" the people of Israel, actually God's people are the living breathing human race that He made whether it be under the Old Testament Covenant or under the New Testament Covenant, the difference is righteous and unrighteous. If people perish for lack of knowledge, they are unrighteous, they are non-believers, they are from **the spirit of error**, they rejected God, and they did not seek nor want to neither find

God in their lives nor accept His Son as their personal savior. Remember 1st John 4:3 ᴺᴵⱽ·

Again, these people *willingly* made their choice. Therefore, people without God's spiritual knowledge of Him will perish because they chose to live in **the spirit of error** of untruth. In reality, what they are doing is worshiping the devil without their knowledge.

p. 93 According to the U.S. Bureau of the Census, the resident population of the United States, projected to 07/30/09 is 307,041,654.

COMPONENT SETTINGS FOR JULY 2009
One birth every.................................. 7 seconds
One death every................................. 13 seconds
World, 6,774,446,627 July 30, 2009

p. 102 The Center for Bio-Ethical Reform, P.O. Box 219 Lake Forest Ca 92609-0219

"CBR operates on the principle that abortion represents an evil so inexpressible that words fail us when attempting to describe its horror. Until abortion is seen, it will never be understood."

WORLDWIDE

Number of abortions per year:
Approximately 42 Million **worldwide!**

Number of abortions per day:
Approximately 115,000 worldwide!

UNITED STATES

Number of abortions per year: 1.37 Million (1996)

Number of abortions per day: Approximately 3,700

p.132 For everything there is a season,
And a time for every matter under heaven:
A time to be born, and a time to die;
A time to plant, and a time to pluck up what is planted;
A time to kill, and a time to heal;
A time to break down, and a time to build up;
A time to weep, and a time to laugh;
A time to mourn, and a time to dance;
A time to throw away stones,
and a time to gather stones together;
A time to embrace, And a time to refrain from embracing;
A time to seek, and a time to lose;
A time to keep, and a time to throw away;
A time to tear, and a time to sew;
A time to keep silence, and a time to speak;
A time to love, and a time to hate,
A time for war, and a time for peace. Ecclesiastes 3:1-8

p. 151 Bob Roberts Jr. "Glocalization" "the problem with the word global, or globalization is "that it says, way over there, which is incorrect. It is way over there and here at the same time, that is why it is glocal, glocalization."

p. 165 Illustration: by the late Rev. Clarence Larkin Est. From his book, "Rightly Dividing The Word" p. 86. Used by permission of The Rev. Clarence Larkin Estate, P.O. Box 334, Glenside, Pa. 19038 **NOTE** this graphic may not reproduce well, some text within the graphic are outside the publisher's guidelines.

p. 169 Teaching on conscience, The Vanishing Conscience, by John MacArthur, 1-800-554-7223 Grace to You.

p. 197 Webster's New World Dictionary of the American Language Second College Edition. © 1972

p. 235 The Narrow Way, Arthur W. Pink

p. 247 Question: "Where is a good place to start reading the Bible?"

Answer: For starters, it is important realize that the Bible is not an ordinary book that reads smoothly from cover to cover. It is actually a library, or collection, of books written by different authors in several languages over 1500 years. Martin Luther said that the Bible is the "cradle of Christ" because all biblical history and prophecy ultimately point to Jesus. Therefore, any first reading of the Bible should begin with the Gospels. The gospel of Mark is quick and fast-paced and is a good place to start. Then you might want to go on to the gospel of John, which focuses on the things Jesus claimed about Himself. Mark tells about what Jesus did, while John tells about what Jesus said and who Jesus was. In John are some of the simplest and clearest passages, but also some of the deepest and most profound passages. Reading the Gospels (Matthew, Mark, Luke, and John) will familiarize you with Christ's life and ministry. They teach us how to live our lives in a way that is honoring to God. When you start reading the Old Testament, read the book of Genesis. It tells us how God created the world and how mankind fell into sin, as well as the impact that fall had on the world. Exodus, Leviticus, Numbers, and Deuteronomy can be hard to read because they get into all the laws God required the Jews to live by. While you should not avoid these books, they are perhaps better left for later study. In any case, try not to get bogged down in them. Read Joshua through Chronicles to get a good history of Israel. Reading Psalms through Song of Solomon will give you a good feel for Hebrew poetry and wisdom. The prophetic books, Isaiah through Malachi, can be hard to understand as well. Remember, the key to understanding the Bible is asking God for wisdom (James 1:5). God is the author of the Bible, and He wants you to understand His Word. It is important to know that not everyone can be a successful Bible student. Only those with the necessary "qualifications" for studying the Word can do so with God's blessings: Are you saved by faith in Jesus Christ (1 Cor. 2:14-16)? Are you hungering for God's Word (1 Peter 2:2)? Are you diligently searching God's Word (Acts 17:11)?

If you answered "yes" to these three questions, you can be sure that God will bless your efforts to know Him and His Word, no matter where you start and no matter what your method of study. If you are not sure that you are a Christian — that you have been saved by faith in Christ and have the Holy Spirit within you — you will find it impossible to understand the meaning of the words of Scripture. The truths of the Bible are hidden from those who have not come to faith in Christ, but they are life itself to those who believe (1 Cor. 2:13-14; John 6:63).

Recommended Resource: What does the Bible Say About...? Easy-to-understand Answers to the Tough Questions by Ron Rhodes

Related Topics:

What does it mean that the Bible is inspired?

What are some different methods of Bible study?

Who divided the Bible into chapters and verses?

Why should we study the Old Testament?

How and when was the cannon of the Bible put together?

Resource: "Where is a good place to start reading the Bible?"
www.gotquestions.org

p. 257 "Do you really believe that what you believe is really real" Is from the 'Truth Project' from the Focus Institute by creator of the project, Dr. Del Tackett

p. 262 This prayer is from a minister named Joe Wright who offered it in front of the Kansas State House in 1996. Although this was prayed for the Kansas State House, it has also been prayed for our nation. TruthOrFiction.com.

p. 265 Jesus is the transliteration of the Heb. "Joshua," meaning 'Jehovah is salvation," i.e., the Savior.' p. 274, Christ, Christos, the anointed One, p.190. Vines Expository Dictionary of the Old and New Testament Words. © 1971.

CPSIA information can be obtained at www.ICGtesting.com
228724LV00002B/73/P